Between the West and Islam

The Tension

Between the West and Islam

September 11 – The Untold Story

by

SHEIKH MOHAMMED NAEEM

ISBN 0-9689551-2-6

Printed in Canada

National Library and Archives Canada Cataloguing in Publication Data

Sheikh, Mohammed Naeem, 1934–
 The Tension between the West and Islam: September 11 – The Untold Story
 By Sheikh Mohammed Naeem.

 Includes bibliographical references and index
 ISBN 0-9689551-2-6

 1. Islamic countries-Foreign relations-Western countries. 2. Western countries-
 Foreign relations-Islamic countries. 3. Terrorism-Religious aspects-Islam.
 4. Islamic countries-Foreign relations-United States. 5. United States-Foreign
 relations-Islamic countries. I. Title.

 DS35.74.U6S48 2004   327'.0917'67   C2004-905120-2

Printed in Canada by: University of Toronto Press, 5201 Dufferin Street, North
York, Ontario, Canada M3H 5T8

Published by Commerce Horizons Inc.
60 Green Lane, Unit 33, Thornhill, Ontario, Canada L3T 7B5
email: sheikhnaeem@rogers.com

Contents

Acknowledgements

The rising hostilities between the West and Islam in the late 1980s and subsequent eruption of war after the 9/11 occurrence in 2001 spurred me to dig out the causes of this conflict, come to grips with the historical background of the crusades against Islam and try to comprehend whether the legacy of these wars was still marring relations between the Western Christian civilisation and the Islamic civilisation.

My quest for answers led me to history and the first modern author that I thought of reading was Karen Armstrong, because I had watched several documentaries on her research into the religious history of Judaism, Christianity and Islam. Her knowledge impressed me, and so I decided to look up her literary work, including *A History of God* and *Holy War: The Crusades and their Impact on Today's World*. Her book *Holy War* particularly fascinated me, since it contained most of the information that I was looking for to understand the current turmoil between the West and Islam. Hence I took many references from this book to arrive at my own assessments on the current situation. I am therefore in deep gratitude to Karen Armstrong and her publishers for putting out such an enlightening historical perspective of the crusading wars and religious history of Judaism, Christianity and Islam that enriches our understanding of the current Middle Eastern crisis.

I had done some research previously to understand the tension between India and Pakistan and the nature of the Kashmir dispute, which was published as my first book titled the *Division of India*. What I was still missing to fully understand Muslim predicaments was detailed knowledge and historical background about Chechnya and the nature of the Chechen dispute. Usually very little details are carried by the Western press about the merits or demerits of the Chechens' strife, and so the common impression in the West is that the Chechens are Islamic separatists fighting a guerilla war against their mother country, Russia. This puts the Chechen struggle in rather a negative light, and so the Western audience is generally unaware of the true nature of the Chechen dispute, how it began and what the

Chechens are really fighting for. Are they separatists trying to break up the Russian Federation or are they freedom fighters struggling to regain their lost liberty and independence? So I decided to acquire knowledge about Chechnya through an account by a reputable Russian correspondent and author named Anna Politkovskaya. Politkovskaya specialises in social issues and has written an enlightening book titled *A Dirty War* about the North Caucasus region in which she brings out the intricacies of the Chechen tragedy and highlights the brutalities of the Russian war. John Crowfoot's translation of her work into English and Thomas de Waal's excellent introduction are also commendable. This book has added to my insight, so I made it a point of reference in my assessments on Chechnya. My gratitude extends to Anna Politkovskaya and her publishers and everyone else associated with her excellent work.

Last but not least my warm gratitude extends to Mr William G. Cooke, who was not only my editor but also a teacher and guide in putting this book together to make it a serious study. Mr Cooke is a retired professor of English language and literature. His knowledge of religions and history was an extremely valuable asset for me, as I was able to draw on him for biblical references pertinent to my train of thought as well as historical facts about the American, European and the Middle Eastern histories. His insight and elucidations of the differences between various denominations of Christianity and the strains on Evangelicalism was particularly helpful to me in interpreting the Evangelical impact on the current Middle Eastern situation. While I have taken help from Mr Cooke gratefully in understanding many intricacies in the historical perspective, the responsibility for views and assessments expressed throughout this book is entirely mine.

I cannot close without saying that I am also enormously grateful to my children and family, particularly my wife, Farzana, for their support and patience in enduring hardships that my commitment to this book may have caused by not leaving enough family-time during the last several years.

Preface

Most of the text of this book was submitted to the 9/11 Commission in April 2004 titled a *Muslim Submission* to present a Muslim point of view on the international situation. Since Muslim concerns do not get due recognition in the media and the popular press owing to the inherent bias against Islam, I felt there is an even greater need today to portray the Muslim viewpoints to create at least some sense of proportion to the prevailing hue and cry over radical Muslim behaviour. My intention is not to condone Muslim radicalism but rather to understand why the Islamic world has become so restive – why so many Muslims are turning to violence and suicidal missions to air their grievances and make political statements. I believe it is critical for the world at large to weigh the Muslim plight assiduously so that a balanced and positive approach may evolve from this study and spur public opinion on both sides to shift their hostile positions in the interest of world peace. Hence I decided to remodel the original draft to present a Muslim perspective on the background of history to come to grips with the current tension that has created warlike conditions between the West and Islam.

There are two ways to look at the Muslim situation. One way, which is currently followed too widely in the West, is to blame Islam endlessly, malign the religion by implicating it in violence, and focus on the Muslims as terrorists bred by their religion. There is no shortage of people in the media and elsewhere pouring out venomous written and spoken material to tarnish the religion of Islam instead of focusing on the misdeeds of particular Muslims. Rather than referring to Muslim acts of terrorism or Muslim terrorism they prefer to speak of Islamic terrorism, as if terrorism were an Islamic injunction. Such advocates seem to have latent hatred stored up in their hearts, which they have now found an opportune time in history to vent. They have seized on Osama bin Laden and Al-Qaeda to give their spiteful sentiments a rationale. There are too many who take this line, but the question is: Have they succeeded in achieving the goal of peace by taking this hostile or hateful approach? If the current plan of action to curb Muslim radicalism is working, then, one may reasonably ask, where is the fruit of success? The plight of our world shows how badly these methods have failed. Nor are they likely to succeed in the future, because they are fundamentally flawed.

Blaming the Muslim radicals and fanatics goes without saying, but I am also deeply concerned about the rise of fundamentalism and ultra-conservatism from the southern horizon of the United States. What is perturbing is that the power of Evangelicalism may have infiltrated into the White House and be using the United States' economic and military prowess to achieve goals that the Evangelical Christian fundamentalists have been aiming at for the past many centuries. These fundamentalists appear to have found partners in ultra-conservatism, and the two now seem to have formed a formidable right-wing or Judeo-Christian force to use the White House to advance its own agenda against Islam. This alliance has become so threatening for the Islamic world that it is now urgent to throw light on the crusading that the Evangelicals are engaged in. It is important to trace historical connections of the Evangelicals with the ancient European Crusaders as well as bring into focus the ultra-conservatives, who appear to have both religious and territorial ambitions in the Middle East.

Retaliatory tactics have so far failed to provide even an interim solution, but a solution is what we must find to restore peace between the West and Islam and establish normality in our world. A fresh approach is therefore needed to come at the Muslim situation from another perspective. This entails examining it more deeply, not only to understand Islam's position on violence, but also to come to grips with Muslim conduct, why a growing number of Muslims behave the way they do. Why are they so restive and why do they engage in acts of violence? What has driven them to such a level of desperation and brought them to such a hopeless crossroads that many are now treading the path of suicidal missions? Understanding the international crisis from this vantage point is both harder and more complicated. Patience and commitment to peace are needed to trace the long historical background and to grasp all the implications that have blended to produce the current explosive scenario. But these menacing implications, however tedious or complicated they may be, must be confronted so that all sides may see the need to revise their hostile positions and work towards peace.

Since the United States of America has now assumed a unilateral role and is dictating its terms and imposing its own version of peace by virtue of its economic and military prowess, no international forum is now left that could independently take decisive action to remedy the ominous situation and restore peace between the West and the Islamic world. The United Nations has been made irrelevant, and the international system of jurisprudence has been disregarded and rendered dysfunctional.

Under these conditions of unilateralism and militarism, Muslims are facing hardships, and the rest of the world is also enduring a great deal of suffering stemming from Muslim restiveness and violent radicalism. The United States, Europe, the Middle East, Southeast Asia and the Far East have all been engulfed in terrorism of one sort or another and innocent citizens are losing their peace of mind as well as their lives. Where do we go from here, and how do we bring an end to this cycle of terrorism, violence and retaliatory violence? Counter-terrorism or retaliatory violence in the name of the war on terrorism has not produced a peaceful climate. The retaliatory approach is not only costly in financial and human terms but is also giving birth to more disgruntlement and spreading more radicalism instead of curbing violence.

The 9/11 tragedy is an excruciating enigma – whodunit? It is important to note that 9/11 is not only a tragic event for the American citizenry, but it is also a trauma in the lives of the Muslims, since they have been made to endure the fallout of this horrific crime and carry its burden. Their religion has been tarnished, and they now receive eerie looks as if they were all terrorists.

The deteriorating international climate has adversely affected the lives of Muslims throughout the world, including the ones living in the West. Muslims are therefore, equally, if not more, victims of the 9/11 plot. Consequently, they are very anxious to know its factual details–how it happened, and who might have schemed it–in order to find a way to cope with it and become part of the solution instead of being branded as the antagonist. Most Muslims are confused and need conclusive answers to these and other questions so they may deal with the 9/11 tragedy in a constructive way.

Already the grassroots majority of Muslims, rightly or wrongly, has doubts about the perpetrators of this crime and views it as another conspiracy by the adversaries of Islam. They suspect that Islam's enemies may have harnessed this incident willfully out of spite, to use as a pretext for waging war against the Islamic world and transforming the fundamentals of the Islamic culture with a view to defeating the polity of Islam. The lack of judicial inquiry and an unsolved 9/11 case lends credence to their suspicion, especially when the Bush administration declined to produce factual details in a judicial manner and based its case merely on hysterical accusations. An independent judicial inquiry would have dispelled the Muslims' misgivings, but President Bush did not favour such an inquiry under either American or international aegis, which has compounded the suspicion that perhaps something is amiss. His unprecedented disregard for jurisprudence does not help a suspecting Muslim, who inclines to believe that the neo-conservatives and Evangelical Christian fundamentalists might be up to some mischief against Islam and now pursuing their extremist policies

behind the smokescreen of 9/11 and in the wake of the war on terrorism.
More than 9/11, the war on Iraq is a much greater cause of concern for the
Muslims, since they fear that the real aim of faith-based President Bush may
be to open the way to conquering the Islamic world and transforming its
religious and social culture. Unless apprehensions of this kind and suspicions about 9/11 are decisively dealt with and removed from the minds of
the Muslim grassroots, the seeds of mistrust will continue to breed hatred
that may turn more young Muslims into hard-line radicals. This is not a
good prognosis for peace.

The hysteria of 9/11 seems to have destroyed all norms of civility and
accuracy. As a result the Muslims are now facing an unprecedented onslaught of inaccurate propaganda against them and enduring harassment
even in ordinary interactions with the Western world such as visiting a
Western country. Karen Armstrong, a renowned author on religion and
history, once thoughtfully said: "It is common in the media or the popular
press to see 'Islam' stigmatised for being an excessively and essentially
violent religion or for being inherently opposed to rationality and progress.
If challenged, it is not unusual for people to look rather puzzled or be-
mused because accuracy is still not exactly the point at issue when talking
about 'Islam'." It goes to show how false Western propaganda has now
made the Muslim ordeal even greater in the wake of 9/11 than many
Americans and other Westerners might imagine.

Hence, while the Western points of view, right or wrong, are widely
propagated by the powerful Western media, very little is known in the West
about the concerns of the Muslim world. What are their issues and grievances that have made them so threatening? There is a need to know this.
And so I became intensely interested in learning how tension between the
West and Islam began and decided to portray the Muslim concerns by
identifying sources of this tension and pinpointing the obstacles that stand
in the way of a harmonious co-existence of these civilisations. The current
state of violence and counter-violence is unacceptable to both Muslims and
non-Muslims alike, and so I began contemplating whether there was any
chance at all of defusing the gripping violence and counter-violence and
what steps would be needed to initiate this. My conviction is that it is crucial
for the international community to know all sides of the equation to be
able to fully grasp our world's woes. So I put much emphasis on sketching
the historical background of the tension and bringing the sources and
obstacle in the forefront to show the nature of the difficulties that we are all
facing in the current turmoil.

This meant that I had to go deeper into the problem, using history as my
guide to learn where the tension began and how it became so gripping that
it is now difficult, even in our modern times of liberalism, to overcome the
menace of faith-based violence.

Since the United States of America is currently a dominant world power, I also decided to look briefly into its historical background to discern how it was shaped and what influences dominate it. and what its economic, political and religious objectives might be. This exercise provides an insight into the composition and characteristics of the United States that now greatly affect our world.

Inevitably my quest also led me to scrutinise religions and faiths closely to learn what roles they might have played in fragmenting human society and generating rivalry and wars, especially between the West and Islam. I was also curious to discern the status and role of God in human affairs and how much of His position has been exploited or abused by humans to serve their territorial and political objectives.

It has been an intense exercise in soul-searching, but it has also been a gratifying experience, since it unfolded the role of the United States as well as unravelling the variety of beliefs that divide humanity and lead into wars. It is amazing how faiths dominate human behaviour, and if they get corrupted for any reason, how destructive they then become. My hope is that reflection on history may inspire all sides to address the roots of hatred and make adjustments in their outlook to give peace a chance to prevail.

It is in the hope for world peace that I decided to project the Muslim viewpoints along with a synopsis of the Muslim predicaments that fuel anger and radicalism. Currently, the Muslims feel alienated and their concerns are either ignored or dismissed on prejudicial grounds. Consequently, their points of view are not considered and they are left outside the fold of the solution. It is necessary to appreciate the Muslims' viewpoints to calm down their emotions and anger and allay their fears, so that Muslims at large may co-operate confidently in establishing a truly peaceful international order. They need a boost of confidence if they are to become unsuspicious members of the international community, and make their proper contributions to solving the international crisis and become part of the solution instead of being dubbed as adversaries.

While I am endeavouring to find basis for peaceful co-existence through learning the sources of tension and hatred and recognising the faulty beliefs, I also realise that I cannot succeed alone, nor could the Muslims achieve peace by themselves. Hence, my objective is to rouse passion for peace widely, so all peace-loving members of the human fraternity may engage collectively in this pursuit. The political leaders do not seem to have a genuine will for peace owing to their entrenched positions on war and imperial domination. Some Western leaders may even be religiously biased and pursuing their religious goals behind the state power of their countries. They need to be reminded of their failed and misguided policies in plain and strong terms. Thus, the onus for changing the current trends and taking initiative to achieve peace rests with the intelligentsia of the international community who would need to address the current wrong policies on both sides and take over the struggle where the political leaders and religious bigots have failed. My hope is that once awareness of the impediments is created, the passion for peace will inspire all peace proponents to join hands and work collectively for the common goal of achieving a peaceful co-existence between diverse religious and cultural civilisations.

However, when discussing religion and politics or intricate matters like peace, some details or even aspect of these topics would be passed over for want of time and space. Nevertheless, I have tried to cover at least the salient points to present a synopsis of historical background of the tension that divides the West and Islam, but most of all my book converges on the pivotal question: Where do we go from here? How could we extinguish the flame of religious hatred and give peace a chance? My book addresses both Western and Islamic audiences in general but American readers in particular and emphasises that in order to see a change in the Islamic world, the West will have to change its own outlook and first deal with its own demons of religious and racial prejudices and imperialistic chauvinism before it can demand a change from the Muslim world. My book ends on the theme of fair and just treatment of all members of the human race, because justice and fairness constitute peace, which is the only sustainer of prosperity and happiness in the human fraternity.

Since peace has been my sole motive, I decided to dedicate this book to the cause of peace.

Sheikh Mohammed Naeem
Markham, Ontario, Canada
October 11, 2004

1

The Background of the Tension between the West and Islam

The tension between the West and Islam goes back to the seventh and eighth centuries and has increased from the eleventh century up to the present time. It began developing in the seventh century, when Islam declared that there is no God except one God (Allah) and that He is alone, neither begotten nor begetting any one, and has no partners. Islam established a supreme and uniquely solitary status for God as the most Merciful and Benevolent Creator and all-powerful Sovereign of the entire universe. Although this Islamic belief in the solitary status of God contrasts with the Christian faith, Islam did not totally reject Christianity, for it accepted that Jesus was a true messenger of the One and Only God and came from the same line of prophets as Abraham and Moses. His disciples were blessed with a Book of guidance, and so the followers of Christianity are also the people of the Book. The major bone of contention between Christianity and Islam is the status of Jesus Christ, but Islam was willing to live with Christianity despite this disagreement, because it preaches religious tolerance and advocates co-existence of faiths. Islam's position on matters of faith is one that others should find acceptable, since it teaches that "Your faith is your faith and our faith is our faith" as declared in the *sura Kafiroon*.

Regrettably, the early Christians in particular did not take such a tolerant view of Islam but took serious offence at its differing view about the status of Jesus. Instead of letting the two faiths co-exist, the Western European Christians of the seventh century and onwards, and increasingly during the reign of Pope Urban II late in the eleventh century, began to denounce Islam as a wicked religion and consider Muslims as evil people. They also criticised Prophet Mohammed (may peace be upon him), calling him a liar and impostor for starting a wicked religion that denied the status of Jesus as the Son of God or God Himself in human form. This was a very unfortunate view. Rather than trying to tolerate another religious doctrine, the early Christians decided to settle the controversy over Jesus Christ's status by waging war and resolved to eradicate this new religion as well as annihi-

late its followers, the Muslims. This approach laid a foundation for perpetual tension and bitterness. The dispute over Jesus Christ's status has
since become the root cause of the tension between the Western Christian
civilisation and the Islamic civilisation that is currently erupting in different
ways.

The Christians of those times also had a bitter complaint against the Jews.
Again, Jesus Christ was at the centre of this bitterness, since the early and
medieval Christians mostly believed, as many still do today, that the Jews as
a people were instrumental in bringing about the crucifixion of Jesus
Christ. Their anger against the Jews was therefore extremely violent. Thus
those early Christians were outraged and deeply embroiled in religious
hatred against both the Muslims and the Jews. On the one hand their
Messiah had, as they thought, been killed by the Jews, and on the other
Islam had rejected the notion of his being the Son of God. Hence, their
hierarchy viewed the situation with indignation and decided to punish both
the Jews and Muslims by brutal persecution and wars against them.

While the Muslims were not easily available for punishment at that time
owing to their statehood and military power, the Jews were more vulnerable
and readily available in Europe, since they had no state or military power of
their own. Thus they were massacred and brutally persecuted in Western
Europe for centuries. They had practically nowhere to turn for refuge and
protection of life except the Islamic states. Thus they came to Islamic Spain,
Morocco, Algeria and other North African Muslim states as well as to Egypt,
Palestine (then under Muslim control), Iraq, Syria and Iran. All Muslim
states without exception provided protection and equal opportunities to
the Jews to live side-by-side with the Muslims. Islam extended its hand of
compassion and humanitarian assistance to an afflicted community. There
was no systemic mistreatment of the Jews as they flourished in the Islamic
Spain, Morocco, Egypt, Iraq and most of all in Palestine under Muslim rule
without persecution or anti-Semitic oppression. Islam accepts the Jews as a
people of the Book, and recognises their right to practice their faith and
live by their own religious and cultural customs. Thus the Muslims did not
interfere with the civic or religious rights of the Jews, nor did they side with
the Christians in persecuting them. Even during the brutalities of the
Second World War, when the Nazis were massacring the Jews, the Bosnian
Muslims took risks to shelter them from the Germans.

It is a great irony of history that the Jews have forgotten so quickly and so
completely how compassionately the Muslims once treated them and how
they provided them humanitarian assistance so they could escape the
murderous pursuit of the European Christians. Bosnia is an even more
tragic case. When Muslims were being massacred and expelled from their
homes in the ethnic cleansing in former Yugoslavia during the late 1980s
and early 1990s, the Jews, who by that time had attained a position of

influence in the international affairs, did not come to their rescue, not even to return the favour that the Bosnian Muslims had once extended to them. In the Islamic world, the Muslims are now on the receiving end of the stick from the warring Western Christians. Instead of helping them to mitigate the onslaught for old time's sake, the Jews have actually joined hands with the Christian fundamentalists, as right-wing neo-conservatives, in attacking and invading the Muslim states by becoming part of the war machine that has bombarded and killed tens of thousands of innocent Muslim civilians. In contrast to the Jews, the Muslims did not join hands with the massacring Christians to wipe out the Jews; rather they helped the victims with compassion. Muslims are justly proud of this heritage, which places Islam in a unique position of compassion in the family of Prophet Abraham's religions. Christians and Jews are ready enough to talk about compassion and humanitarianism, but all too often it is quite another matter when it comes to demonstrating the compassion practically. Muslims not only claim to be compassionate, but they also demonstrated their compassion and humanism practically by opening their countries to protect the oppressed Jews right up to the sixteenth century. Not that the Muslims are now looking towards the Jews to come to their rescue; the point is that the influential Jewry seems to display a lamentable lack of any sense of moral obligation. This is an important piece of history that must be mentioned in the context of present world affairs, especially to the Jews. Today the Jews have joined hands with the Christians in attacking Muslim countries, killing innocent Muslims to gain a tract of land. They have occupied the Palestinians' lands and brutally suppressed the population, demolishing their homes and driving them literally to the wall. The Jews have forgotten completely that the ancestors of the Palestinians once provided them protection from the hounding Christians. What an irony that they are now massacring the descendants of the very same people who were once their benefactors! The brutal treatment of the Palestinians betrays a lamentable ingratitude and an utter failure of moral responsibility.

But to return to the study of the Christian onslaught, as was said earlier, they were not in a strong position to take action against the Muslims as they did against the Jews. However, the balance of power changed with the advent of the Scandinavian Viking warriors who invaded Western Europe in the ninth century and had overrun much of northwestern Europe by the end of the tenth century. The Christian leaders fretted about going under subjugation to these pagans and worried that they might erode the population's Christian faith. Consequently, while accepting the Viking political domination, the Christian religious leaders began working on these warriors to bring them into the fold of Christianity. The Vikings themselves were eager enough to assimilate into the local religious and social culture so that they could control the population from within and rule without local resentment or insurgency. Hence, it was mutually beneficial for the Viking warriors to enter into the fold of Christianity and establish their rule as Christian knights and kings. Their conversion not only averted the threat of paganism but also provided Western Europe with a ferocious military power that the Christians had been lacking.

Thus the Viking warriors eventually took a new shape and emerged as Christian crusaders. Although the concept of 'Holy War' existed prior to the Vikings when it was used by Charlemagne against the Saxons, the marriage of Vikings with Christianity reinforced the notion of holy war that the Christians waged against the Islamic world. Owing to the Vikings' military power and their new role as Christian crusaders, the Christians committed unspeakable atrocities against Muslims in their frenzy to annihilate the evil people, which they had not before been able to do. History is full of accounts of the crusaders' wars, narrating how much blood the holy warriors spilled. These barbarous brutalities and the enormous bloodshed of the Muslims have made many good-hearted Christians ashamed for what the crusaders did.

But massacre and bloodshed is not all that they did. As knights and kings and rulers of Christendom along with the Pope, the clergy and all kinds of preachers, the ruling crusaders sowed the seeds of permanent hatred of Islam and despite of the Muslims in the hearts and minds of the European populations. The propaganda from the pulpit with its incessant denunciations of Islam set an extremely tainted view of the Muslims so deep in the psyche of the Western European Christians that it has since become an integral part of the Western frame of mind. While the clerics were spreading their spiteful view of Islam from the religious platform, the kings were using their state power to spread an indelible rancour that now seems almost impossible to erase from the minds of many Westerners. As in the course of many centuries the heirs of crusaders took yet another identity and became colonialists and European imperialists, they deployed their growing military and economic power to suppress the Islamic states and Muslim populations even more brutally. Thus the Muslims were hampered in transforming their states socially, economically and industrially as the Western countries were doing. The iron hand of the imperialists was a major factor in keeping the Muslims backward, but their own repressive elements, mostly under the patronage of the West, were also responsible for thwarting their progress. What is more painful is that, despite astronomical social, economic, educational, industrial and technological progress, the West has not been able to discard religious bias and the spiteful attitudes toward Islam that were inculcated into its frame of mind many centuries ago by the crusaders and perpetuated by the imperialist monarchs. This hatred shows its ugly face in many and sometimes innovative ways. The born-again Christians, the Evangelicals and other Christian fundamentalists who have come to power from time to time have kept the flame of hatred burning by showing disrespect for Muslim rights or issues and using economic and military power to defeat the polity of Islam. As can be seen in Afghanistan and Iraq, their objective seems to be to transform the Islamic religious and cultural heritage so that the commitment or adherence of the populations to Islam will weaken and one day they may adopt Western values in the name of modernity. Accordingly, the occupying forces of the Muslim world have forbidden the population to form Islamic governments, to pave the way for Western values in the name of democracy and modernity. If the American Evangelicals are trying to impose their version of Christian values in the wake of Western values, then it is not clear how far their values and their allies' values in other Western countries are genuinely Christian. Thus they may end up in creating a set of values that has no moral or spiritual basis at all.

Regrettably, the tension of faith that started almost a thousand years ago has not subsided, however much progress our world may have made in other fields. The Christians have always had the upper hand owing to their beliefs in wars and militarism as they, indeed, still do today. In spite of liberalism and waning religious fervour in the Western world, the world has not seen a real change of heart towards Islam. It shows up in different negative ways in dealing with Muslim issues, and this acrimonious attitude perpetuates tension between Christians and Muslims.

In the face of these many difficulties, we need to explore a feasible middle-of-the-road approach in order to extinguish this old flame of hostility. Both sides have to learn from scratch the benefits of religious tolerance and cultural co-existence and, most of all, adopt the attitude of "live and let others live." The responsibility for a change always rests with the bigger partner, who carries the greater burden of obligation to show accommodation and make a gesture of goodwill. Thus, through amenability, the West can take out the heat and initiate respite from the current hostilities by engaging in greater interaction of scholars and enlightening the intellect of the public on both sides to stimulate religious and cultural tolerance. This may be a slow process, but it could help to erase the old scars of hatred. Sadly, it is the exceptional and occasional fundamentalists that come to power in the West that spoil the chances of a change. Equally, it is an occasional fanatic from the Muslim world that ruins prospects of peaceful negotiations. Both parties keep reverting back to the old habit of hostility. The West, being the stronger of the two, ignores the rights and issues of the Muslims and suppresses their populations by the force of its economic and military power.

Thus, from the days of crusading, the Napoleonic invasion of Egypt and the British and French attack on the Ottoman Empire beginning in 1917, the Anglo-French invasion of 1956, and now the American onslaught on the Islamic world in the twenty- first century have kept the flame of hatred burning. Persistent Western invasions keep the old tension between the West and Islam alive. The Muslims react violently, and the vicious circle of violence and counter-violence continues. How to break this circle, and especially change the focus of the Western combatants to end scorn against the Islamic social and religious culture, is now a challenge for all good-hearted Christians and Muslims. As was said earlier, peace is a collective endeavour and needs participation by all peace-loving citizens alike, including the Jews, Christians and Muslims, to end the current hostilities in a fair and just manner.

2

Islam's Position on Violence and Terrorism

The religion of Islam neither condones violence nor promotes terrorism in any shape or form. Islam, in fact, prohibits its followers from resorting to terror or violence to resolve social or political issues. Numerous examples can be cited to elucidate Islam's position. First, there is the example of the Prophet himself when he gave instructions to Ziad, his freedman, while sending him on an expedition to Syria against a threatening Christian ruler: "He told them to fight in the cause of God bravely but humanely. They must not molest priests, monks and nuns nor the weak and helpless people who were unable to fight. There must be no massacre of civilians nor should they cut down a single tree or pull down any buildings."

These instructions of the Prophet are binding on Muslims for all times. While Muslims are forbidden to engage in acts of violence and terrorism, they are not denied the right to defend themselves against aggression by appealing to arms against transgressors. Critics take this as Islam's injunction for war and cite Sura *Anfal* and *Tauba*, chapters 8 and 9 of the Quran, as evidence that Islam approves killing opponents wherever they may be found. This is a case of reading the Suras out of context and misinterpreting the text, which is not only true for some critics of Islam but also true for many Muslims who misinterpret these Suras and abuse the injunctions to justify their fanatical offensive actions. The point is that self-defence even by armed resistance is a right of every society, and Islam, too, upholds this right for its followers. Sometimes self-defence becomes preemptive, and at other times it requires brutal force, depending upon the circumstances. Islam permits these tactics of warfare against those who may have violated peace treaties or committed atrocities against Muslims by expelling them from their homes, denying them their livelihoods and denying them freedom to practise their religion and cultural customs. There is no denying that these injunctions have been abused by fanatical Muslims for aggressive purposes, just as fanatics in any other religion and culture abuse the precepts or prohibitions of their religions.

When the Sura *Anfal* and *Tauba* are read in full context and against the background of the circumstances under which they were revealed, it becomes clear that they are no different in character or intent from any other injunction supporting the universal right to oppose transgression. Where Islam differs from other cultures is that at no time does it allow its followers to inflict harm in any way on non-combatant unbelievers, or their animals and other property. Even combatant transgressors, when they surrender or cease fighting, are to be treated humanely. Such transgressors may be freed from captivity after they renounce aggression and pay war reparations (*Jazia*), which may take the form of monetary payments or be made in other kinds to benefit the Muslim community, such as imparting education or helping the Muslims to improve their social infrastructure. To imply that the Suras *Anfal* and *Tauba* superseded the Prophet's earlier gentle position is not right, as was demonstrated by Saladin, who practised the Prophet's tradition in the twelfth century, long after the Suras *Anfal* and *Tauba* had been revealed.

Saladin's conduct in war, which a Western reader can easily recognise, illustrates that Muslim warriors were still bound in the twelfth century by the earlier injunctions of the Prophet and continued to deal with their adversaries clemently and humanely. How Sultan Saladin abided by the Islamic tradition in treating the vanquished clarifies any suggestion that the Suras in question superseded or nullified the earlier Islamic injunctions of merciful and humane treatment of the adversaries. Accordingly, whereas the Christian warriors of the First Crusade had filled the streets of Jerusalem with Muslim blood up to the knees of their war-horses and mercilessly slaughtered tens of thousands of Muslims, Saladin did not take revenge when he victoriously entered Jerusalem after defeating the crusaders. He not only forgave the Christians, but he also allowed them to go on living in their districts and communities and carry on with their social, economic and cultural lives. Thus Muslims, Christians and Jews lived in Palestine in harmony and co-existence once Saladin had established a just and humane Islamic State.

Without going into the details of the crusader wars, it is sufficient to say that Saladin's ultimate victory did not come from defeating the army of King Richard I; rather it came from a remarkable show of compassion, clemency, forgiveness and respect for human life. King Richard did not give up fighting because he was too ill or had other state business to attend at home. The fact that he was twice close to capturing Jerusalem, and chose not to do it, indicates that he must have been overwhelmed by Saladin's conduct and decided that waging religious or ideological war was futile. He saw the future in peace and realised that peace could offer a cordial and compassionate co-existence of diverse cultures, which is what seemingly changed his mind. When he came into closer contact with Saladin, he also saw the real face of an Islamic warrior and the true nature of the religion of Islam. It seems to have dawned on him that Islam was not a wicked religion, nor were the Muslims evil people. Hence he opted to make peace with the Muslims and paved the way for a harmonious co-existence of Christians and Muslims. His treaty of peace in 1192 A.D. with Saladin was a landmark achievement of clear thinking and compassion between Christians and Muslims.

King Richard concluded this treaty not so much as an English monarch but as the head of a united Christian crusade, which comprised all the countries of Western European Christendom; effectively it was Christendom's treaty with the Muslims. So, all Christian monarchs and countries were also morally and technically bound by its terms. However, the Christians did not all view it as such, and under the pressure from the Pope the Holy Roman Emperor Frederick II reluctantly launched a new crusade in 1228. The Muslim ruler of the time was understandably indignant, but he preferred to resolve the crisis by negotiations and accepted Fredrick's proposal to make Jerusalem an open city for followers of all three religions of the children of Prophet Abraham. Thus peace was again restored by negotiations, which lasted until 1239 when a contingent of Christian troops broke the truce by attacking a peaceful Muslim caravan moving up the Jordan Valley towards Damascus. This second infraction by the Christians infuriated the Muslims and the Khwarismian Turks reacted violently and captured Jerusalem in 1244. Further minor crusades, including the one by the English King Edward I in 1272, continued until Mameluke Sultan Arghun drove the crusaders out of their strongholds in Palestine in 1291. The Holy Roman Emperor was bound to honour King Richard's treaty, and King Edward I was also technically bound, but in both cases little or no respect was shown for the peace treaty. The Muslims on the other hand demonstrated their commitment to and preference for treaties in keeping with the teachings of the Prophet, who had showed them how to resolve disputes by negotiations and honouring treaties.

After the failure of the crusades, the Muslims regained control of Jerusalem until it passed to Britain by yet another violation of Richard's treaty in 1917, when Britain attacked and captured Palestine.

Throughout the period of their ascendancy the Muslim leaders amply demonstrated their preference for negotiations and peaceful resolution of disputes by truces. Even though provoked by many breaches from their antagonists, they did not respond or resort to acts of terrorism as part of their warfare tactics. Their abhorrence of terror and violence and rejection of revenge killing of fallen adversaries is a shining milestone in their history. They also demonstrated their trustworthiness in abiding by the terms of the treaties and truces that they concluded with the Christians. Regrettably, it was the Christian military orders and kings that showed little respect for treaties and truces, as they routinely violated their agreements. Their conduct was regrettable because it undermined Western credibility and eroded the Muslims' confidence in their trustworthiness; ever since, it has been a source of mistrust and an obstacle in the way of establishing congenial relationship. Islam has particularly taught its followers to honour treaties and truces, which it regards as essential for a harmonious civilisation comprising diverse faiths and cultures. Thanks to the Muslims' trustworthiness and their adherence to treaties, Christians and Jews have lived peacefully under their ascendancy not only in Palestine but also in other Muslim countries.

However, the same cannot be said about the Christian or Western leadership. It is difficult to imagine how the West can pride itself as civilised when it flouts the basic precept of civility, which is credibility or trustworthiness. As can be seen from the historical track record surveyed above, lack of such credibility has always been a problem for Christendom. It remains a problem for the West even to this day as can be seen from its policies in Afghanistan and Iraq. By violating the peace treaty of 1192, the West not only disturbed peace between the Christians and Muslims, including the Jews, but it also opened the doors for the old tension to re-grip the Islamic world, which is clearly evident in our own contemporary times. There is a dire need for the West to cultivate the habit of credibility and trustworthiness to support its claim to be civilised in the true sense of the word.

3

The Origins of Terrorism in Muslim Culture

Since Islam did not promote terrorism and Muslim rulers did not practise it, how did violence and terrorism creep into the Muslim culture as we see it today? The origin(s) of the phenomenon of contemporary terrorism that increasing numbers of Muslims are now practicing therefore needs to be explained.

Again, a reflection on history shows that the first time Muslims ever came face to face with terrorism was during the crusaders' invasions beginning in 1095. As was shown by Saladin, Muslims did not adopt their tactics of violence or terrorism or retaliate in the same kind.

The second time that Muslims encountered terrorism was in the fourteenth century, when the barbaric Mongols invaded the Islamic world and ransacked Iraq. Some Muslim clerics, including some scholars of that time, tried to find Islamic justification for retaliating and paying the Mongols back in their own kind. But there was no religious ground to justify such cruel retaliation, even though some zealous clerics might have used rhetoric in extremely trying times to incite the fallen Muslims to fight back in the same way. In any case, their exhortations had little effect and remained just inflamed rhetoric. The retaliatory passion also faded away once the Mongols had surrendered before the power of Islam and embraced the religion of One God. Thus the Muslims did not resort to Mongol-type terror or violence as tactics in retaliation. They used their spiritual talents to overpower the enemy.

It is fair to say that the Turks, who came down out of Central Asia (from what is now Uzbekistan) and took control of the countries at the eastern end of the Mediterranean after the fall of Saladin's dynasty, did not display the same chivalry and magnanimity as Saladin did. Thus it is true to say that the European Christians are not the only people who persistently fail to live up to the teachings of the religion they profess. Turkish conduct in the Balkans and eastern Anatolia was an example how some Muslims have also failed to live up to the teachings of their religion. Fortunately, the Turkish

episode is an isolated incident in Islamic history. The Turks, who descended from the Mongols and were influenced by their ancient culture of
brutality, seem not to have experienced true conversion to Islam or attained full appreciation of the Islamic teachings of merciful and humane
treatment of the vanquished. While the Turks practised some acts of violence in the Balkans, the Muslims as a body were not engaged in any kind of
terrorist or violent activities.

The third time the Muslims came face to face with terrorism was in the
early twentieth century, when the British used Arab hands to perpetrate
violence and acts of terrorism against the Ottoman Empire. The Arabs'
succumbing to the British and consenting to use their tactics of terrorism
was perhaps the greatest setback to the Muslims in all Islamic history.

With the rise of European imperialism and colonisation from the sixteenth century onwards, Islamic civilisation seems to have gone into a
serious remission or slumber, since there were no forward movements or
upward strides in the Islamic world. It was a strange display of inertia by the
followers of a dynamic religion and vibrant community. Somehow Muslims
became passive and indifferent to developing their societies and to their
future as a viable and progressive community.

After the achievements of the Golden Age the steep decline of the
Muslims raises questions about what happened to them and how they could
slide to such low levels as we see today. Briefly, there are two main reasons
for the Muslim downfall. First, the Mullahs, the so-called Muslim scholars,
began emulating the Western Christian priests and pastors in the eighth
century in Spain to control the population and dictate state affairs from a
religious perspective. Steadily they began interpreting the Islamic laws from
the point of view of controlling state affairs as well as the population, as
opposed to helping them in the dynamic and revolutionary spirit of Islam.
Thus the Muslim societies were pulled back and made no progress. Second,
the Muslim rulers also went back to the tribal practice of controlling their
societies, which brought back the old Arabian custom of despotic domination and gave birth to a degenerate rule of governors who claimed to be
caliphs but in fact were quite the opposite. These despots, too, emulated
the Western form of kingship and created hereditary monarchies, which
put the state reins in the hands of a few families. As a result, the mass of the
people were cut off from developing their own social, economic and civic
lives on modern patterns compatible with human progress. Consequently,
the dynamic character of their society was thwarted, and the vibrant Muslim
communities went into a serious recession that made them not merely
dormant but also regressive.

This Muslim passiveness seems to have encouraged the European imperialists in the late nineteenth and early twentieth centuries to think that the
stagnant Islamic world was theirs for the taking. Britain and France had set

their sights on the Arab world for mixed reasons of economic exploitation and imperialistic domination. Stagnation in the Islamic world and political fragmentation between the Arabs and the Turks enabled the British and the French to bring down the decadent Ottoman Empire after the First World War and share its spoils in the Middle East. The Ottoman Empire had been fragmenting since at least the 1830s and the First World War only speeded up its disintegration, but the onslaught by the British and the French effectively ended it. This was a double-edged development. On the one hand it ended the Islamic form of government, the Caliphate, and on the other it brought new territory under European domination. It also opened door for other opportunities that the British Prime Minister Lloyd George may have been contemplating for some time, such as the text of the Balfour Declaration.

Thus it was greatly tempting for Britain to come into action and devise a belligerent strategy against the Ottoman Empire based on using the Arabs to perpetrate acts of violence and terrorism so as to destabilise the Caliphate in Turkey. Various steps were taken to accomplish this, including exploiting the instability that the young Turks had created in their revolt against clericalism and the Sultan's hidebound autocratic government. Other measures included using the rebellious Arab Bedouin tribes against the Turks by training them in the art of violence and terrorism. The Bedouins' collusion with the British for subversive activities was the first major incident in Islamic history when Arabs would actually use acts of violence and terrorism to effect political changes. Britain was a world power and well accustomed to toppling or destabilising foreign governments. So it deputised Colonel Lawrence, later known as Lawrence of Arabia, to go to the desert, assemble the disgruntled tribes and train them in the art of sabotage for the purpose of destroying the government in power by acts of subversion. Thus Colonel Lawrence played the role of a master terrorist and initiated extensive training of the Bedouin tribal chiefs, including Malik Abdul Aziz along with other tribal chiefs of shady and greedy reputation. The Bedouins learned how to make bombs and blow up government buildings, railway tracks and supply convoys, which killed numerous government employees including civilians. Thanks to the training and leadership of Colonel Lawrence, many Bedouin tribal chiefs became accomplished saboteurs and terrorists, proficient in the subversive activities that eventually brought down the Ottoman Empire.

The Sultan's decision to side with the Germans in the First World War made the Ottoman Empire a clear target of the Allies. Accordingly, in 1915, after the Ottoman Empire had entered the war on the German side, the Allies, including Tsarist Russia, signed a secret treaty in London mapping out the spheres of influence that they expected to have in the former Ottoman lands after they won the war. Basically, that treaty assigned what became Iraq, Transjordan, and much of Palestine to Britain; what became Syria and Lebanon to France; southern Turkey to Italy; and to Tsarist Russia, Constantinople and Turkish Armenia in outright possession and the rest of northern Turkey as a sphere of influence. After the war the Western powers regarded the treaty as a dead letter as far as Turkey proper was concerned, because Italy had done nothing to earn its share and they refused to deal with the Soviets, whom they regarded as a mob of gangsters rather than a proper government. Some commentators say that Lenin opted out on his own accord, but others point out that he was never given the chance to take over Turkey proper. Even if he had been interested in acquiring northern Turkey, he was in no position to do so since he had his hands full trying to secure his authority throughout Russia itself.

In the Arab lands of the former Ottoman Empire, however, Britain and France basically carried out the partition they had agreed to in 1915. Besides Transjordan and Palestine, Britain also took charge of Iraq, from which Kuwait was carved out and made into a separate state. France took over Syria, from which it carved out a new state of Lebanon for the Christian Arabs. Both Britain and France vivisected Iraq and Syria respectively to weaken these countries territorially and economically so that the Policy of Islam might not resurge from these two fomer bastions of Islamic power. As far as the Arabian Peninsula was concerned, Britain decided to maintain the Sharif of Mecca, Hussein, in power in Hijaz and made two of his sons the first King of Iraq and the first Emir of Transjordan as a consideration for their part in bringing down the Ottomans. A new emir loyal to Britain was installed in Kuwait. The Gulf states were allowed to remain in the hands of the local rulers, who were mostly pirates robbing the passengers of the Hajj pilgrimage and commercial traffic from India. Since Ibn Saud, Malik Abdul Aziz, had played a major role in waging war and carrying out acts of terrorism against the Ottomans under the guidance of Colonel Lawrence, he asserted his right to rule over Hijaz, which Britain allowed to pass into his hands in 1932. France, on the other hand, had earlier extended its influence in North Africa by seizing Islamic states such as Morocco, Tunisia and Algeria.

A governor of the Ottoman Empire, named Mohammed Fuad, was administering Egypt, but he was disloyal to the Sultan and aspired to break away from the empire to establish his own rule over Egypt. He was conniving with Britain in many ways to weaken the Ottoman Empire, so that when the empire would crumble, Britain would reward him a domain of his own in Egypt. When the time came, Britain placed Egypt under his control by making him king of Egypt. His son and successor was the notorious King Farooq, who became Britain's strong ally against Muslim nationalism and kept a watchful eye on Al-Azhar, the Islamic institution of learning, to make sure that it played no part in the revival of Muslim nationalism or Caliphate.

Egypt's despotic rulers still carry on suppressing the *Akhawane Muslaimeen*, the Islamic Brotherhood, just as Britain had set the pace long ago, which is now a huge source of unrest in Egypt.

Thus with the demise of the Ottoman Empire the Islamic world was divided and mostly shared by Britain and France, though the Soviets also inherited the Caucasus, Azerbaijan, and Central Asia from the Tsars. Hence the future of the Islamic world depended how these occupying powers treated them. The immediate benefit for the West was the disbandment of the Caliphate form of Islamic government, which was a severe blow to the polity of Islam. The long-term benefit was that the Islamic world was destabilised and put into the hands of despotic rulers who retarded the growth and development of the Islamic countries to perpetuate their brutal and exploitative regimes.

As far as Turkey proper is concerned, Kamal Ataturk had already begun doing what the Allies would have liked to do themselves, that is to undermine the seat of the Islamic government and uproot the influence of clericalism. Ataturk was averse to clericalism and theocratic administration. He wanted to modernise and reinvigorate his country through drastic changes. However, in his frenzy or aversion of the Islamic system, he ended up initiating a radical revolution instead of adopting a systematic process of reforms to overhaul the antiquated system. Consequently, instead of curing the disease he ended up killing the patient. His interference with the religious practices of the masses disenchanted them and created a gap or rift between the ruling elements and the population.

Since the Turks had settled down at the far eastern end of geographic Europe, Ataturk and his protégés considered themselves as part of Europe. Hence they began adopting European secular cultural customs after their military takeover to fully integrate into Europe. However, a large section of the population had not given up on its commitment to Islam, and so they were not fully transformed as Europeans, nor has Turkey been recognised or accepted by Europe as part of the European Community. Consequently, Turkey is caught in an identity crisis, because it is neither European nor has it retained its Islamic identity. The Turkish military dictators and technocrats have taken away its Islamic identity but the Europeans have not yet agreed to give it a new identity as a secular European nation. Turkey is now in a state of confusion, which is why the Europeans refer to it as Europe's sick man.

The military rulers are not prepared to let the population have its aspirations, and the population is equally not prepared to fully give up its religious heritage. As a result there is an ongoing conflict between the state of Turkey and the people. The technocrats and military dictators who replaced the theocrats of the past now run the state in the old repressive and reactionary style. Consequently, Turkey is embroiled in internal strife that has thwarted its social and economic progress.

Teaching the art of terrorism and training the Arabs in subversion and opening the door for Ataturk to carry out his attack on the polity of Islam was not all the mischief that Britain did in the Islamic world. The severest damage was to patronise the cruel and oppressive tribal chiefs, who were notorious highway robbers, power-hungry and grotesquely brutal and greedy. These brutal rulers had two objectives in mind: first, to protect the interests of their masters who patronised them, and then to serve their own greedy ends by terrorising the populations. Keeping the people backward and illiterate was therefore essential. Consequently, the entire population in the Arabian Peninsula went through a most excruciating period of suppression at the hands of their own brutal rulers who were assisted by the West, especially after the discovery of petroleum reserves in the 1930s. When Britain and France left off trying to control the Islamic world after the Second World War, the United States took over the task. So the citizenry of the Islamic world has never in modern times had a real chance of free and independent growth according to its religious and cultural heritage.

These kings and emirs went further to grip the populations tightly by exploiting Islam, so that the religious sentiments of the populations might not turn them against their régimes. So, they made a pact with religious leaders such as Mohammed Abdul Wahab in Saudi Arabia, whereby the management (or suppression) of religious affairs was assigned to the clerics with a proviso that they would not interfere in the state affairs of the kings and emirs. At the same time the kings undertook not to interfere in religious matters. Thus the task of controlling the populations was divided. While the kings pursued their own goals of exploitation and living immoral lives, the clerics got down to the business of interpreting Islam according to their own definitions, so they could use religion as a pretext for suppressing the population. This is how Wahabism was born to dominate the Arab world with strict primitive rules. The underlying idea was to clamp down the population or overburden them with antiquated edicts and regressive rules, so that they would have no outlet for moving forward to a life that might give them greater political, social and economic freedom, which might in turn threaten the despotic kingdoms.

Religiously speaking, Wahabism has no place either in Muslim society or in Islam itself because of its regressive approach to life. Muslims used to have a vibrant society owing to the dynamic teachings of Islam, which sought continuous changes to improve life from bad to good or from imperfection towards perfection. Islam does not promote regression, but the entire philosophy of Wahabism is based on creating regression and stagnation by imposing antiquated stringent rules. Wahab had no real credentials as a religious teacher except for the authority vested in him by the Saudi kings, who used his regressive and antiquated mentality to protect their kingdom. If all things had been equal, Wahabism would have died a natural death. But thanks to the British and later American support for the house of Saud, especially after the discovery of the oil reserves, Wahabism flourished and served its purpose of keeping the population clamped down. Consequently, the Arab world experienced an unprecedented and devastating suppression at the hands of their own internal forces as patronised and shored up by external powers.

It must be emphasised here that Islam neither reared these dictatorial kings and other repressive rulers who are currently dominating the Islamic countries, nor were they nurtured in any way by Islamic traditions. They did not come from any Islamic institutions or *madarsaas,* as the Western critics would like to imply. Simply put, these oppressive despots are the creation and products of the British imperialism in the first place and subsequently nurtured and groomed by the United States.

The Western media, including many Western intellectuals, unjustifiably blame Islam for the misdeeds of these autocratic régimes without admitting their own share of the blame or recognising that the West should own responsibility for their misdeeds since it was the West that actually installed these brutes to start with.

What we are seeing in the Arab world today is an explosion of revulsion at the prolonged repression that was inaugurated by Britain and later backed up by the United States when it acquired an interest in the Middle East as spoils of the British Empire after the Second World War. The current turmoil in the Arab world did not stem from *Jihad* or any form of Islamic instigation. Rather it is the manifestation of a revolt against the roles that the British and Americans had been playing in aiding and abetting the dictatorial kingdoms and sheikdoms that subjected the populations to such brutal repression. Had Britain not supervised or done what it did during 1915-1932 and had the United States not carried on with wrongheaded British policies, then we would not see such a turmoil and its related terrorism in the Arab world or violence from the Arab people.

The greatest Muslim encounter with terrorism actually came about in the 1980s in Afghanistan, where once again the West needed Muslim hands to carry out its scheme of terrorism to accomplish its political goals. The Muslims had been used once before to bring down the Ottoman Empire; now they were needed again to deploy acts of violence and terrorism against a new target, the Communist Soviet Union.

It is important for the American public to know how the Western superpowers, including the American administrations, had been capitalising on terrorism and using Muslim manpower to carry out their schemes of subversive activities to safeguard their political and economic self-interest. If this fact of history is fully appreciated and recognised by the American people, then they will be able to comprehend how and from what source the phenomenon of terrorism arose, and how this brigade of terrorists came into being that is now so acutely threatening them. A full realisation of the facts might induce them to switch their focus from looking outward to looking inward to control the menace of terrorism and its related problems. This might throw a totally new light on the question who really is the Master Terrorist and what the disease of terrorism originates from. The tragic saga of Afghanistan is not only heartbreaking but is also a bizarre demonstration of how the Western powers used terrorism and brutal violence to achieve political victory over their archenemy.

By the late 1950s and 1960s the Soviets had begun to pose an economic threat to the West. They were using their huge resources of slave labour (made up of German prisoners from World War II and the large number of their own people who managed to offend their government) to make cheap manufactured goods, which they then sent abroad to undersell the Western countries, particularly in the developing countries. This, in essence, was Khrushchev's threat "We'll bury you." The response of the Western countries, and the U.S. in particular, was to escalate the Arms Race and the Space Race and to get the Soviets bogged down in Afghanistan–all with a view to forcing them to divert most of their industrial resources to producing arms and rockets and keep their people poor, in hopes that eventually the people would rise up and overthrow their government. It took thirty years, but in the end it worked.

Briefly recounting the part played by the Muslims in materialising the Western goals, history tells us that when the Soviet Union succeeded in putting a puppet Communist régime in Afghanistan in the mid 1970s, the Cold War between the East and West became a fumingly Hot War. However, both the United States and the Soviet Union were determined not to fight against each other openly, because they rightly feared each other's destructive powers. America needed a subordinate third party to engage with the Communists and bleed them militarily and economically to bring about their downfall. Sadly, this subordinate third party was the Muslims, and the Americans made the world's poorest country, Afghanistan, the battleground between the East and West. The tactics of this war were based on acts of violence and terrorism, which the Muslims were required to carry out to provoke the Soviets.

This is how it all happened. The Russian-backed Communists of Afghanistan toppled King Zahir Shah in the 1970s, and Noor Mohammed Taraki, a diehard Communist, formed a socialist government in Kabul under the protection of the Soviet Union. The Americans were enormously displeased, but the Muslim world was also outraged that Communists had taken over one more Muslim state. While the Muslims were fuming with anger, the Americans went to the drawing board to chalk out both a short-term and a long-range strategy to deal with the Communists. It had always been their policy somehow to erode Communism, and now they saw an opportunity to fulfil their long established policy. The timeframe was 1977-78 and President Jimmy Carter was in the Oval Office. His national security adviser was a former Harvard University Professor, Dr Zbigniew Brzezinski. Apparently, he was assigned the task of building a war plan not only to fight the puppet Communist régime in Kabul, but also to drain Soviet material and manpower resources in the long run. His mandate seems to have been to plan war in Afghanistan in such a way that America would not be seen as directly involved but American military and financial resources would be used from behind the scenes to support the war against the Communist Soviet Union.

Brzezinski was a brilliant strategist, blessed with a highly imaginative intellect. Accordingly, he, with the help of many other brilliant colleagues in the Defence and State departments along with the talent and resources of the intelligence service, devised a sophisticated war plan. His strategy was not only to end the Communist régime in Kabul but also to provoke the Soviet Union to invade Afghanistan and thus wade into a protracted war in Afghanistan. This was a twofold attack on Communism, and, as it turned out in the end, a great success. Brzezinski is said to have taken credit for luring or provoking the Communists to invade Afghanistan, which eventually became their graveyard.

The premise from which Brzezinski appears to have been working was the Brezhnev Doctrine that President Brezhnev had proclaimed in 1968. The Brezhnev Doctrine laid down as a Soviet principle of international law that the Communist Bloc had the right to intervene where internal and external forces hostile to Communism tried to turn the development of a socialist nation toward capitalism, a situation that was seen as threatening to all Communist nations. Brzezinski could see an opportunity of provoking the Soviets to act upon this doctrine by planning a guerrilla war (terrorism) against the Taraki regime in Kabul, which Moscow would view as a hostile act to turn the development of a socialist nation towards capitalism. If all worked according to plan, then the Soviets would be obligated under the Brezhnev Doctrine to invade Afghanistan. The Americans could then engage them in a protracted covert war that would drain the Soviet military and economic power.

Hence Brzezinski got down to building an Afghan force to start a war of terrorism against the Taraki régime, using subversion and violence. Many Afghans came forward to fight Communism. Hafizullah Amin led this band under American guidance and supervision. They were mostly planting bombs, blowing up communications and supply depots as well as targeting military establishments. Since it was a war of terrorism, the Taraki régime could not withstand it. Taraki was eventually toppled and killed by the commandos of Hafizullah Amin, who was then able to set up an American sponsored régime in Kabul in 1978. As Brzezinski had planned, the Soviets made the biggest political blunder in their history by invading Afghanistan in 1979 and thereby got entangled in a much larger war than they had ever imagined. The Soviets might never have thought of invading Afghanistan at all, but given the Brzezinski scenario they were almost compelled to do it. As envisaged, the Communists fell into the trap that Brzezinski had so brilliantly laid.

He in turn recognised their response as the greatest opportunity for America to drain out Communism. It would not be a small operation like the one used to oust Taraki. Although essentially this war plan would also be based on acts of violence, terrorism and subversion, it would have to be a much larger operation involving a much greater force backed by abundant military and financial resources. Brzezinski apparently received pledges of full military and financial support for his plan from the Carter administration, but what he also desperately needed was a huge force of ferocious fighters who would have a motive for fighting the Communists. Deploying American soldiers was out of the question. For one thing, the American public would not support the idea; and for another, that would have openly engaged America in a war against Russia. Hence third- party manpower had to be procured and an exciting motivation had to be given to make these warriors fight tooth and nail against the Communists. No one could fit the bill except the Muslims. If they could be aroused in the name of Islam and inspired with the spirit of *Jihad,* they would form the best fighting force that America could hope to assemble.

Thus, in the name of Islam and exploiting Islam, Brzezinski turned his eyes towards the Muslims and began luring them to come to the rescue and free their Muslim brothers of Afghanistan from the occupation of the godless Communists. Brzezinski recognised that he would also need tremendous co-operation from the Muslim states to mobilise the Muslim fighters and that inspiring the Muslims in the name of Islam and *Jihad* was the only sure way to create an intense war climate. The Muslim world in its own right was already furiously outraged by the Soviet invasion of Muslim Afghanistan and hence became a willing candidate to back Brzezinski. But while he was putting together all pieces of his war plan, as luck would have it, President Carter lost the election of 1980. This meant that Brzezinski would also lose his position, and so his plans for the Great War were in jeopardy.

However, after the transfer of power in Washington, President Reagan quickly recognised the scope and potential of Brzezinski's strategy. He designated Bill Casey, the new Director General of the Central Intelligence Agency, to take over all Brzezinski's plans and carry through his strategy along with any improvements that he might think necessary. Before leaving office, Brzezinski seems to have made some fundamental decisions for Casey. The first was to use the "Islamic Card" by giving this war an Islamic connotation and so attract Muslims from all over the world. Accordingly Brzezinski called all those warriors who came forward to fight the brave Mujahideen of Islam. Until then, the fighters against Taraki had only been called the Afghan fighters, but now the terminology changed, and Islam was brought into the picture by calling these fighters the Mujahideen. Brzezinski initiated this terminology; otherwise Muslims had not used this term for many centuries. The second thing that Brzezinski did was to revive the spirit of *Jihad* throughout the Muslim world. The concept of *Jihad* had been used and abused sporadically by various Muslim warriors locally without injunction of the *Ummah;* it is indeed open to exploitation, as we see today in the case of bin Laden, just as the fervour of other religions is open to exploitation in other cultures. But as a Muslim national endeavour of defence or liberating an Islamic state *Jihad* had been practically dormant since the days of Saladin in the twelfth century. Since then it had never been widely propagated until Brzezinski gave it currency in order to arouse Muslims right across the spectrum of the Islamic world. Thus *Jihad* revived again with American backing as Muslims began chanting its slogan throughout the Islamic world and responding to the call even from the shores of the West, and Mujahideen began pouring in from all corners of the world, including the United States, Canada, Britain and Australia. Such an overwhelming response to the call had not been seen since the days of Saladin.

The third project that Brzezinski bequeathed to Casey was to build an Islamic force of at least 35,000 Mujahideen and find a suitably prominent Muslim leader to lead this army. It goes without saying that America was to fund this war and meet all its requirement for arms and weapons.

General Zia ul Haque was ruling over Pakistan. He was already heavily under American influence, so his co-operation was swift. Casey had to work his way to muster the support of other Islamic states, but it proved not difficult to get. According to the historical accounts, he went to Saudi Arabia, where he met his counterpart, Prince Al-Faisal Turki, and solicited his support for raising the army of 35,000 Mujahideen and a prominent Saudi prince to command them. According to reports, the Saudis co-operated in every way except providing a commander from the royal house; they did not want to be seen fighting openly against the Soviet Union. However, Turki introduced Osama bin Laden to Casey as a promising young man who had some leadership qualities. We may note in passing that Turki and bin Laden had been friends, and so we may fairly assume that Turki was glad to put forward bin Laden's name. Bin Laden was aged 23 and had no military exposure or, for that matter, any leadership experience. The other person of any significance introduced to Casey was a Palestinian by the name of Abdullah Azam, who was an academic and a charismatic teacher at the Jeddah University. He had great skills in communication and a profound knowledge of Islamic history and was also a great organiser and strategic planner.

Abdullah Azam proved to be a great asset, since he successfully managed the Office for Services in Peshawar, which was technically a recruiting centre for the Mujahideen. During all this time, the drums of *Jihad* were beating in all corners of the Islamic world and Mujahideen were coming from all over the world. The greatest number came from Saudi Arabia because of the interest taken by the Saudis, but Yemen, Egypt, Morocco, Algeria and Pakistan and many other countries also filled the ranks. It is important to note that American officials were behind the campaign of drumming up the spirit of *Jihad* and mobilising the Muslim fighters in the name of Islam by calling them the Mujahideen of Islam. Today the American administration may view *Jihad* and Mujahideen with aversion and distaste but yesterday American officials were in the forefront in beating the drums for spurring or inspiring the same phenomenon throughout the Islamic world. How ironic! Anyway, Casey was able to put together all the elements of Brzezinski's plan, and so the army of the Mujahideen, some 35,000 fighters, was deployed to start the war against the Soviet Union. How this war was won is now history.

At the end of the war, the United States emerged as the chief victor, but there were other beneficiaries, too. Strangely, they were never named, because they did not want the credit, as in the case of General Zia and his fellow Pakistani generals and some Saudis, for fear of dire reprisals from the Soviets. Names of others, especially the Afghan fighters, seem to have been suppressed for fear of extending the momentum of the *Jihad* to freeing other oppressed Muslims in other situations. Thus the primary heroes, such Pakistan's General Gul Hamid, Afghani warrior Gulbaden Hikmatyar Khan and Ahmad Shah Masood and so on, were obscured and secondary or even lower-ranking warriors were artificially set up in their places. Osama bin Laden was such a secondary warrior who was made a hero of the Afghan war, although Pakistani military sources say that he was a minor player and a retired agent of the British security service who had been involved in training the Mujahideen. Those sources did not remember ever seeing bin Laden during this war.

To conclude this part of the study, we can see that the Muslim engagement in acts of violence and terrorism was never inspired or initiated by the teachings of Islam or the Quran. All the terrorism that Muslims were thus far engaged in was instigated by either the British or the Americans. The current outcry about Osama bin Laden's acts of terrorism is directed at Islam to tarnish it as a religion based on violence. The truth is that Islam played no part in creating bin Laden, nor is he its product; he was nurtured, trained and groomed entirely by the Americans. Any complaints about his conduct should be addressed to America, because the United States officials are the ones who created this menace.

As far as the overall question of terrorism is concerned, this study should have made it clear that Islam has made no contribution to spreading this menace. Properly speaking, there is no such thing as Islamic terrorism or Islamic terrorists. The British and the Americans are the ones who implicated Muslims in subversive and terrorist activities under varying pretexts to serve their own political and economic self-interest. They are the ones who ought to be blamed for developing terrorist schemes and spreading terrorism around the globe. Ironically, people like General Gul Hamid, Hikmatyar Khan and Ahmad Shah Masood were suppressed so they might not become problem for the United States in the future. Now Osama bin Laden is a case that turned sour for them. They are taking out their anger on Islam when they should be looking inward at their own mistakes and accepting moral responsibility for cultivating the seeds of terrorism among the Muslims.

These are important historical details that the American public need to take into consideration to properly assess the source and extent of terrorism. Blaming a third party simply because their own scheme of terrorism has turned against themselves will not solve the problem of terrorism. More importantly, accepting responsibility may help the American public to look inwards for solutions instead of waging wars all over the world. It may also inspire them to look deeper into the actions of their own administrations, who appear to be using the security laws to hide their wrongful, even criminal, acts.

Restiveness among the Muslims springs from unjust treatment of their issues, illegal occupation of their lands and denial of their social, economic and political rights. The Muslims are now struggling to recover their lands and regain liberty and freedom from the occupiers. The grim fact is that their struggle is branded as acts of terrorism but the perpetrators of injustice and usurpers of their rights and lands receive no condemnation at the international level. This is the real tragedy that lies behind the obvious perils of terrorism.

4

The Role of the United States in International Affairs

The people of America, having worked so hard to make their country such an outstanding success, deserve to play a leading role in international affairs. In view of their all-round progress, the rest of the world has also begun to look up to them for leadership. Sadly, performance by successive American administrations has been less than world-class. Not only have they let down the American people in many domestic matters, but their imprudent foreign policies and aggressively self-serving enterprises have also been disappointing on the international scene.

Academically speaking, American society is not easy to understand. While the Americans have many commendable qualities – they are hardworking, enterprising, innovative and show generosity in times of natural calamities, for which they deserve credit – there are also irksome traits in their attitudes towards others that generate distaste with their overall leadership at home and abroad. There are many complexities and visible tensions such as racial prejudice, economic disparity and a noticeable violent strain in their society that create stresses for the American citizenry.

Economic self-centredness can be brutal and often breeds corruption, violence and even crime. Corruption can go quite high in the social and political system. In many cases high officials, reputable professionals and businessmen and women are found involved in unethical and nefarious activities. American values, in which Americans take great pride, are also not immune from violation. Individual freedom and civil liberties can be set aside and the principles of democracy can also be flouted. Democracy itself becomes a victim when it is abused for completely opposite purposes or to accommodate the overbearing will of the rulers. Its ups and downs can be seen in how elections are contested, how votes are counted and how the power of the media is used to propagate misleading impressions only to win elections and not necessarily for the guidance of the nation. This partisan outlook may help a particular party in the short run but ignores the rightness or wrongness of issues that hurt America in the long run.

When one watches American debates or reads about their views or sees their intellectual trends, one gets a depressing feeling at seeing how narrow their perspective is or how little they know about outside facts and how preoccupied they seem to be with self-interest. They seem totally nonchalant towards the rest of the world and even towards their own underprivileged citizens. They may talk a great deal about human rights and peace and put on all the fanfare of the modern electronic media, but in substance their talk often proves to be just that, or else another means to support their own point of view or self-interest.

The Americans as a nation appear remarkably unconcerned about what goes on in the rest of the world. That is partly a carryover from the days before modern communications, when they really were isolated from most other countries. But it is largely because they are so self-sufficient, both economically and culturally, that they do not think they need to know what goes on elsewhere.

Undoubtedly, self-interest is a natural tendency, but when one claims to be a world leader, then one is obliged to strive for a wider outlook. What are the strains on the American society that make America self-serving and a hard partner in the international community? There appear to be three broad areas in the American consciousness that disturb the world equilibrium and even world peace; namely the economic self-centeredness, foreign-affiliated policies at home and abroad and the impact of the religious convictions of the domineering segment of society. Americans also appear to others as a violent nation. Their chief pro-gun activist, actor Charlton Heston, acknowledged the violent nature of his countrymen during an interview with film producer Michael Moore.

Historically, the American character took shape under the influence of European immigrants, who flocked to the New World of America in search of a better economic life. The Highland Scots and Ulster Irish, who are Protestants and regard themselves as British, settled the upland parts of the southern seaboard states in large numbers in the late 1700s. They and their descendants who migrated west formed quite a significant element in the settlers of the "Bible Belt" of the modern U.S. and are largely responsible for the Evangelical strain in the southern population. But the northern Evangelicals derive chiefly from the Puritan English colonists who settled in New England in the seventeenth century or from the large numbers of Germans who settled in Pennsylvania before the Revolution or immigrated directly to the mid-western states after independence. The Catholic Irish also came in huge numbers, but only after the Potato Famines in the 1840s. It is also plausible that the Danes or Vikings, who had settled down in the northern and eastern regions of the United Kingdom and spread their own warmongering culture in Scotland and Ireland, may have affected American culture indirectly when their descendants came to the New World.

It seems that religiously the Puritan English colonists have impacted America more than any other strain. It is therefore important to learn more about the Puritans, who they were and how they have impacted America's religious leanings. We shall make use of historical facts and the insights of Karen Armstrong, taken from her book *Holy War,* to discuss the Puritans in the next several paragraphs.

Puritans go back to the old days of crusading of the eleventh century when the Western Europeans were fortifying their Christian identity and regarded Muslims and Jews their adversaries. The crusaders were fundamentalists and struggled to establish the Kingdom of God so that they might live under the Biblical laws. After the crusading ended in about the fourteenth century the crusaders dispersed and took new identities but mostly retained their crusading spirit.

Many became secular and joined the armies of the kings to become the forces of imperialism and carried on with their crusading tradition in conquering the Third World. Others who were committed to religion became missionaries of different denominations and carried on their crusading spirit to spread their faith.

Those who held on to the pure belief that was fundamentally true to the Old Testament (Judaism) were called Puritans. This new attitude was aimed at returning to a simpler religion of direct intimacy with God without the intervention of priests or rituals. The Puritans considered themselves as the new chosen people and based their faith on the old covenants, as had the Jews. Henceforth they began identifying themselves closely with the Jews and gave their children Jewish names like Samuel, Amos, Sarah or Judith. They also believed that they were living in the Last Days and that all Jews would embrace Christianity before the Second Coming of Christ. Since the Puritans did not believe in priests as intermediaries in spiritual fulfillment, they became Nonconformists and rejected the authority of the Anglican bishops. Because of this attitude they were deemed a threat to the religious establishments, which could spread to harm the authority of the king. Their defiance became such a problem that King James I and Archbishop Laud decided to take harsh measures against them. King James resolved to persecute them severely and even expel them from the country. Hence it became dangerous to be Puritan in England. Many Puritans fled to Amsterdam and formed a tight community there living according to their own religious beliefs. Others stayed on to confront the establishment in different ways. This was the beginning of a new holy war that the crusaders were so accustomed to. They considered the state establishment as the enemy of God so they were fighting against it in the old crusaders' spirit. Later in the course of British history the warring Puritans became the army of Oliver Cromwell and turned their holy war into the Civil War.

While the majority of the Puritans remained in England to continue fighting, some decided to migrate to pursue their religious beliefs in the

New World of America. Some of those expelled by King James also joined them. Their decision to come to the United States would later overwhelm world history, as they would be able to impact Middle Eastern politics in a profound way from the echelons of American prowess as we see today. Thus, as one deliberates on the various impacts on the American society, the impact that the Puritans brought to bear upon America is the most defining one as it affects the world politics. Hence not only did the crusading spirit of the Puritans impact America, but it also saw an increasing influence of Zionism.

The Puritans first arrived in America in 1620 and called their settlement the Plymouth Plantation in New England. Historically the Puritans are from the stock of the ancient European Crusaders and took a new identity of the Pilgrim Fathers in the United States. Soon they turned to their old instincts of crusading like the chosen people, the Jews, and began establishing their colony, which they called the "English Canaan", and gave their settlements biblical names such as Hebron, Salem, Bethlehem, Zion and Judea. However, the native Indians were an obstacle in the path of their growth, and so they decided to deal with them with hostility. Their legacy of crusading and Zionism led them to ruthless methods against the Pequot Indians during the 1640s as they overpowered them and took their land in the same spirit as Joshua did in Canaan. Their conviction of living in the Last Days and deep faith in Jesus' Second Coming gave them a feeling as if they had a special reason to come to the New World. Thus they made America the new centre of Christianity that would hasten the Second Coming. This would explain why the zeal for Jesus' Second Coming is more dominant in America than in Europe. The Puritans have since taken newer shapes in America and are now the resurging from the South in the same old crusading spirit of their forefathers. This would explain why some of the modern presidents with religious inclinations such as Ronald Reagan and George W. Bush have often used the term crusading to describe their policies and actions.

The Puritans and the Jews had been deeply compatible from the beginning of Puritanism. Their affinity continued and flourished when they met in the New World. The first Jewish settlers arrived in 1654 and settled in the Dutch colonial town of New Amsterdam, but they did not enjoy full citizenship rights until the Dutch town fell to the English Puritans in 1664 and became New York. The Jews living there were given full rights of citizenship, which laid the foundation of American Jewry. The Jews fitted perfectly in the American congregational system. Hence an alliance was formed between the Christian and Jewish Zionists that would later impact Middle Eastern and world politics. Since the Puritans were moving into the New World in a crusading spirit, they spread their influence to many other parts of the country. The northern Evangelicals were derived from them, while their influence also penetrated in the south with other Evangelicals.

These influences have shaped a specific American character that has two distinct attitudes: first, a favourable one towards the Jews and second, a rather dim and hostile one towards Islam in general and Arabs in particular. As a result of the American bias in favour of the Jews, the United States continues to feel strongly about Israel and this fervour has greatly increased with the rise of a new wave of American Christian fundamentalism, which is aggressively Zionist. It is now showing its impact as a power bloc in presidential elections designed to help Jews settle in Israel and fulfill the biblical prophecy about the Second Coming and redemption of the sins of Christians. Penetration of the Christian fundamentalists in the Republican Party to pursue this goal is blatantly visible in the administration of President Bush Junior. But many years before him the Democratic President Jimmy Carter had also touched upon America's attachment to Israel, apparently for the same religious reason of fulfilling the biblical prophecy. In a speech before the Knesset in 1979, he said:

> Seven Presidents have believed and demonstrated that America's relationship with Israel is more than just a special relationship. It has been and it is a unique relationship. And it is a relationship, which is indestructible, because it is rooted in the consciousness and the morals and the religion and the belief of the American people themselves...
>
> Quoted from *Holy War* and originally taken from Sharif,
> *Non-Jewish Zionism*, p.135

As a result of such unflinching commitment to Israel by both the Christian and Jewish Zionists the United States has disqualified itself from playing an objective role in finding a just solution of the Middle Eastern disputes. This would explain why there is no progress either in the United States or at the international level toward resolving the Palestinian issues. It is not that the Palestinian issues are practically insoluble; it is the lack of will on part of the United States to be considerate to the Palestinians that has made these issues insoluble.

Puritanism, which is heavily inclined towards Judaism, and its derivatives such as the Nonconformists and Evangelicals steer America's foreign policy and reinforce its commitment to resettle the Jews to hasten Jesus' Second Coming. This zeal originates from an interpretation of the prophecy that became current after the Hebrew text of the original Bible was translated with the help of Jewish scholars after the Reformation. Although the actual text of the Bible was not altered, the surrounding interpretation was innovative. As a result of this interpretation both the Evangelical fundamentalists and the Jewish Zionists are doing everything in their power to resettle Jews in Palestine, even by displacing the Palestinians, since according to their interpretation the Second Coming cannot happen until that task is fulfilled. Consequently, there is enormous bloodshed and upheaval in the

Middle East resulting from this effort. While the legacy from Puritanism provides America the crusading spirit of the Middle Ages, Evangelicalism has penetrated into the White House to wield political power that several presidents, including the current President Bush, have been using as *resurging crusaders* against the Palestinians in particular and the Islamic world in general to make the Biblical prophecy come true. The consequences of such religious zeal have made America an ominous superpower as we see in its role in today's international affairs.

Other impacts also originated collectively from the immigrant population that prospered in America and emerged as powerful Americans. With their growing economic power and the crusading spirit of the Puritans, the new generation of Americans waged a war of independence with the same zeal as earlier puritans had done against the British Monarchy as part of Cromwel's army. The British and the loyal colonists fought back, but they could not match their opponents' determination and lost the war, leaving the New World largely in the hands of the Americans.

The violent and lawless streak that one finds in the American character has much to do with the character of society as it developed first in the colonies before independence and then on the "frontier." The original colonists on the Atlantic seaboard all established reasonably ordered, internally peaceful and effectively governed communities. But virtually from their first arrival they were at intermittent war with the Indians. They could only expand by driving them out or killing them off. As soon as they expanded into the hill country away from the coast, the settlers found themselves remote from their governments and largely left to their own devices, both for defending themselves and for settling their quarrels. This became even more true in the new states that were settled after the revolution in the lands west of the Adirondacks; until the railways began to be built in the 1840s and 50s, those areas were remote from the central government and developed rather as communities of equal, free, self-reliant farmers or craftsmen who all knew how to use weapons and resorted to them with very little provocation. They became used to righting their own wrongs, peacefully if possible but violently if necessary. Rather than appealing to some higher authority, they admired the kind of man who was most successful at handling matters in their own free and self-reliant way. The influence of the frontier Indian wars, coupled in the south with the slave-labour system, made them develop with a strong fellow-feeling towards their own kind of people (Whites) but little or no compassion or pity for others (Black, Indians, or Mexican half-breeds). These traits persist very strongly in modern White Americans, outside the educated urban classes who used mostly to run the national government.

The freebooting strain in the Americans also has to do with a persistence of the spirit of the English "sea-dogs" or buccaneers who founded some of the colonies. They, too, saw the world as open to them, through their command of the sea, to get rich on, either through trade or through plunder. The Americans are rather like the British were while the Americans were still their colonials; one might say that the Americans never really made the transition from commercial hegemony to political imperialism. Having been colonists themselves and successfully freed themselves from the rule of their mother country, they have a deep-seated conviction that actually ruling over foreign peoples is wrong; but that in no way stops them from exploiting them for their own advantage and enrichment. And since they will not take direct responsibility for ruling the people they wish to exploit, they follow the alternative method of supporting, or if necessary installing, compliant local régimes, without much concern for their character. In fairness, the liberal educated urban Americans have been troubled by this for generations. Their weakness, however, is their naïve belief that, left to themselves, other peoples would behave just the way they do themselves and hold all the same values. So, where the unscrupulous Americans are all in favour of shoring up people like Pinochet and Batista, the more idealistic ones can usually be got to support efforts to get rid of rulers like Saddam or Castro, without giving much thought to who are going to replace them or whether the new rulers will treat their subjects any better.

Bearing in mind this brief discourse of historical background will help us understand how the Second Coming of Jesus became the unifying factor of the Christian fundamentalists and the Jewish Zionists who are both now working to resettle Jews from all corners of the world in the whole of Palestine. Part of their thrust to assist the Second Coming is to transform the East by converting all infidels to Christianity, which is what the Bush coalition with other Christian leaders is currently trying to accomplish in the Middle East. This study will also show how the culture of violence and self-centredness penetrated into the American psyche and became part of the American way of life and why there is so much crudeness and arrogance in the United States.

So the American culture of cowboyism and the gun-slinging of the Wild West was born. The rule of unfettered freedom and the unbounded right to carry firearms only helped the strong to suppress the weak and exploit the vulnerable. Thus a new kind of civilisation began developing as the United States of America and emerged on the Western horizon. Suppressing the natives, breaking land treaties and disregarding agreements, mistreating the slaves and racial hatred, arrogance and injustice to fellow human beings came with the newfound wealth that the settlers had acquired in the New World and became part of the American frame of mind.

Victory in the War of Independence gave birth to a new confidence in the Americans. In addition to their newly acquired wealth, they now also began to feel the strength of their military prowess, especially after having defeated powerful imperialist Britain. So the Americans started showing their muscles to their neighbours, first towards the Canadians in the War of 1812 and then towards the Mexicans, which sparked the American-Mexican war. By this time the Americans had become powerful and decided that it was in their national interest to annex California and Texas, which were taken from Mexico by force. The philosophy of "our national interest" was thus born and the seeds of American militarism were also sown. Later they flowered to become an integral part of the American culture. Their growing wealth and expanding militarism gave rise to a new craze, as Americans were now itching to make their mark on the international scene. The First World War was their chance to enter the world arena, but they had to have a reason or cause to enter the war. The opportunity came with the sinking of American ships by the Germans because they were carrying food and goods to Britain. Once President Wilson Woodrow decided to enter the war, he also played up an earlier incident of 1915 in which the British liner *Lusitania* was sunk off Ireland by a German submarine, killing 1198 passengers, including many Americans. Loss of American ships and lives gave the United States a reason to join the war and deploy their wealth and military prowess as a show of their strength. In fact the technique of using loss of American ships and lives as a pretext for war is even older than the incident of the *Lusitania* tragedy. The United States' excuse for declaring war on Spain in 1898 was that the U.S. battleship *Maine* was blown up in Havana harbour (while Cuba was still a Spanish colony) under what remain very mysterious circumstances. Thus American administrations discovered a long time ago that tragedies can be used to manipulate public opinion to serve political ends. Victory in the First World War boosted American morale as a powerful nation and also earned them the appreciation of the Europeans, who were happy to have found a rich and powerful ally who could come to their aid in difficult times. Thus realising the military prowess and importance of their role in the international conflicts, the Americans began building even more military capability, for which they had all the resources.

By the time the Second World War came, the Americans were much stronger economically and militarily. But, again there was resistance at home against war as the America First Committee opposed U.S. participation in the European war. The attack on Pearl Harbor, however it happened, was seen as an opportune incident that cleared the way for the United States to join the war. This was a prolonged and colossal war in which the U.S. played a major part. Consequently, the victory brought major credit to the U.S. in international standing. So America emerged from the ruins of the Second World War as a new leader of the world.

While American participation in the Second World War helped to achieve victory, it also created a certain amount of resentment among the British and French, who disliked having to rely on the Americans and, when push came to shove, take orders from them. After the war the Americans basically used their predominance in the alliance to undermine the standing of both Britain and France as great powers, notably at the time of the Suez crisis. Many people of British stock feel even today that they sacrificed their blood, treasure, and power to free the world from fascism and then got shafted by their allies.

As a result of American predominance, the rest of the world may also feel resentment of another kind because it is now under the wings of a world leader that not only lacks maturity and wisdom in human affairs, but also is intensely biased to the detriment of the Muslims. The fact that self-interest, unilateralism and militarism overwhelm its culture is another irksome characteristic.

The history of the United States dates back only a few centuries, and it has yet to go through the same process of evolution as other civilisations and world powers have. Its psychological makeup is derived from its cultural history as it strives to impose domination, exploitation and usurpation of the rights of the weak and vulnerable. Its techniques have changed in that it does not colonise in the territorial sense, but it makes its clients its economic vassals and controls them with economic leverage. Its methods of domination and exploitation have also been modernised, in that they are now carried out in the name of "our vital interests", as if it is their right to encroach upon other peoples' rights and violate their sovereignty to achieve these so-called vital interests. America's fulfilment of these vital interests is, in effect, the same as the plundering that European imperialists had practised in the past. The mentality of the Wild West, the gun-culture and disregard for other peoples' rights has become the usual American way of dealing with the rest of the world. Thus our world is still ruled by the customs and practices of the European Dark Ages in uniquely modern dress. There is no sign of improvement, owing to the unilateralism and militarism that Americans now persistently deploy to dominate the world scene.

A history of a few hundred years is simply not enough credentials for assuming world leadership. This is not sufficient time for America to have erased the memories of the baggage of the Dark Ages that the European immigrants brought with them. Neither it is enough time to come out of the "frontier" mentality that Americans had grown accustomed to while fighting against the Indians. Its leaders had not had time to refine their policies sufficiently to lead human society without trampling over other nations. They lack comprehension of what is fair and just and appear to have no intention of respecting the sovereignty, rights or aspirations of other nations. All that seems to matter to America is its economic superiority and military domination. There is no room for truly compassionate wisdom and humanity, but there is plenty of room in their culture for greed and weapons to perpetuate economic and military superiority. Living in a moral and spiritual vacuum the Americans appear unable to grasp that there are loftier ideals than their narrow materialistic goals, and other ways to be magnanimous and great than just throwing around the weight of dollars and mighty guns. It is deplorable that, after spending so much aid money and spreading charity, the Americans are not spoken well of, but rather even hated, in almost all parts of the world, including many parts of Europe. But this state of affairs is all too natural, because nobody likes to remember that he is in somebody else's debt.

Arrogance and persistent mistreatment of fellow human beings, dating back to slavery and segregation times, demonstrate double standards in the American frame of mind. It has evidently not yet rid itself of racial bigotry, since many of its political leaders still harbour hatred of their fellow human beings. The recent Trent Lott fiasco is a living proof of how the yearning for segregation persists in some political leaders. Lott, a leader in American politics, lamented that his favourite racist candidate could not become president of the United States in 1948, and that all the problems that America has faced since would not then have happened. When defeat of segregation is still lamented and racial bigotry lives on in political and lawmaking circles, how can America claim to be the leader of all the world's people? Granted, Lott lost his position, but his statement showed that the flame of racial hatred has not entirely died in American political circles.

Under half a century or so of predominant American influence our world has suffered injustice and disregard for the rights of nations and individuals in spite of claims to human rights and freedom and independence in the Third World. Much of it has been inflicted with American knowledge and some with American acquiescence. It is truly a misfortune of our world that such an immature nation, which indeed remains more of a melting pot than a nation, has taken over the reins of global leadership. Hitler and Nazi Germany may be blamed for provoking the Second World War, which left France, Germany and Italy incapable of sustaining global responsibility as well as opening the door for the American world domination. Once the war was over, the government of the United States followed policies in conjunction with the New York bankers that deliberately manipulated world finances to deplete the value of the pound sterling in order to impoverish Britain and make it get out of Palestine and India. Economically, Britain was so badly devastated that it could no longer sustain its rule over both Palestine and India and had to get out hurriedly under American political and economic pressure. Consequently, these territories were relinquished rather haphazardly, resulting in chaotic bloodshed and unfair disposal. Europe may be blamed, however, for not bouncing back in recent times to assume a potent share in global responsibility that would have tamed the Wild West and restored a balanced order on the world scene.

Europeans are relatively more mature, as they have gone through many stages of evolution. They have fought many wars within their own continent during the course of their evolution as nations. They have seen the ugly face of wars when tens of millions of their innocent citizens were brutally killed and their economies and territories were devastated. In particular, the colossal damage to humanity and property during the last two world wars has made them realise the futility of wars. After the Second World War, the Europeans changed their stance to defence only and began chanting the songs of peace and non-violence. They now look for peaceful resolutions of contentious problems instead of jumping into wars. In contrast to Europe, the United States has not truly encountered the ugly face of war, since it has never lost tens of millions of its innocent citizens or seen the colossal damage to economy or country that Europe has faced many times. This may explain why the United States does not really understand the cost of war and prefers wars to peaceful resolution of conflicts.

The Iraq war is a good illustration of the difference of mentality between Europe and the United States. There is a great deal of misconception in America about the role that Europe played in the war in Iraq. Americans are upset that Europe, especially France and Germany, did not stand by them in this war. Some Americans have been ungenerous in criticism and accused Europe of betraying America in its moment of crisis. There was no shortage of words to remind Europe how America had come to its aid during the two world wars and played a leading role in saving it from fascism, Nazism and destruction. Americans were expecting a payback, and when that did not happen, their reaction turned peevish and even uncouth. Most Americans were unable to understand why France and Germany did not support them when Great Britain and Spain were on their side. What was missing is that only the prime ministers of Britain and Spain supported the war but the populations of both countries remained intensely opposed to war. The Spanish voters showed their displeasure against their prime minister in the elections and the British voters are now waiting for their chance to express their opinions.

The point that the Americans were missing is that France and Germany could not regard this war as a defensive measure when the evidence for Iraq's alleged weapons of mass destruction failed to measure up and hence in their view Iraq posed no immediate threat to either Europe or the United States. President Bush's war rhetoric was unconvincing and made him look like a resurging crusader who was determined to wage war on Islamic civilisation and thereby revive an era that Europe had forsaken long ago. Europe is now much more realistic and fully understands the cost of wars in terms of human lives and damage to countries and prefers peaceful means for settling international issues. Europe has also come to realise that clashing with another civilisation is of no avail, since it would neither produce any transformation of culture nor lead to peace. The Europeans had dispensed with the notion of crusading to transform Islamic civilisation centuries ago, but the rising war cries from the Bush administration against Islamic civilisation make it seem as if the descendants of the crusaders are now resurging from the American horizon and rekindling the old flame of religious hatred. Europe has passed beyond this phase of history and put the hateful notions of crusading against a religious civilisation behind; it is now looking for a new world where all civilisations can live side by side in harmony and peaceful co-existence. This is the new philosophy of Europe and slowly and steadily it is inching towards this goal.

It is not disloyalty to America or a rift within the Western world that separated Europe; rather it is the rejection of the crusading war that President Bush is waging. Europe is confident that as soon as America acquires enough maturity to abandon the path of war and embrace the European philosophy of co-existence with other civilisations in a new world of peace and harmony, the gap will be bridged again. In contrast to the American view, the European outlook on the world community is much healthier than it ever has been before.

Rising American militarism is a threat to human civilisation because the Americans use military force to settle international disputes instead of taking a judicious and compassionate approach in a peaceful and civilised manner. They have now invented deadly war machinery that could kill humanity on a massive scale. They have no qualms about dropping cluster and other types of bombs to kill innocent human beings, because they think they can excuse their conduct by describing the loss of lives as "collateral damage" as if human beings were lifeless entities. They have demonstrated their deadly skills to impress others with how brutally they could crush humanity to perpetuate their superiority. It was America that dropped atomic bombs on Japanese civilians and napalm bombs and poisonous gas in Vietnam to maim and kill humanity at random and buried Iraqi soldiers alive, besides killing a retreating army and taking countless innocent lives in bombarding civilian targets. Besides furthering their political and economic self-interest, the Americans have now invaded Iraq to alter its Islamic culture and civilisation and to redraw the regional map. They talk about the graves that Saddam Hussein had dug, but they seem unconcerned about the fresh graves that American soldiers are digging in Iraq as a result of their invasion. There appears to be no remorse for the toll their military action is taking on the lives of the Iraqi civilians.

They call all this a duty to peace and freedom. They are building the morale of their soldiers, and propping up their chivalry, by describing their expedition as a mission to free the people of Iraq from dictatorship. An air of bravery and valour is thus attached to the war against Iraq. But in truth there is no bravery or valour in attacking a crippled nation that had been

losing tens of thousands of its children every year to malnutrition and
sickness, whose population is grossly impoverished and whose army had
been stripped of all effective weaponry with which to defend itself.

There may be other historical trends to explain the nature or character
of the American national inclinations. However, what is more troubling is
that there are no signs in American society of any effective tendencies to
curb or reduce the practice of these pernicious traits. Instead of dissuading
the population, the American leadership, particularly the policymakers,
seem to be making sure that self-interest and overbearing power (sometimes violent power) become the hallmarks of the nation rather than
incidental economic and political needs. As history tells us, a prominent
American official, George Kennan, who was head of the State Department
policy-planning staff, laid down a most far-reaching and explicitly defined
self-centred policy after the Second World War in 1945 that has since
become the cornerstone of American goals. He defined American foreign
policy and said:

> …"We need not deceive ourselves that we can afford today the luxury of
> altruism and world-benefaction…We should cease to talk about vague
> and…unreal objectives such as human rights, the raising of the living
> standards, and democratisation. The day is not far off when we are going
> to have to deal in straight power concepts. The less then we are
> hampered by idealistic slogans, the better." Kennan went on to explain
> "that one of the main concerns of the U.S. policy is the "protection of
> our raw material'". "Who must we protect our raw material from?"

Already it is becoming clear that America is meticulously adhering to the
Kennan doctrine and dealing with the rest of the world in straight power
concepts. American slogans about human rights or raising living standards
or the democratisation of other countries are increasingly becoming exposed as ploys for protecting sources of raw materials. America's current
involvements in international situations demonstrate that Kennan's doctrine of power concepts and protection of "our raw materials" remains a
rigorous American policy objective, whatever other factors and considerations may also have come into play to augment it.

Many Americans frown when their foreign policy is criticised and assert
their right to follow whatever policy they may choose. That might be true if
America were not a world leader, but when it asserts itself in the name of
the international community, then it loses its privilege as a private country.
Its policies and actions are no longer its own private business; rather they
are also the concerns of the rest of the world that it claims to lead. As
satellites of the leader, the rest of the world has a right to question him,
because he asserts that he is their leader, too. One cannot be a world leader

and then choose to ignore world opinion. It is necessary to emphasise this point because many Americans reject outside criticism of their policies and insist on following a unilateral track instead of working within the international framework.

Having stated this perhaps painful truth, we may proceed to examine American foreign policy in greater depth. While the international community may tolerate, though not condone, the economic exploitation of others and grabbing of raw materials, it cannot ignore or condone the political ramifications of American foreign policy, because they affect the lives and livelihoods of others throughout the world. Therefore it is appropriate to question the wisdom or the basis upon which America has built a foreign policy that so adversely affects some members of the international community. As a world leader, America cannot avoid this scrutiny; and even if it wishes to, the scrutiny is already going on.

The fact of imbalance in American foreign policy is not under debate, since outside America it is universally acknowledged. What is in question is how this profound imbalance has come about and who formulates this unbalanced policy. Looking at Kennan's doctrine, his motivation was mainly based on economic exploitation, for which he was prepared to use force and set aside being altruistic and trample over human rights and other idealistic considerations. But the current trends show that Americans have since embraced even more damaging ambitions in their foreign policy, which are profoundly affecting the lives of so many millions of people in the smaller and weaker countries that have accepted satellitehood under American world leadership.

When we cast our probing eyes over the foreign policy, we see a certain pattern as well as certain faces that are at the centre of the policymaking machinery and are easily recognisable by the public. These include Dr Henry Kissinger and Dr Zbigniew Brzezinski, a former Harvard University professor. More recently the assertive Paul Wolfowitz of the Defence Department and his colleague Richard Perle, a former head of the Defence Board, who was dubbed by some Americans the Prince of Darkness, have also been making important contributions in framing overall American policies. On the intellectual front academics like the Harvard University Professor Samuel Huntington are said to provide the academic cushion to the foreign policy, working in conjunction with the main proponents. For example, the article "Clash of Civilisations" was a disappointing essay in which an eminent professor of Harvard University spent energy on harping on clashes, when he could have spent the same effort to better effect by suggesting ways to eliminate or reduce the clashes. In retrospect it seems like a harbinger of what was coming within the next couple of years, as if the ground were being prepared for the American public to accept the clash when it would occur. There are, of course, other personalities in the

government machinery from similar and other backgrounds that also help
in propelling the policy. The media, both electronic and print, also provide
support, but the striking thing is that many media pundits and owners also
come from the same or similar backgrounds to some of the main formula-
tors of the policy. Hollywood does not want to be left behind either, as many
film directors and producers pick up the theme of the policymakers and
help in its propagation by producing films that are visibly biased.

When we scrutinise these and other policymakers in order to grasp what
impels them to devise the kind of policies they produce, we see their minds
are tilted in only one direction, contrary to America's role as world leader,
which ends up in producing an extremely flawed product. When we further
look into the policymakers' backgrounds in an attempt to understand how
their mind works, we see many of them have foreign affiliations and
commitment to one particular foreign country, which might help to explain why they fashion a slanted policy. As was explained earlier, the
Christian fundamentalist derivatives of Puritanism augment the efforts of
the foreign-affiliated policymakers to realise their own religious convictions. Hence there is a twofold pressure on policymaking that creates the
tilt. When we see the policymaking from this perspective, it becomes clear
why the resulting policy is so imbalanced. One would have thought that a
world leader would have a multi-faceted world policy commensurate with
its obligations to all members of the international community, but this is
not so.

Given that so many key proponents in the U.S. policymaking cell have a
Jewish background, it becomes valid to ask whether American policy is
being diverted to serve Israeli interests. Admittedly, it is natural for the
American Jews to help Israel in every way, but America is not a leader only
for the Jews or Israel. It claims to be a world leader, so its policies should not
be directed to serve only one particular interest; they have to be balanced
to serve the interests of all countries of the world. Since this is clearly not
the case now, the question arises whether a certain group within the
American policymaking machinery is manipulating it to create this imbalance. If so, then the foreign-affiliated policymakers would be in a clear
conflict of interest that could lead them to abuse their positions in the
government to advance their own causes. In the interest of probity, such
suspect policymakers should be made to withdraw from the foreign-policy-
making cell for the sake of restoring balance in American policies. Otherwise, America's own policymakers will seem to have hijacked American
economic and military power to serve their foreign-affiliated interests.

All recent American administrations have had a singular outside input
from one particular predominant community, which is counterproductive
to America's role in international affairs as a world leader. If the United
States wishes to play a congenial and compatible role in international

affairs, then it needs to enlarge its panel of advisers, so it has the benefit of advice from experts with background in all parts of the world. The status quo obviously does not help to make the United States a congenial and harmonious world leader.

Principally, these may be taken as America's internal problems, but the outside world also has interest in this matter, because it affects the world scene, particularly the well-being of communities and nations in other parts of the world. It is time for Americans to realise that Israel is not the only other country in the world and Jews are not the only people that need their support and protection. Others, too, need protection and fulfilment of their religious and cultural aspirations and are looking for world-class leadership. It is unacceptable for the world leader to have ties with only one country at the cost and detriment of others. If America chooses to continue to adhere to a one-sided policy, then it will not be respected as a world leader, but only as an American or pro-Israeli leader.

Accusations of unhealthy or undue Jewish influence over America or abuse of American power by the Israeli lobby are not new. America's high priest and social leader, Dr Billy Graham, was also at one time deeply perturbed by this problem: so much so that he took it up with President Nixon, because he feared that it might harm the country in the long run. Normally, this kind of conversation is highly confidential and private, but Nixon had it recorded on his infamous tapes, which were subsequently released to the public. That is how Billy Graham's concerns about excessive Jewish influence became public knowledge. Nixon was clearly taken aback and said in somewhat exasperated tone something like "Oh boy, I can't say that, though I believe it." Anyhow, he declined to do anything about Dr. Billy Graham's concerns. Nixon's response is a typical example of how American politicians fight shy of confronting the problem of abuse of American power for furthering the cause of Israel or the pervasive influence of the Jewish community over American society, for fear of being branded anti-Semitic. America has been sweeping this problem under the carpet for too long, but it cannot be swept there any more, since it has now grown into a wider problem creating conflict of interest on the international scene.

The unwillingness of American politicians to face this problem can be explained by their self-interest in power and position. They may see confrontation with a powerful lobby and its many sympathizers as threatening their positions. Hence they shun any suggestion, however appropriate, for rectifying this situation, since they sense that it would alienate the majority of Americans, who have a strong sympathy for the Jews because of their terrible sufferings in the Second World War. American politicians also realise that any adverse comment or action may stir up the forces of the media or the powers of the financial tycoons and the ferocity of the propaganda brigade against them to undermine their political careers. Nixon's evasive remarks showed how he was unwilling to deal with a situation that has increasingly become a problem not only for America but also for millions of other citizens who live under the umbrella of American world leadership.

Thus we can see that framing of a judicious and equitable American foreign policy has been a difficult task. That is a serious concern from the national and international standpoint that needs serious consideration to restore balance in America's foreign policy, so that American leadership may become equitable and compatible with the country's international role and world leadership.

A policy does not become imbalanced or obnoxious by itself; someone has to fashion it in that way. Who does so, and why? This is food for thought for the American people. As for the rest of the international community, they find it essential for the Americans to take internal measures to rectify this imbalance, so that their role in international affairs may become congenial. The current situation fills many parts of the world with confusion, discontentment and disappointment and creates a depressive feeling that the leader of our world has proven to be of a much lower calibre than we deserve.

5

President Bush –
Where is he Coming From?

Where President George W. Bush is coming from? What are his ambitions? What is his calibre and background to lead America and then, by virtue of the American power, become the world leader? These questions need to be answered, so that a clear picture may emerge of the characteristics and aims and ambitions of the current world leader.

The personality of President Bush is intriguing, since he appears to hold back something about himself and his political ambitions. We cannot recall any significant statement of mission that he made while electioneering in 2000 except a resolve to end the rule of the Democratic Party. He did not spell out what his personal ambitions or long-term political objectives were or what his presidency would be all about. Intellectually, he has been found lacking in astuteness and even in knowledge and information, which becomes painfully obvious from time to time in his speeches. Even though the White House professionals control the damage, the unease about President Bush's calibre and ambitions lingers on. He does, however, demonstrate a strong religious conviction and often refers to God and "calls", as if he is in communication with the Almighty and pursuing presidential policies according to His calls.

What was it that he wanted to accomplish from his presidency? Is it political ambition in the normal sense of the word, or are there some deeper religious goals that he may be trying to achieve from the echelons of American power?

Looking back, we learn that as governor of Texas, when he first decided to seek nomination for the presidency, he called his friends from the religious community, the preachers and pastors and so on, and told them that he has been called to seek a higher office. It strikes one as a rather strange reason to become president of the United States, and what is even more surprising is that he claimed to have called on the religious community for advice and support in a political venture instead of turning to the usual political pundits for consultation. Deciding to seek an enormously powerful office on the notion of a "call" was not only extraordinary but also a foreboding step. Who called him; was it God? If it were God's call, then one might ask: Is President George W. Bush working on the notion of calls that he might be receiving or presume to be receiving from God from time to time? Hence the premise of his governance or the policies that he follows as President of the United States may be deeply rooted in his own religious beliefs. If so, then logic or rationale may have little or no part to play in his government policies, because religion and logic, unless carefully balanced, can clash with each other and render the believer irrational. Many critics have already discovered that President Bush is less than an astute leader, and if he is under the influence of irrational religious notions, then he could prove to be a big liability internationally and an extremely worrisome world leader.

Having taken office, he at once faced a tense international climate owing to the violent activities of some Muslim radicals. The Evangelicals had long considered Muslims as the evil people and Islam as a wicked religion. Some of his Evangelical supporters who came to his presidential inauguration even said so openly, but political expediency led President Bush to downplay their comments by saying that those were not his beliefs. Anyhow, combating terrorism gave him opportunity to deal with the evil people in the name of war on terrorism and also perhaps opened a door for realising overall Evangelical policy against Islam. Given the roots of President Bush's churchly support, it seems conceivable that the Evangelical agenda might be his secret passion, too, which he is not able to pronounce openly owing to political considerations, but for all practical purposes he is pursuing it as the mainstay of his presidency. The fact that he has surrounded his office with numerous conservative and fundamentalist Evangelical Christian advisers gives the impression that he is taking their advice in developing and pursuing fundamentalist policies of Evangelicalism. Dr Condoleezza Rice is an influential and notable adviser, but she is also the daughter of a Methodist preacher who seems to have had quite an influence over President Bush in his religious life. The daughter may share her father's views, which would explain why she is such a close adviser and deals with the president as if she were a member of the family. It has been said that she visits him on his ranch and mingles with his family in a way that is quite unusual for a member of the presidential staff. One could infer from these conspicuous surroundings and the influence of Evangelicals that President George W. Bush might be striving for some far-reaching goals of the Evangelical movement through his presidency. Annihilating the evil people and eradicating the wicked religion could well be part of his overall covert strategy. Or again, the main ideas and policies of the Bush administration may come from strong men like Dick Cheney and Donald Rumsfeld as well as from the devout Evangelicals, and President Bush may be their "front man" for selling those policies to the electorate.

As it happens, Bush's main preoccupation as president has been the gruelling task of combating terrorism. Terrorism is indeed a serious matter, for it profoundly affects the American way of life; but without being callous or ignoring the pain and grief that 9/11 has caused to so many American families, we need to face the serious possibility that this tragic event is now being exploited by the fundamentalists, or by those within the administration who wish to appeal to fundamentalist voters for their own purposes. Therefore, while recognising that it is essential to combat terrorism, we must remain vigilant to be certain that President Bush is not in any way, knowingly or unknowingly, serving the ends of the hawks or the militant Evangelicals or making their goals his own undeclared objectives in the wake of his war on terrorism. It is necessary to keep this possibility in focus, given his particular church background and the influence that hardliners and Evangelicals seem to have over him. His one-track policy of belligerency against the Islamic world in the name of war on terrorism is, accordingly, alarming.

Keeping President Bush's policies and actions in focus can be a difficult undertaking, since he does not exactly open up to give the American people a real sense of the purpose of his presidency. He does not pay as much attention to social and economic matters or the health care and other issues that directly affect the lives of the American people. One could argue that he inherited a nasty problem of terrorism, so he is entirely preoccupied fighting it. However, his war on terrorism has now become questionable in the light of the Presidential Daily Briefing of August 6, 2001. Anyway, his single-track posture on terrorism may be one explanation for not attending duly to other important areas, but it cannot be the full explanation of his policies. Could terrorism be a pretext or platform that he is using to pursue priorities dictated by his religious affiliations? This might explain why his policies are so single-track.

Even after giving President Bush the benefit of the doubt, his single-track policies still do not clarify what he is really striving to achieve. As far as combating terrorism is concerned, there are right ways and wrong to tackle it, depending upon whether one really wants to bring an end to this menace or just play around it for other covert purposes. What is obvious so far is that the actions taken by the Bush administration have not truly helped to curb terrorism. There may be some temporary lull, but the danger is constantly looming. While some places may have become secure, there are other places that are not. His approach has actually escalated the fear and intensity of terrorism, which is growing day by day, and this misplaced strategy raises alarm that perhaps something else is in the works in the wake of the war on terrorism. While it is important to destroy the operating cells or bases of the terrorists, the right way would have been also to pay attention to the causes that generate or fuel terrorism. Confining the action to beating up the evil people or trying to transform Islamic religious and cultural traditions through military power lends credence to the thesis that President Bush may be using terrorism as a pretext to enforce overall Evangelical objectives of transforming the wicked religion and converting the evil people. His policy of lashing out at the Islamic world fits more closely with the Evangelical agenda rather than with curing the disease of terrorism.

Today, we are in a better position to trace the intricacies of President Bush's policies than we were two or three years ago. The hysteria, fear-mongering and propaganda that gripped the entire world after 9/11 significantly impaired Americans' ability to evaluate this situation properly and rationally. However, hysteria has now subsided somewhat and people are in a better position to assess the war on terrorism, especially as the facts are slowly emerging through many sources, including the witnesses.

Briefly, recapitulating what has recently transpired, we learn that combating terrorism was also a hot issue in the Clinton administration. However, in spite of limited action such as bombing the Al-Qaeda in Afghanistan, President Clinton neither took any decisive military action, nor did he address the true causes of terrorism, which are the grievances of the Muslim world. He did try to settle the Palestinian problem, but he failed to exert enough pressure on the Israelis or give the Palestinians substantive incentives to make the sacrifices required for a compromise. President Clinton was also handicapped during the last leg of his presidency by the sex scandal and looming threat of impeachment. Therefore, much could not be expected of him, though he may have had plans and wished to attack the terrorists. The embarrassment of hitting a pharmaceutical plant in Sudan was bad enough public relations for a hamstrung president, who could not afford to misfire again or create further embarrassment for his government.

In any case, his unfulfilled plans were handed over to the incoming administration of President Bush. This is where the complications started. Was President Bush truly interested in tackling terrorism or was he using the situation for realising his undeclared objectives? Could it be that he has a map of the future in his mind and tends to make his *ad hoc* decisions accordingly? If he were determined to tackle terrorism, then there was enough on the table for him to make a strong move. For example, the incident of the *USS Cole* happened in 2000, and yet the Clinton administration had taken no action, in spite of verification by the intelligence services that it was an Al-Qaeda operation. This was a readymade opportunity for President Bush to spring into action. Had he done so and also gone after bin Laden in a determined way in the spring or summer of 2001, then the chances of 9/11 happening would have been greatly reduced, if not altogether eliminated. Al-Qaeda would then have been seriously crippled from undertaking any further major operation.

But Bush's lack of response to the *USS Cole* incident, when coupled with lax security measures, gave wrong signals to the terrorists. Not only was there enough on the table already for President Bush to come into action, but the intelligence community was also raising red flags that something ominous (big) was in the air that needed the president's attention. The infamous PDB is now lending further credence to suspicion that perhaps President Bush was waiting for a huge tragedy to happen, so that he could then take a mighty action to realise his undeclared goals. Even though he was warned about the possibility of hijacking U.S. planes, he did not consider it threatening enough to warrant an alert for the aviation authorities or mobilise the security service to launch special surveillance of Arabs moving around the country in groups. From his nonchalant response to this PDB, one is driven to conclude that perhaps it was considered more beneficial, for the sake of a wider war against Islamic civilisation, to let the attack happen instead of stopping it. Richard Clarke, a former head of counter-terrorism, also gave sworn testimony to the effect that the Bush administration did not seem concerned enough to take any precipitate action or pay timely attention to the Al-Qaeda threats.

Could the reason for this non-combative posture or lack of a sense of urgency have been intentional rather than incidental? Are we seeing a re-enactment of the Pearl Harbor scenario? Is it plausible that President Bush is taking such a stance on his own, or someone puppeting him? These are hard questions and need serious answers, because so much is at stake, not only for the Americans but also for the rest of the world.

It is now crucial for President Bush to come clean and testify publicly under oath to clarify why he did not act in a timely fashion and what he was doing during the first eight months of his presidency and where his attention was focused during that period. He should also be asked to explain why he diverted resources to attack Iraq when Saddam Hussein was not an imminent danger or threat to the United States compared to Osama bin Laden. His daily diaries or briefings could throw light on his schedule and priorities and explain why no active attention was paid to bin Laden's threats in the spring or summer and particularly between August 6 and September 11. A full clarification of President Bush's focus of attention during the first eight months of his presidency is critical to understanding why 9/11 was not thwarted. Testimony by a president under oath is not new or contrary to presidential privilege; President Bill Clinton was called to testify under oath on a much less serious matter and he agreed to comply. There is no reason why President Bush cannot do the same, especially when the issue is enormously serious and involves the loss of some three thousand American lives. As that of a religious man, his testimony under oath would be particularly meaningful.

There is no wisdom in avoiding public testimony on grounds of presidential privilege, even though it might supposedly compromise his executive prerogative. The issue at hand clearly outweighs the presidential prerogative. Otherwise, suspicion will continue to grow in an even more damaging way that perhaps he did have a plan to use the impending tragedy for the purpose of a larger war against Islam. From studying the eras of Presidents Reagan and Bush Senior, it is clear that the Pentagon officials had long been prompted to initiate war against Islam. Could it be that President Bush Junior combined his own idea with the Pentagon officials' vision of war and was holding back his action for an opportune time to start a war that would go beyond Al-Qaeda and further than Afghanistan?

From President Bush's actions one gets the impression that his long-term foreign policy is not at all well thought out. This reinforces the belief that he might be acting as someone's front man. For example, Rumsfeld could be the one who pushed the president to war on Iraq, since he clearly espouses an extremely interventionist foreign policy. Business associates (Halliburton) from Bush's days in the oil business could be another influence pressing the president towards war, since they would presumably welcome a chance to get control of the Iraqi oil fields. Lastly, President Bush may also be influenced by his co-religionists, accepting the interpretation of Biblical prophecies that is current in the U.S. Evangelical circles and thinking it gives him a kind of rough map of what is going to happen, and then tend to make his decisions accordingly; or else his chief advisors may know the prophecies and the accepted interpretation and use the knowledge to get President Bush to do what they want. These factors may explain why President Bush's actions are so scattered and why he jumps from one situation to another without properly dealing with the first one. As far as his own intellectual calibre is concerned, he had been found lacking in astuteness, which explains why his policies are not logical or rational.

What is puzzling is that President Bush was not lacking energy or enthusiasm for military action; only his focus was premature and in the wrong quarter. A former Secretary of the Treasury, Paul O'Neill, noted that right away from January 2001, President Bush was talking and targeting Iraq for war. As is now transpiring from various intelligence reports, there were no credibly urgent threats from Iraq, whereas there were real threats from Al-Qaeda. Retaliation on account of the *USS Cole* was also pending and required urgent attention. It is therefore puzzling why President Bush would concentrate on a less threatening Iraq compared to the more threatening and pressing menace of Al-Qaeda. Shifting focus from Al-Qaeda seemed absurd unless there was a hidden agenda.

President Bush's preparation of war against Iraq as early as January 2001 actually gives out the secret of his undeclared objectives of waging war against the Islamic world starting with the transformation of Iraq. Rationally speaking, he ought to have listened to the advice of his security specialists and attended to Al-Qaeda first and maybe then address the problem of Iraq. But the problem with President Bush seems to be that he was not working on a rational basis; rather he was under many pressures, as out-lined above, including the pressure of the "call", which seems to have precluded rational thinking from his thought process. Thus, it could not have been the strategic rationale, but religious emotions and other strains that distracted him from a real problem towards an imaginary or secondary problem. As it happened, choosing Iraq for attack in fact spilled the beans of his secret strains. In the end there were no weapons of mass destruction and the president failed to demonstrate how Saddam Hussein constituted a threat to the United States. Without a justifiable cause, one has to ask what was the point in attacking Iraq?

When pressed hard to explain why he did not focus on Al-Qaeda right from the start in January 2001, President Bush explains that he had no specific intelligence reports about any imminent attack on the US soil to warrant specific action. Hence no alarms were sounded to alert the airport security and other security branches. His response has since become con-troversial in view of the PDB. It is a bizarre logic to say that he would act immediately if he knew about specific attacks but otherwise would not even consider taking precautionary measures.

With regard to Iraq, President Bush has also been quoted as saying that he has done nothing different from what President Clinton had intended doing. What he has not told the American people is that President Clinton rejected launching a military assault against Iraq because he had no valid pretext to do so. What held Clinton back from attacking was lack of credible grounds. He knew that the American public would not support military action without a compelling reason, which he did not have. As we saw earlier, Clinton was also preoccupied with a sex scandal and already embarrassed by having attacked what turned out to be a pharmaceutical firm in Sudan; he did not want to open another front against himself without a credible reason. When President Bush came to office, he seems to have had different reasons to attack Iraq, but he, too, had no credible grounds for initiating the attack. He inherited this dilemma of the missing pretext from Clinton. Nevertheless, he seems to have been under so many pressures, as mentioned above, that he decided to act regardless of any reason, and thus consumed or diverted American resources from the real enemy by inopportunely concentrating on Iraq. His officials were also pushing him to attack Iraq, in keeping with their own plans for a wider war against Islam carried over from the Reagan era. Producing false or at least misleading information about Iraq's WMD may have been their part in pushing the president to go after the Islamic countries one by one. Mean-while, the nineteen hijackers under mysterious guidance found the United States an open field and inflicted the tragedy of 9/11. The so-called foot soldiers, a dozen or so, entered the U.S. from various points at the very last stage. Had proper vigilance been put in place at the airports in response to the PDB of August 6, they might have been detained and the plot of 9/11 uncovered.

Whether opening this window of opportunity for the hijackers was incidental or intentional is a disturbing question that needs thorough probing on its own. Could it be that President Bush knew what was coming and purposely did not attend to it so that the disaster would give him a much larger and global pretext to realise the Evangelical plot against Islam? This is another disturbing question that the 9/11 Commission needs to investigate. It is not enough to say that the available information was incomplete or vague. It was the president's responsibility and Condoleezza Rice's duty to go back to the intelligence sources and demand elucidation of their warnings to form a better idea for what was going on. To date there is no information on whether the White House made any attempts to obtain such clarification or further explanation of the points raised in the PDB of August 6, 2001.

Even after 9/11 had happened and the United States had destroyed the backbone of bin Laden's organisation in Afghanistan, President Bush still did not give undivided attention to uprooting Al-Qaeda completely to bring a sense of security to America as well as to the rest of the world. As of this writing, bin Laden has not been captured and Al-Qaeda appears to be alive and well, as can be seen from the tragedy in Spain in March 2004. But those facts merely supplied the Bush administration with more reasons for perpetuating its actions against the Islamic world in the name of the war against terrorism. Opening a second front in Iraq without first properly securing the Al-Qaeda front is another example of irrational actions by President Bush.

When opening his war front against Iraq, President Bush claimed that it was also behind the 9/11 attack and that Saddam Hussein was a supporter of bin Laden. As soon as this claim was made, American critics refuted it and pointed out to President Bush that there was credible evidence that bin Laden and Saddam Hussein were both personally and ideologically opposed and were highly unlikely to be colluding. The 9/11 Commission in a recent interim report has also affirmed that there was no evidence of Iraq's collusion with Al-Qaeda in the 9/11 attacks.

Still when he finally attacked Iraq in March 2003, he had no valid reason to justify the invasion. Nevertheless, he decided to go ahead, presumably hoping that either his words as president or the fear-mongering generated by media hysteria would help to carry him through this expedition. How he went from citing one excuse to another is already well known. In the end he took a regrettable unilateral action when the international community would not agree with his reasons to start the war against Iraq. His case is like that of a mischievous boy, who churns out story after story to get out of trouble, but at the end has no more stories to dodge either the headmaster

or his father and gets caught. Similarly, all President Bush's stories have
now run out, but he is still holding back the true reason.

What was the point in attacking Iraq? It seems to be so irrational and
bizarre that President Bush dares not admit it. His hedging the issue
suggests that his religious convictions and association with the Evangelical
fundamentalists may have led him to wage this war for religious reasons. He
may have attacked Iraq hoping to open a door for attacking other Islamic
countries on one pretext or another to eventually defeat the polity of Islam.
For obvious reasons President Bush would never admit that openly, which is
why he has been going in circles, hoping that in the end the American
people will stop asking for the reason and take his word for it that Saddam
was a vicious man who had to be removed by force. The American public
may indeed put this matter behind them and get on with life, but the
international audience cannot let it go, because if President Bush is waging
war on religious grounds, then he may continue it against other Islamic
states in his next term, if he gets one. Therefore, from the point of view of
international peace, it is crucial for President Bush's motives in attacking
Iraq and possible future war plans to be fully investigated and grasped, so
that he may be prevented from launching any more such onslaughts.

It is the same situation as when a suspect leads the investigating detective
in circles with story after story to avoid the truth, but the investigator does
not relent and opens a much wider circumstantial probe to discover the
truth. Eventually he succeeds in putting two and two together.

Following this procedure, a wider personal and circumstantial probe into
President Bush's personality should be undertaken in pursuit of uncover-
ing the truth or the point of his war on Iraq that he has concealed so far. A
leading article in the *Newsweek* magazine of March 10, 2003, titled "The Man
of God", provides a good insight into President Bush's frame of mind and
his overall approach to presidency, which may be used broadly in discern-
ing the truth about his decision to attack Iraq.

Reviewing the characteristics of President Bush broadly, we can learn
from the *Newsweek* article that he is a Man of God, as he has declared,
"behind all of life and history there is dedication and purpose, set by the
hand of a just and faithful God." On his desire to seek higher office, he said,
"he had been called to seek higher office." He has also said, "our nation is
chosen by God and commissioned by history to be a model to the world
justice."

What we see here is a man who admits to having received call(s) that may
be akin to dreams or even hallucinations and goes on to shape his own life
as well as his presidency according to these "call(s)." He has been described
as a born-again Christian. His statements give the impression that God is in
communication with him and telling him what to think of himself and what
to do in life. This would appear to be the basis upon which he assesses his

capabilities and formulates his political policies. That being so, one would have to be concerned that President Bush follows policies that may have no foundation in reason or logic but stem from the "call(s)" or dreams that he may have had from time to time. This could be a good feeling for him, but making decisions on the perception of divine guidance could also be a dangerous thing unless one is an accredited prophet of God, because the risk of obsession arising from unfounded godly dictates is very high. David Kuresh also acted on the notion of dictates from God and created the Waco tragedy. If the president of the United States also acts on similar notions of calls from God, then he could bring about a global tragedy. What David Kuresh did and how he ended up is frightening, but what an American president could do based on supposed supernatural revelations could be catastrophic for world peace. The tragedy of Jim Jones is another example, as he persuaded scores of men and women to drink poison and end their lives because this was the supernatural dictate that he perceived himself as having received. It is truly frightening how supernatural notions can impair the faculty of intellect. One has to be careful about godly messages. Unless one is a known prophet, the probability of one's mind churning out irrational notions under varying levels of mental stress is quite high. This is why we consider it a danger for the rest of the world when the so-called Man of God is allowed to shape his presidency on supernatural notions or perceptions of his religious faith. Such perceptions can close one's mind on divine grounds and thus lead one to an obstinate path without regard to reason or logic.

Nobody can be expected to set aside his religious convictions when acting in a public capacity, but it is fair to expect the president of the United States to use supernatural notions peacefully for the good of humanity, as opposed to believing that wars can achieve the same goals. President Bush's convictions that the hand of a just and faithful God was guiding him when he felt called to seek higher office, or that the American nation is chosen by God or commissioned by history to be a model to the world of justice, becomes problematic, since he accepts the Evangelical notion, derived through Puritanism from Judaism, of a God whose supposed "justice" really involves "playing favourites". Genuine belief in "a just God" can be very beneficial and lead to many good things, but the belief that "a just God" is the God of war, vengeance and partisanship can preclude the believer from seeking peaceful solutions to world problems and alienate him from the reality of diverse religions and cultures due to an impaired faculty of logic. As was said above supernatural notions are acceptable only in prophets, but if political leaders start claiming telepathy with the Higher Being and use their political and military powers to implement their so-called supernatural notions, then the world runs the risk of reverting back to the old religious rivalries and holy wars. There are serious problems in accepting policies of a modern-time president who admits to being influenced by so-called supernatural notions and could be seen to work with obsession in an obstinate way.

With regard to President Bush's "calls" we might venture to suggest that his election victory in 2000 could not have been a result of a summons from the Higher Being, since it was so flawed and dubious. His claim that God has chosen American standards of justice and morality as models for the rest of the world is also questionable, because there are many flaws in both the justice system and the morality of Americans. There is much to be desired before American standards could be taken as models for the rest of the world.

The point is that if President Bush is not put to the test of fact, he might allow his fundamentalist mind to be influenced in other matters, too, that he has not told us about or not ready yet to tell us about it at all. One concern is the belief of certain Evangelical Christians in Last Days and the Last Emperor, what has been called the "dream of the Last Emperor of ancient prophecy who would conquer the East and force the return of Christ and the Last Days upon the world" (quoted from Armstrong's book *Holy War*). We hope that this is not another of President Bush's supernatural notions or call(s) giving him the feeling that he might have been chosen to be the Last Emperor according to supposed biblical prophecy. It is a serious concern. Certainly he is now acting like an emperor and could not seem to care less either for world opinion or even for international or domestic law.

Christians differ widely over how to interpret prophecies of the "Last Days." Without going into the technicalities of the traditional account of the Antichrist or the King of the South and the King of the North, suffice it to say that President Bush may have a tendency to see himself as a Last Emperor and think he has a roadmap to the future furnished by the Biblical prophecies in the light of his actions. It seems all too plausible that he or the pastors he listens to have correctly identified the King of the North of the Book of Daniel with the ruler of Mesopotamia but failed to understand that the prophecy of chapter 11 of Daniel, which plays a great role in Evangelicals' attempts to forecast the "Last Days", deals with wars between the Ptolemaic rulers of Egypt and the Seleucid rulers of the Fertile Crescent, over two thousand years ago, and cannot be trusted as a guide to how events will unfold now.

The complexities of the belief in the Last Days or the Last Emperor may explain why President Bush has made no clear pronouncement on his position as an Evangelical believer and leader, and thus seems to have been going in circles about his position or his reasons for going to war in Iraq. He might be too embarrassed to admit that he has had another "call" to conquer the East and bring about the Last Days as supposedly prophesied in Daniel.

These suspicions grow when we learn that President Bush talked about attacking Iraq even before the U.N. inspectors undertook examining its weapons inventory. Again, while the intense work of the inspectors was underway, he had already begun dispatching the U.S. army to the Middle East. His advance preparations for war and disregard of the inspectors' verdict would suggest that, as far as he was concerned, the "call" had been made and everything else was simply irrelevant, regardless of fact or logic. His one-sided decision and advance preparation for war on Iraq falls more in line with his "call" than with any strategic rationale. Hence he was not ready to wait for a factual report or appropriate consensual action, perhaps because of the inner pressure of the call. All this would suggest that, as far as he was concerned, the war was a foregone conclusion arising from his religious convictions, regardless of the outcome of the inspections.

Later, it would emerge that the intelligence reports upon which he supposedly acted were also questionable. Whether such misleading reports were fashioned at his behest or his advisors' for other reasons is not yet known, because the matter is still under investigation. What we do know is that President Bush was firmly committed to waging this war one way or the other. He could not have done it without being convinced that the hand of "a just God" was guiding him. Had he been working on a realistic basis with logic and rationality, then he would have waited till the proceedings of the Security Council were completed and he had a final report of the inspectors at hand. The fact that he began preparations to attack Iraq even before the inspectors could complete their work supports the assessment that he was internally pressurised, perhaps by a self-conceived supernatural call, and so had no choice or time for any other option except to yield to the call. The call, according to the assumed interpretation of the prophecy, is to conquer the East. So, his determination to attack Iraq is a strong indication that he may have presumed himself to be the Last Emperor and thus gone ahead to conquer the East regardless of facts, international law or world opinion. Otherwise, one would have to ask what was the rush for war, when the issue of disarmament could have been resolved peacefully by taking a little longer time. He was in such a mad rush that he neglected to plan this war properly, as can be seen from the current state of chaos in Iraq.

President Bush's rush for war is the key to understanding his undeclared motives. He tells the American people consistently that Saddam Hussein is or was a threat to America, so he must be removed dead or alive. Saddam's perceived stockpile of weapons of mass destruction was effectively used to frighten and even manipulate the unsuspecting and rather ill informed American public. It was a good ploy to generate public support, but the fact of the matter is that Saddam Hussein was too crippled, exhausted from two long wars of ten years each, almost fully disarmed and simply too demoralised and old to pose any real threat to America. His country was ravaged, his people were heartbroken, and the morale of his scientists was shattered.

How could such a broken leader or shattered country be a threat to America? President Bush has failed conspicuously to persuade his critics how Saddam Hussein was a threat to the United States or the world. Undoubtedly he deserved to be removed, but invading or occupying Iraq in the way that was done could not have been undertaken without some other covert or ulterior motive.

The current controversy about the justification for invading Iraq reinforces the thesis that as far as President Bush was concerned, conquering the East was the dictate of the "call." He just had to go for it, regardless of facts and figures concerning the culpability of Iraq or even proper planning of the war. There are now serious allegations in both Britain and the United States that some information was even fabricated, or at least coloured up, to frighten the public in both countries so that a case could be made to attack Iraq. Both Blair and Bush are now in hot water for misleading their people. Bush's story is the same old one of weapons of mass destruction and a threat to America, which does not interest anyone any more, even the Americans. No matter how much both Blair and Bush may hide their real reason for attacking Iraq, facts are now surfacing to belie their professed claims and demonstrate that there may well have been a hidden agenda that these two leaders have not come clean about.

To judge by the momentum that President Bush has created, he appears all set to invade other Islamic countries, which he calls autocratic and unacceptable in modern times. Surprisingly, he has not taken a similar position against the Castro régime in the American backyard. His real reason for targeting the Islamic countries does not stem from the goodness of his heart towards the Muslim populations but is rather to fulfil his own bigoted faith-based agenda of annihilating the 'evil men' and transforming the 'wicked religion'. When we put them to the test of reality, we shall find that the welfare or well-being of the Muslims is not the mainstay of his policies. President Bush portrays himself as a Man of God, but his actions show that he is in fact a Man of War in the true crusaders' tradition. Crusaders also used to consider themselves as Men of God but pursued the vocation of war.

Sadly, we are living in an unjust and unfair world where people practise deception with words. In these modern times there are smart lawyers, skilful and controlling psychologists and shrewd bureaucrats and clever policymakers who are masters at juggling words and twisting and turning or spinning situations only to outwit their own unsuspecting public and exploit the political system. This might also be the case with the Bush administration, which has at its disposal so many imaginative and brilliant war architects who could construct any number of scenarios to suit their purposes.

Analysing Bush's professed policy of liberating Iraq, one has to wonder about his words and ask how has he become so concerned about the freedom and democracy of the Iraqis and the rest of the Muslim world. Reflection on the history of the past thousand years shows that Christian rulers have seldom been sympathetic to Islam or the Muslims; they have mostly considered the Prophet of Islam a liar and impostor and labelled Islam as an evil and wicked religion. Some of Bush's own Evangelical supporters have said the same. It seems surprisingly inconsistent that an Evangelical like President Bush is now fighting to bring liberty to Muslims and wishing economic and material success for them. Is this truly a change of heart, or is it a new manifestation of the old passion of converting the infidels in a uniquely modern way? If so, newer and fancier words like modernity, liberalism and secularism are merely being used to cloak the old goal of converting the Muslims. The intent does not seem to be so much to build healthy Islamic societies so that Islamic civilisation may also survive in honour alongside other civilisations as it is to change the character of the Muslims and transform their societies into ones based on Western values or Christian traditions.

From a Muslim point of view President Bush cannot be a friend of Islam or Muslims when he seems determined to transform Muslims and alter the character of Islam. According to the *Newsweek* lead story, "after Iraq he promises to transform the Middle East into Utopia." What utopia, one might ask?

Utopia is an idealistic scheme needing ideal conditions to accomplish it. It is easier said than done. Since President Bush promises to transform the Middle East into Utopia, one has to ask whether he has first succeeded in establishing the conditions that are needed to realise such an idealistic scheme. Winning the hearts of the people of the Middle East is an obvious prerequisite for ideal conditions, but going to war, dropping bombs and bringing destruction and devastation will neither create ideal conditions nor win any hearts. The Iraqi people have not forgotten how President Bush Senior attacked and slaughtered their sons and brothers in 1991, how tens of thousands of Iraqi soldiers were then buried alive in trenches by the U.S. tanks in spite of their white flags, and what destruction his bombing brought to civilians in Baghdad. The ongoing sanctions and continuous bombing and destruction of Iraq are no signals of love or peace for the Iraqis. Secondly, what can America offer Islamic civilisation by way of utopia? Is it to replace Muslim culture with American social, sexual and behavioural immorality and introduce all those American cultural ills that have become problems even for American citizens? There is no precedent of trust between Christian rulers and Muslim subjects, so why should the Muslims now trust a faith-based Evangelical president, especially when he appears to be one of those fundamentalists who hate Islam and wish ill to the Muslims all the time? A Western Evangelical Christian ruler could bring no utopia to any Muslim society, for he lacks the fundamentals for bringing anything to any country except serving his own bigoted religious objectives and self-centred economic goals.

President Bush talks about ushering liberty by removing the autocratic governments. But he forgets that the system of autocratic rule in the Islamic world was in fact installed by several Western powers separately in different regions of the Middle East after the First World War. The present pack of despotic kings and dictators is a legacy of the system that the West had imposed on the Muslim world. The United States took over charge of these despotic régimes after the Second World War, nourishing and fortifying them to serve American interest (oil) in the region. America, in fact, brought new dictators as presidents to the forefront to serve its interests and also eliminated the ones who had changed their minds. The hanging of a former Turkish Prime Minister, Adnan Manderes, the replacement of Dr Sukarno by General Suharto, the murder of King Faisal, the execution of Bhutto, and the blowing up of General Zia's plane were not small historical mishaps. They have a suspicious air or appearance of having been engineered.

To criticise the Islamic world or blame Islam for the misdeeds or atrocious conduct of the current pack of despots is totally unjustified, because neither the Muslims nor Islam brought these brutes to power. If there is any blame arising from the misdeeds or oppressive régimes of these despotic rulers, then it ought to be directed to Britain and the United States because they are the ones who brought them to power in the first place. There is no justification for attacking the Muslims or the Islamic world on account of their atrocious conduct because they are not the products of Islam.

Anyhow, President Bush now wants to oust them and undo the work of so many Western and American leaders. This is unbelievable. Who is going to look after American interests if full democracy is restored and the people do not want to deal with America or the West at all? Already a mini-example of real democracy in action can be seen in Turkey, where the people do not like American imposition and so refused permission to use their land for military operations against Muslim Iraq. How would President Bush or any Western power deal with decisions taken democratically by Muslim citizens that went against Western interests? Could America or the West live with such democratic decisions? America has thriven on dictators and puppet rulers installed and supported by the CIA, so how could it do business in the Islamic world without them? In a truly democratic Middle East the people would have nothing to do with American or Western policies, especially now that the recent hostilities have seriously damaged chances of a cordial relationship. Iraq is a good current example of non-cooperation with the United States for the same reason. How would President Bush build trust with the Muslim world when he is bent on transforming its religious and social culture? If America continues to follow George Kennan's doctrine, the benefit of the people of Iraq will neither be in its interest nor reflect its policy.

Although freedom and democracy seem to be the two main themes of President Bush's claim to wish to benefit the Iraqi people, he has flouted the very fundamentals of democracy and freedom by denying Iraqis the right to choose their own form of government or frame their own constitution without American interference. According to the directive issued by President Bush, the Iraqis can take only what is dictated to them, as dictatorial decrees are now the new norms of democracy and freedom. Hence the Iraqis could only have a government by the will of the Americans, by the imposition of the American administration and for the benefit of the United States. The notion that a democratic government is of the people, by the people and for the people is no longer valid in President Bush's definition of democracy. The slogan of transforming the Islamic world in the name of freedom, liberty and democracy is without real substance. Liberal ideas are being used merely as modern tools to weaken Muslims' faith, so that getting them to adopt Western ways of life, akin to Christianity, may become easier. What has happened in Iraq is not true liberation from dictatorship but rather the beginning of an attempted diversion from Islamic civilisation to a "modernity" based on Christian values. This is the true agenda of the Evangelicals and President Bush may just be striving covertly to implement it using American economic and military power.

This thrust can be seen from what happened to the Iraqis immediately after the American occupation. There was an outcry in the press, both American and international, that thousands of Evangelicals had descended upon Iraq with the message of the Bible to convert the Iraqis to Christianity. It was reported that the chief organiser of this gigantic mission was the very son of Dr Billy Graham, and that many other Evangelicals funded the mission to transform Islamic culture in Iraq. While the country was still in a state of war the Bush administration helped these missionaries to enter Iraq and start their work of transforming or converting the population. Consequently, thousands of American missionaries were knocking at the doors of the Iraqis, giving them free copies of the Arabic version of the Bible and inviting them to embrace Christianity as the solution of all their troubles. The press dubbed it a spiritual invasion of Iraq on the heels of the American military invasion, which in fact reveals the true nature of the invasion of Iraq. Attacking the spirituality of the fallen Iraqis was the worst thing that any victorious ruler could allow so soon after the military occupation. But President Bush is not a normal president; he has a covert objective, which was why his administration allowed American and some European missionaries to enter Iraq despite the dangerous and risky conditions. Sending missionaries at such a critical time shows what the Iraqi war was all about.

The Iraqis were in a state of shock from the war and the grief of discovering the mass graves of their relatives. This was neither the time nor the circumstances for anyone to attack their spirituality. Their lives had been shattered. All civic amenities were disabled and the population faced hunger, disease and acute misery. They had no employment and no infra-structure to support civic life. The engineers and technicians had not arrived yet to restore water supply and electric power and the hospitals had not yet received medicines and equipment, but the Christian missionaries had landed in their thousands to distribute the Arabic version of the Gospels to spread their faith. The Iraqis were not amused and took it as a serious affront to their religious beliefs, which is why they do not trust America, nor do they wish to co-operate with it.

The mission of bad conscience started by the American Evangelicals has served no religious purpose because of its distasteful nature. It succeeded only in annoying the Iraqis, as it hurt their religious feelings, increased local tension and made Iraq even more unstable. The recent attacks on Christian churches were regrettable and deplorable but they seemed coming in view of the provocation by the Evangelical missionaries. This Evan-gelical offensive against Iraqi spirituality is an affront to decency and social morality, which deserves condemnation by good-hearted Americans.

America has now embarked on changing régimes to transform the reli-gious culture of other nations. President Bush has set the course to replace Islamic civilisation with Western civilisation based on Christian values. This is not what America used to be about. This country was built on the foundation of freedom; people had freedom to choose whatever way of life they might want to live, so long as they allowed the same freedom to others. If the Muslims want to live under an Islamic form of government, then they, too, ought to have the right to adopt it. This is the essence of democracy and freedom. Granted the Muslim societies do not have experience of running and living under democracies, so they would face enormous chal-lenges in building a democratic infrastructure that would function in modern times. Undoubtedly they would need help from the international community, but the prerogative of choosing the type of government they would have is entirely theirs. It is not for an outsider to go around changing régimes, imposing foreign forms of governments and altering the Middle Eastern religious culture. This is contrary to America's own values of liberty and freedom of choice. What moral authority or permission from interna-tional law has America or Britain got to impose changes against the will of any people?

Changing lifestyles and imposing particular forms of doctrine or chang-ing régimes used to be the profession of the Soviet Union. Thanks to President Bush, America now appears to have embraced the Soviet traits and begun emulating Soviet practices by invading other countries and taking away the rights and choices of their people. One has to wonder since when America has become Soviet-minded? What President Bush is now doing in Iraq is a serious breach of freedom. It is not for any outsider to change a régime or tell the people how to live their lives, or require them to become Western or give up their own religious and cultural heritage. This is an absolute no-no in our modern world, which professes to be based on tolerance of cultures, religions and the social and governmental practices of other people, so long as they are not flouting any international law. Only the people themselves can make their own choices and decide to live under whatever system of government they may wish. Let changes or revolutions evolve from within and not be imposed from outside as the Soviets used to do. What President Bush is doing in Iraq is akin to what the Soviets did in Hungary in 1956 or in Czechoslovakia in 1968. Americans denounced the Soviet invasions, but now they are being asked to swallow the invasion of Iraq because their own government has begun acting in the Soviet fashion. This is an enormous decline in American values, and President George W. Bush ought to be held accountable for introducing Soviet tactics into American politics. To dominate the world by undertaking Soviet-style invasions and threatening the social, cultural and religious values of others is a frightening departure from true American values and tradition.

If it becomes necessary to help a nation to regain its freedom, then there are other means available to accomplish this goal. One is to provide constructive assistance so the people may oust their despots. But, as was stated earlier, the problem is that the West itself grooms these dictators, and supports them, so how could the population oust them? The people of Iraq are only witnessing the replacement of a régime without seeing the real benefits of freedom of choice.

The truth is that removing dictators is not so much of a problem for the Muslim populations because the people could replace them, as the Iranians did in 1953 when they ousted the tyrant Shah. The hurdle is the United States since it uses its secret services to neutralize peoples' freedom efforts just as the CIA did by overthrowing Dr Mossadaq's revolutionary government and executing his brilliant Prime Minister Dr Fatami. What is now happening in the Islamic world behind the smokescreen of changing régimes is an attempt to change the very values and culture of Islam without effectively changing the nature or character of the dictatorships. One form of dictatorship is now being replaced by another. In both cases the people are denied the freedom of choice. Their constitution is being framed with outside interference, and they are being told how to live their lives. The result is that the Iraqis are violently refusing to accept this form of dictatorship.

What the antagonists of Islam or those who are trying to transform the Islamic culture forget is that Islam is not a man-made ideology like Communism that could be defeated or disbanded. Islam is a divine religion based on spirituality and its followers are deeply committed in heart and soul to practising not only its rituals but also its code of life. However, President Bush wants to impose Western or Christian modes of life on Muslim societies. All good Muslims must resist this, and it may end up by creating much greater chaos in our world than we have today. Besides his thrust to change régimes and social and religious cultures, President Bush is in fact striking at the roots of diverse civilisations and negating the very essence of freedom of choice. His closed mind on religious grounds cannot see the beauty in diversity. He wants to transform everything into a monotonous and dull universality of his own version of Christendom, because he seems to have no tolerance for diverse religions or diversity in cultures or civilisations.

President Bush's policy of interfering with the Islamic states and altering the socio-religious setup of Muslims is counterproductive. It needs to be stopped. The American people are the only ones who can make this happen and avert the looming clash of civilisations by changing their own régime instead of watching régime changes in other countries. President George W. Bush is eroding diversity from human society by trying to transform Islamic civilisation by the force of military power. He has trampled on international law by disregarding the principles of jurisprudence and made American law the law of the jungle by discarding civil liberties and the rights of individuals. He has turned human beings into animals by treating the captives in subhuman fashion and brought back the rule of might as in the Dark Ages, which crushed the civility that numerous reformers in various parts of the world had striven so hard to achieve. Worst of all, he has begun to adopt and use Soviet practices contrary to genuine American values. He has sacrificed the fundamentals of the American constitution, which upholds the freedom of choice of individuals and nations. He is using force to deny Muslim societies their choice and using deceptive words like modernity and liberalism to change the Islamic countries to win the crusaders' war against Islam.

It may be remembered that after the religious revolution and civil wars in Europe many victims of religious persecution escaped to the New World to make their new homes and centre of religious activities there. With due respect to the sentiments of the people of America, history tells us that many of these refugees proved just as intolerant of views that differed from their own as their persecutors had been of their own opinions; in colonial Massachusetts, for instance, Anglicans were punished for observing Christmas and Quakers were burnt at the stake. Although in times these new Americans adopted a new life and assimilated into their new environments, their zeal for crusading in one form or another did not subside with time. It was passed on from generation to generation, and now it has grown into a

formidable force, especially in the south. Even President Bush characterised his war on terrorism as a crusade against the evil people. His staff
cautioned him about what he was saying, so he quickly retracted the word
crusade, but the cat was already out of the bag.

The rising religions fundamentalism and right-wing conservatism from
the southern horizon of America suggests that our world is seeing the
resurgence of the old crusaders in newer forms. What they were barred
from doing in the Near East in the Middle Ages they now appear to be
restarting from American soil, rekindling the old flames of hatred of Islam.
The Evangelicals in the American south have now mostly joined the Republican Party to pursue their goals from a political platform rather than
through the churches. Perhaps this would explain why there are scores or
even hundreds of born-again Christian fundamentalists in the main political stream of the United States, forming the backbone of the Republican
Party. Normally it would be of no concern to anyone, but if the political
power of the United States is used to propel a crusade against Islam, then it
becomes a matter of concern not only for the people of America but also
for others. As in the past, crusading is sure to disturb world peace. If not
checked it may do so all over again, using newer methods and newer
pretexts to practise the same old warmongering. The plight of the world
during the last few years tells us that we are already in the midst of such
turmoil. This is a matter of great concern for all peace-loving people all
over the world. Our world must not slip back into religious hatred or
religious wars. Our world has gone a long way towards becoming civilised,
and we cannot afford to take chances to allow resurgence of the old
crusading forces from the American horizon.

Only time will tell the true nature of President Bush's character, whether
he is a genuine reformer of human society and a brave combatant of
terrorism or an Evangelical zealot fulfilling the mandate of the old crusaders in a uniquely new way. Time will also tell whether he went to Iraq as a
friend of the Iraqis to give them true and genuine freedom, so that they can
work towards achieving their own aspirations, or whether he went there on
totally false pretexts with an Evangelical agenda in mind to play his crusading role to conquer the East as the Last Emperor and force the Last Days
upon earth. Time will show why he ignored warning signals about Al-Qaeda
and what were his reasons for not taking timely action to thwart the 9/11
attacks.

These mysteries are now slowly unraveling. The WMD fiasco is the real
crunch of what President Bush is all about. His shifting of positions to
sustain a non-existing pretext have become ludicrous as he is now justifying
the Iraqi war after the fact on Saddam Hussein's perceived intentions as
opposed to facts on the ground. After Hans Blix's preliminary report and
Dr Kay's final determination that WMDs did not exist it became clear that
further searching for them was of no avail. Yet the Bush administration

dispatched Inspector Duelfer, a serving CIA official who had been a member of the previous inspection teams and familiar with the fact that WMDs did not exist, to somehow find them. It was not only a puzzling move but also suspicious for what could Duelfer find that both Blix and Dr Kay said did not exist? Even Duelfer seemed doubtful of his assignment, but the administration's strategy in sending him on the expedition appears to be motivated that he might give a new twist to the threat of WMDs that would at least provide the president with a fighting chance to rebut his opponents during the election debates. True to the expectations of the administration this CIA official brought into discussion a completely new and bizarre twist to the WMD story by saying that Saddam Hussein had intentions of restarting his weapons program as soon as the U.N. sanctions were lifted. The inference or the insinuation of Duelfer report is that at that point in time Saddam Hussein would have passed these weapons to organisations like the Al-Qaeda. This was enough ammunition for President Bush to stick to his guns as he coined Saddam Hussein's unattested intentions to collaborate with the terrorists as "a threat" and availed himself of yet another irrational pretext to justify attacking Iraq. His jumping from one pretext to another and even clinging on to a seemingly contrived straw alludes that something is amiss in his own intentions that he is not coming clean with.

Lately President Bush had also been accusing the Muslim fundamentalists saying that their ideology (religion) is terror based, and that they are attacking the U.S. because they hate "our freedom." We beg to differ with the president and draw his attention that it is not a situation of ideological or religious belief of Muslims in terror as the president alludes; rather it is radicalism and reactionary behaviour of Muslim activists that emanates from overall unfair and unjust treatment of their issues by the world community. To mix radicalism with ideology or religion tantamount evading the real issues and misleading American public opinion. It is also wrong to suggest that Muslims hate American freedom. What we are seeing in their restiveness is not ideological hatred of freedom, but a reaction to unjust and imbalanced policies of the West.

The American public needs to take these issues into consideration and realise that resolving international crisis depends essentially on three factors, namely the diplomatic channels, use of wisdom, impartiality and justice and lastly the military power can also come into play to enforce the regime of law in human society. In the current situation President Bush does not have open diplomatic channels with the Islamic world; wisdom and impartiality are also missing from the scene. So all that President Bush is left with is military power, but peace cannot be achieved either by force or merely by uttering hollow words or sketching blank roadmaps. The American public needs to impress upon their president to change the course of war that he is so adamantly staying on because war cannot achieve peace. Peace has it own rules that need to be embraced and given a chance.

6

The Causes and Effects of Unrest

We hear so much about the effects of terrorism, violence and counter-violence, but we see no steps taken to discover the causes and control the source of this menace. The thought of a disaster occurring in our surroundings adds to an already stressful lifestyle. This is a serious situation. It calls for concerted international action to discover why there is so much violence and how it could it be controlled. The United States spends billions of dollars to deal with the effects of violence, but it makes no real effort either to learn about the root causes or to remedy these causes and so avoid the affliction of the effects.

The United Nations also pays no attention to the causes, even though international peace and the well-being of all communities in the world are its primary mandate. It has made no effort to inquire why the Muslims have become so restive and dangerous. Nor has it appointed any commission of inquiry to look into the Muslims' grievances and recommend measures to deal with their frustration and cool down their tempers in a civilised and just manner. Merely harping on effects and doing nothing about the cause is both illogical and suspicious and certainly not conducive to peace. The missing American endeavour to restore a sense of fairness in the Muslim world and the international apathy towards their issues are major sources of disappointment in the Muslim world.

The phenomenon of injustice and the resulting violence is not new. These failings had been with humans from the beginning of times. But after having come so far and passed so many milestones, our civilisation should have overcome these perils. At least these failings ought to have been reduced, especially when we claim that our civilisation has made gigantic progress in education, astronomical achievement in science and technology, and above all in the development of civilised societies and the evolution of human rights. Yet our world is suffering an unprecedented and unsurpassed magnitude of violence and counter-violence. Where is the fruit of human progress? Instead of moving forward, the human race has regressed in the realm of peace, tranquillity, fraternity, equality in justice and social and economic well-being.

For the Muslims the decline had been proceeding steadily from the beginning of the last millennium, but it took a nosedive in the twentieth century under Western ascendancy. The saga of Muslim suppression did not end with the First World War. The changes that took place after the Second World War maintained pressure on the Muslims. When the British Empire faded away, Western colonialism resurfaced in a new form as the United States picked up the spoils, inherited the British legacy and began practising its own brand of imperialism. Regrettably, the Western religious faith had not always taught its followers to treat other human beings justly without religious prejudice. Consequently, followers of the Evangelical faith do not appear to be spiritually trained to treat people of other religions fairly. When these religious forces acquire state power they become even more aggressive and arrogant and use modern tactics to pursue their prejudiced goals. Victimising the Muslims comes as second nature to them.

The Muslim population are not oblivious to what is happening to their causes. Despite the neglect of their concerns by successive administrations, the Muslim intelligentsia, the political and economic leadership, continued to hope and believe that friendship with America was still the best bet for progress and advancement of the Muslim world. So, almost the entire leadership in the Islamic world continued to rely on America, despite warning signals that Evangelical influence had gripped many Americans with anti-Islamic sentiments that had been imbedded in their minds by faulty media and biased religious and social propaganda. However, for all the Muslim leadership's leaning on America, Muslim concerns rarely get their fair share of support from the United States, which goes on breeding discontent and disgruntlement. What is worst is that Muslims feel that besides exploiting their natural resources, the United States government manipulates them, even uses them for fighting its wars, but never truly supports them or their causes.

The cumulative effects of neglecting Muslim issues had been building resentment for a long time. But the Muslims did not decide to jump into the guerrilla warfare or acts of terrorism spontaneously. They first tried to seek justice for their causes through the civilised means of international channels. Their cases were heard, debated, considered and then formulated in the shape of U.N. resolutions setting out procedures for resolving the disputes. The initial U.N. resolutions held out hope of resolving the Muslim disputes peacefully. However, when the time came to implement those resolutions, they were betrayed. The U.N. passed two resolutions on Kashmir, but the then Soviet Union vetoed the proceedings and blocked their fulfilment. As a result, the Kashmir dispute has lost all chances of a peaceful resolution. Consequently, tens of thousands of innocent lives have since been lost because of military aggression by India and armed resistance by the Muslims. In the case of Palestine, the United States uses its veto privilege whenever Israel is pressed by the international community to comply with the resolutions. As for Chechnya, Russia does not allow this issue even to be placed on the U.N. agenda. Worst of all is the tragic silence and apathy of Western intellectuals, authors and commentators, including the media, who simply do not talk about the failure of the international system to provide justice to Muslim causes in any effective or constructive manner. There even appears to be a concerted effort by the media to ignore Muslim causes. Apathy on part of the Western powers in fulfilling their share of the responsibility towards the Muslims is a contributory factor in the loss of world peace. They criticise the Muslims for being restive but choose to ignore the causes of their restiveness. This then fuels Muslim emotion and generates even more frustration and resentment among the radicals.

Without condoning violence as a means for resolving disputes or making political statements, the need for a change in the American attitude as well as the attitude of the international community cannot be emphasised strongly enough for the sake of world peace. Muslims are a significant part of this world. They, too, need peaceful environments for their own prosperity and progress. A just and healthy treatment of Muslim issues is, therefore, crucial not only for the sake of world peace but also for Muslim peace. Muslims' rights, hopes and aspirations cannot be brushed aside forever under the guise of a war on terrorism. The international community has an obligation to address Muslim issues and investigate Muslims' legitimate grievances and the causes of unrest. Merely harping on effect seems a waste of time and energy since it does not produce the desired result of peace. Paying attention to the causes and taking action to eliminate the sources of disgruntlement could produce the peaceful world that we are all striving for. Transformation of their religious culture is not what the Muslims need; they need a transformation in the world's attitude towards them.

Since the United States is now at the helm of world affairs, it is appropriate to arouse American public opinion so that the world's leading nation may realise the need for and importance of addressing the causes of unrest, not merely attending to the effects.

7

The Muslims' Predicaments and their Ongoing Strife

Now that we have come to recognise the importance of knowing the causes of Muslim restiveness, it is essential to look into Muslim issues more deeply, if we are to comprehend their merits and see how they contribute to aggravate Muslims' resentment and frustration.

Besides their grudge about social and economic exploitation of their resources by internal and external forces, the Muslims, by and large, agitate over three major examples of international ill treatment. As is widely known, these three problematic issues are:

The Palestinian Riddle
The Kashmir Dispute
The Chechen Saga

The Palestinian Riddle

The Palestinian issue is the key to world peace, so this dispute requires an in-depth examination, not only to comprehend all the elements of this intricate question, but also to explore how the riddle might be solved. It is called a riddle because of the history of this tract of land. One party claims its ownership on religious grounds based on a commandment of God, while the other party presses its rights on grounds of ancestral heritage. Both claims are made with enormous passion and emotion.

The Israelis have brought religion to the centre of this argument and cited God Himself to support their claim. Since Palestine has become an issue of passion and emotion throughout its history of thousands of years, it is crucial to understand the history of this region to grasp how these passions and emotions were born. As was stated previously, when passions and emotions are involved, the faculty of logic and reason gets impaired; so analysing such situations becomes both complex and controversial. Nevertheless, the challenge of analysing the Palestinian riddle must be taken up,

in order to establish at least a sense of sagacity that might help cool the
passions and emotions to pave way for untangling this enduring intricacy.
Since all arguments in this case are based on religion and history, we must
delve into these topics from those perspectives to assess what can be done
now to convince the conflicting parties that, in spite of their faiths and
beliefs, there is room for adjustment. Thus going into the historical background of Canaan is crucial to grasping the root cause(s) of this riddle.
Tedious as it may be, it is the only route to developing a realistic formula for
tackling the Arab-Israeli dispute.

Historically, the Jews are not natives of Canaan or Palestine. Hence their
claim is not based on grounds of ancestral perpetuity; rather it is based on
religion as a commandment of God, who is quoted as having given this land
to the Jews as their Promised Land. The dispute is over whether God
granted exclusivity to the children of Israel or whether there was room for
other native people or nations to co-exist with the Israelites in peace and
harmony. It should also be kept in mind how God was using Canaan as a
territory first for Prophet Abraham and then for his progeny. Was He using
it to provide protection for His favourite people from atrocities and persecution in both instances, or was He turning this land into a Holy Land that
would later become a battlefield or bone of contention between the natives
and the newcomers? Circumstantially it would appear that the immediate
problem that God was set to resolve in both instances was to provide
protection for His chosen people, and so it would be logical to view Canaan
or Palestine as a place for peaceful co-existence rather than a battleground
for spiritual domination. It is important to approach the purpose of God
through logical appreciation; otherwise, there is a risk that someone might
abuse God's name for territorial or political purposes.

All the three branches of Prophet Abraham's people–the Jews, Christians
and Muslims–believe that God directed first Prophet Abraham and then
the children of Israel to enter Canaan to avoid brutalities, so their presence
in Canaan is undoubtedly at God's Will. What cannot be independently
ascertained is whether God ordered the Israelites to kill and drive out the
native inhabitants and take over the land exclusively for themselves. It may
be granted that the present-day Torah contains such commands and the
Christian and Muslim scholars who interpret history of the Israelites in the
light of the Torah have the same understanding that annihilation and
extermination of the Canaanites is at God's commandment. However, this
view or interpretation cannot be claimed as totally free from bias or misin-
terpretation. Hence it is important to rely on God's overall attributes to
seek guidance on whether such a brutal treatment of the Canaanites could
really be God's commandment or whether it is an example of human
venture in tampering with the word of God to serve one's own ends. How
would God's attributes of mercy, forgiveness, compassion, love and care for

all humanity fit in with the commandment to kill and drive out the original inhabitants, the Canaanites?

Rationally it does not seem like a just way for God to solve one problem for the Israelites by creating another one for the Canaanites. Surely God is wise and all-knowing and fully aware that humans may easily resort to bloodshed if some are given authority to kill and expel others. To say that God is Almighty and has the power and prerogative to do whatever He pleases, including inflicting injustice and inhumanity on some human beings, is really stretching the point of God's Almightiness. He is indeed Almighty and has the right to do whatever He may please but in spite of His unlimited powers He has rules and principles under which He runs His universe and conducts His business. Without rules and strict principles He would become unruly and so create the danger of chaos in His Kingdom. Furthermore, to say that the Canaanites were grossly immoral people, and as punishment for their idolatry and horrible crimes such as sacrificing their children, God ordered the Israelites to kill and drive them out of Canaan would be irrational because God's method of dealing with immorality is through reforms and education and not by killing and destruction. There are, of course, examples in history showing that God destroyed people and nations, especially the example of the people of Sodom, who had rejected their prophets and transgressed and totally rebelled against all norms of decency and human dignity, so that God used His prerogative of destroying them. But these were extreme situations and God continues to have this prerogative to destroy future people and nations when they also become total transgressors and incorrigible. However, before God resorts to this extreme action He does give them opportunity to mend their ways by first sending prophets and reformers to them. When God decides to enact His wrath to totally destroy a people, He then uses natural forces such as floods and earthquakes etc. But when the situation is not totally hopeless Gods uses His chosen people and reformers to guide the wrongdoers and gives them ample opportunity to right their wrongs. In the case of the Canaanites, it is not clear from either the historical accounts or the scriptural descriptions that they had reached such a point of no return to human decency that they had to be killed and driven out as the only way of dealing with them. Their religion was paganism, just as many other people followed their own customs. The practice of sacrificing children was also widespread. The Pharaohs were killing newborn boys and the Arabs were killing their newborn baby girls. If these were adequate reasons to destroy a nation, then many nations in the region would have been annihilated. Prophet Mohammed also faced the immorality of the Arabs since they, too, were killing their newborn baby girls. But he did not resort to violent action against the Arabs; rather he cured this disease by education and reform, which is truly the way of God for dealing with such abhorrent customs.

It all began when Prophet Abraham (may peace be upon him) was chosen by God to spread the message of One God by rejecting the idolatry that had gripped human society. Hence Prophet Abraham undertook a vigorous campaign against idolatry and preached the religion of One God. This endeavour got him into serious trouble even with his own father, who was one of the main crafters and suppliers of the idols. Prophet Abraham was persecuted and harassed for rejecting the ancient custom of worshipping idols. Nimrod, who was king at the time, put him in a fire to end his new religion. However, God rescued Abraham from fire and persecution and then advised him to migrate to another land, Canaan, and carry on his religious mission there. Consequently, Prophet Abraham left his ancestral home in Ur of the Chaldees in what is now Iraq. Subsequently, God referred to Abraham as his friend for the work he was doing. Technically, Prophet Abraham was a refugee who migrated at God's Will to another country to escape atrocities and persecution. He brought his wife, Sara, with him, but they had no offspring; so Prophet Abraham took a second wife, Hagar, who bore him a son named Ishmael. Later Sara also gave birth to a son of her own named Isaac. However, Sara and Hagar had family squabbles, so Abraham took Hagar and Ishmael off to another place, which is now known as Mecca in Saudi Arabia, and kept Sara in Canaan. Hence Arabs and Israelis are the two branches of Abraham's posterity, one stemming from Ishmael, who are the Arabs, and the other from Isaac, who are the Jews. Ironically, in spite of such close blood relationship, the Arabs and the Jews are now each other's bitterest enemies and miserably fail to co-exist as two branches of the same family. Isaac's son was Jacob, who was particularly liked by God and given the second name of Israel. Hence his posterity are known as the children of Israel, who are the present-day Jewish community.

Later in the course of history, the Jewish descendants of Prophet Abraham described Canaan as their Promised Land given to them by God and began asserting exclusive claim over it on religious grounds. Prophet Abraham had made no declaration laying exclusive title to Canaan, but the Jews rely on God's promises to Abraham as recorded in Genesis 12.7, 15.18-21, and 17.8. They also cite 21.12-13, where God tells Abraham that Isaac, the ancestor of the Jews, is his true heir, though Ishmael, the ancestor of the Arabs will also be provided for. Again, in 35.12 God promises the land of Canaan to the descendants of Jacob (otherwise named Israel) to the exclusion of Abraham's other descendants. From these passages the Jews and other later offshoots of Judaism such as the Puritans, Nonconformists and Evangelicals have deduced that God has given the Jews an irrevocable title deed not only to the whole of the Holy Land (Canaan) but also to Jordan, Lebanon, and Syria as far as the Euphrates. The counter-argument that that would be unfair and therefore contrary to God's justice simply doesn't trouble the Jews and their Evangelical supporters. According to their theology, God arbitrarily blesses some individuals and nations and condemns others, but to say that He is therefore not just is blasphemous. As they read Genesis, God arbitrarily favoured Isaac over Ishmael and Jacob over Esau, not because they were more virtuous but simply because that suited His plans. Similarly in Deuteronomy, Moses is represented as reminding the Israelites more than once that God did not choose them to possess Canaan because they were better people than the Canaanites but simply because He had promised Abraham, Isaac, and Jacob that their descendants would have it (e.g. Deut. 9.4-5). These passages are accompanied by others where Moses warns them that they will lose the land again if they forget God (e.g. Deut. 6.12-15). But as far as most Jews and Evangelical supporters are concerned, mistreating other people who live in the Holy Land is not disobedience to God, because He repeatedly commanded them to kill or drive out the original inhabitants. That is why they are so eager to identify the modern Arabic-speaking population of the Holy Land as descendants of the Canaanites, overlooking the fact that they probably also descend, at least in part, from Jews who converted to Christianity in ancient times and whose descendants either kept that faith or converted again embracing Islam. Their argument that the Canaanites were immoral people and so deserved to be killed does not hold true today since the modern Palestinian Arabs are all either Muslims or Christians and do not worship heathen idols or sacrifice their children. Modern Jews cannot claim the same sanctions for dispossessing them as they did against the Canaanites.

These are some of the essential elements of the Jewish and Evangelical Christian beliefs about the Jewish claim over Palestine. There is no disagreement that God indeed brought Prophet Abraham to Canaan and also showed the children of Israel the way to a safer place where they were promised a life without being persecuted. However, the inference that God had given them exclusive rights or even ownership of this land is contentious as it is not substantiated by either God's own attributes or the declarations of Prophet Abraham.

While we are bound by respect for other people's religious beliefs and their scriptures, we cannot help testing the above elements of faith on the anvil of rationality because they affect the rights and lives of others. It becomes a matter of concern for other communities and religions when these edicts proclaim that God has disinherited Ishmael from being Abraham's heir and that God has also commanded the Israelites to kill or drive out the original inhabitants from Canaan. Had the Jewish faith been self-contained without encroaching upon the rights of others, no one would bother about what they might believe in or what their scriptures might say.

Since the Jews believe that Canaan is exclusively theirs by virtue of God's commandment, their very philosophy and view of the nature of God and His attributes come into question as to whether He really is "a just God" as the Jews and their Evangelical supporters claim or His image has been somehow distorted to justify a land claim. Can God really be a just God, when He is portrayed as so blatantly unjust with regard to Canaan and its people and Ishmael? Religious philosophies must have a sense of proportion and conform to logical understanding; otherwise they may lose credibility. While faiths may be corrupted, the doctrines of religion cannot avoid rationality or logical definition if they are to be accepted as a divine word of God. If we take this approach, then we must question where the justice is when God repeatedly commanded the Jews to kill or drive out the original inhabitants of Canaan, demolish their homes, seize their livelihoods and subject them to the severest oppression. If that were truly the commandment from God, then manifestly God would fail His own test of justice. This cannot happen, because God is perfect and beyond any shortcomings. If He claims to be a just God, then He will be just in all circumstances and not forsake the precepts of justice in one case and enforce it in another. This would be tantamount to a double standard. Thus logical analysis of the Jewish position on Palestine suggests that there is something seriously amiss in their belief system.

The other side is that before Prophet Abraham migrated there were already inhabitants in this land, the native Canaanites, who had been living there from dawn of history. They practised paganism and had an established socio-religious civilisation of their own. Economically, they were self-sufficient as farmers and shepherds. They were not at war with God and mostly lived a peaceful life according to their own customs. Undoubtedly they practised many immoral customs but that was common in the human society of that time. So they lived a lifestyle like most other ancient people and also did war from time to time among themselves. In any case, they did not oppose Prophet Abraham's arrival and there was no conflict between the natives and the new immigrants except that they differed in matters of faith. Prophet Abraham preached his religion of One God, which many natives embraced, but there were no religious wars or persecution of either party by the other. Jacob and his sons and their offspring continued to live in this peaceful environment of co-existence.

When Canaan was hit by a severe drought that brought acute food shortages, misery and hardships on the population, the children of Israel decided of their own freewill that it was not advantageous to continue living there; so, the whole body decided to leave Canaan and migrate yet another time. This time their destination was Egypt, which was more prosperous and offered a brighter economic future. No one expelled the Israelites from Canaan; rather they forsook it on their own for a better life in Egypt.

They adopted Egypt as their new home and country and indeed prospered there, moving up in society and gaining high positions in the kingdom, especially during the administration of Prophet Joseph. They lived in Egypt successfully for several centuries without interruption or returning to Canaan to regain their residential status or maintain their claim over Canaan as their Promised Land. In practical terms, their long and protracted departure diminished their links with Canaan as their homeland.

Everything went on just as human civilisations are supposed to go on. The notion of Canaan as being their Promised Land or a safe haven and place of refuge had faded away as the Israelites had found another home in Egypt and were busy enjoying a new prosperous and successful life there. However, things went sour in Egypt. After having acquired success and prominence in the society, the Israelites somehow lost favour with the Pharaohs. Whatever the reasons were, the Pharaohs were enormously displeased with the children of Israel and decided to take harsh measures against them. It is well known how brutally the Pharaohs treated the Hebrews and that they put them in severe bondage. The Hebrews had no way to escape the oppression; so they appear to have renewed their contact with God in the name of their ancestors and prayed for help to save them from the savagery and inhumanity of the Pharaoh. God's mercy thus came into play, and the most Merciful and Beneficent God summoned Prophet Moses to take the children of Israel back to their original place of refuge, Canaan, so that they could again live in peace and harmony there. How Moses freed the Israelites from the bondage and extricated them from Egypt is well known.

However, it is noteworthy that even after Moses had gone to Mount Sinai to receive the word of God, some members of the Israelite caravan recanted their loyalty to him and crafted an object from their ornaments, a bull-calf, and began worshipping it instead of the God of Abraham and Moses. Worshipping a bull-calf was common practice in those days, so it was easy for the Hebrews to go back to the old custom. When Moses saw this transgression upon his return he was enormously upset and angry at such perverse behaviour. Anyway after he forgave them the expedition moved towards Canaan, the ancient Promised Land of security. There were many difficulties and disagreements among different tribes of the Hebrews as to how they would enter Canaan. Some were too tired and exhausted to go any further, others were afraid that Canaanites were too powerful and kill them in no time. Hence they were arguing with Moses, asking for help from his God to first clear out the Canaanites from their Promised Land so they could enter without fear of losing their lives. While the arguments were still going on, Prophet Moses passed away. His demise created an acute vacuum in leadership. The military leader of the expedition, named Joshua, then assumed the leadership and continued the journey. He also became custodian of the tablets that Moses had brought from Mount Sinai. The demise of Prophet Moses at that particular time was perhaps the most unfortunate and profoundly significant event in human history, because it opened the door for a controversial character to assume the leadership of the Israelites. It changed the dimensions of Middle Eastern politics forever and laid the foundation of an enduring strife from which our world is suffering even to this day.

Joshua was a military leader and his goals were completely militaristic. He had also emerged from the brutalities of the Pharaohs and been exposed to savage treatment and understandably did not want his people to go through that experience ever again. He was following the instructions from God to bring the Israelites into Canaan but the tactics he used were very questionable. It seems that he agreed with some of the tribes that it was essential first to kill and drive out the Canaanites and then establish the state of Israel, so the children of Israel could live under their own rule without falling under the domination of others that might treat them with savagery and harshness. What better place for making a country of their own than Canaan, the Promised Land? Thus, while the expedition was still on its way to Canaan, Joshua's intentions had changed, and he began planning a new strategy of taking over Canaan as an exclusively Hebrew territory by killing and driving out the Canaanites. However, at the same time, he was also aware that the natives of Canaan had a strong civilisation of their own and would resist any military takeover of their land. While the Canaanites might not have opposed the return of the Hebrews as refugees, they were naturally not going to allow a territorial takeover without a hard fight. Consequently, Joshua realised that he would need to build an army and prepare the Israelites to fight for a homeland. This was not easy, since the Israelites did not want to fight at all. For one thing, they had fewer resources; and for another, they were too fatigued and demoralised from their arduous journey, so it was hard to turn them into a fighting force. From their point of view, it seemed that they would consider themselves lucky if they could find a place to live and start life all over again without having to face brutality again. The thought of engaging in an uncertain war under those conditions was not popular. Many tribes wanted God to fight on their behalf and secure the land so they might enter without struggling for it. However, God had ordered the Israelites to make an effort to enter Canaan, and Moses had said previously that God had permitted the Israelites to resort to defensive war in the event their entry was resisted by the Canaanites.

The Quran has also described the journey of the children of Israel and their dilemma of how to enter Canaan. According to sura *Baqara* verse 245 the children of Israel were permitted to kill in the cause of God, which Muslim scholars interpret as the first *Jihad Fisabilillah* that authorised the Israelites to kill the idol-worshipping and immoral Canaanites if they opposed their re-entry. Being *Fisabilillah* meant that this war was restricted by the rules of God, which only permit wars in self-defence. The inference is that the children of Israel were stimulated to enter the assigned land and were permitted by God to kill if their entry was resisted by the Canaanites. The interpretation that this was a blanket permission to annihilate the transgressors and free the Promised Land of the idol-worshippers and immoral inhabitants is not consistent with God's character of forgiveness and mercy to reform the wrongdoers. Furthermore the children of Israel were made "a light and example" for the rest of humanity by virtue of their chosen status, so they carried an even greater burden to inculcate education and reforms instead of exterminating the misguided or wrongdoers. They were given permission for a defensive war but their primary duty remained to readopt the Promised Land and live there as a light and example for the others.

Section 4 of sura *Maida* in verses 22 to 29 provides more information about the return of the children of Israel to the Promised Land. First it tells how Moses reminded his people of the blessings that God had bestowed upon them when He produced prophets among them, made them kings and gave them what He had not given to any other among the peoples. They were then commanded to enter the Holy Land, which Allah had assigned to them. They were warned not to turn their backs ignominiously; otherwise they would be overthrown and ruined. But the children of Israel declined to proceed because they feared that the people living in this land were exceedingly strong and might kill them. They were not willing to enter until God made these people leave first. But, despite their unwillingness, there were two persons among the God-fearing men whom Allah had bestowed His grace who said "assault them at the proper gate. When once you are in victory will be yours." This was a response proposed by two men who were in the group of men of Moses who were discussing ways to overcome the fear of the strong people of Canaan that had gripped the Israelites. Moses admonished the Israelite tribes to put their trust in Allah if they had faith in Him. However, they did not heed and insisted that Moses and his Lord should fight the kings of Canaan and when it was free of the strong people they would then enter the assigned land. Otherwise they would remain outside and never be able to enter to the end of time.

It is clear from the Quranic version that the children of Israel were indeed commanded by God to enter Canaan because it had been assigned to them as a place of peace and refuge. They were even encouraged by two men from Moses' group to force their entry and resort to a defensive war in case of resistance as Moses had already said. Their refusal to comply with the command of God was tantamount to rebellion against Moses as well as God. It is important to note that according to the description in sura *Maida* the notion of driving out the strong people, the natives, persistently came from the Israelites, who kept demanding that Moses and his Lord should kill them and drive them out before they would enter the Holy Land. Killing or driving out the strong people was not a commandment from God, but rather a demand from the children of Israel; the Quran describes it as a rebellion and represents God as consoling Moses not to sorrow over these rebellious people.

The two men who had suggested assaulting the Canaanites at the proper gate were proposing to break the stalemate that the Israelites had created for entering the Promised Land. Again it should be noted that the notion of "assault" was not proposed by God; rather it was the suggestion of two men who were trying to break the deadlock. It is presumed without evidence that one of these men was perhaps Joshua, who took the notion of assault further and turned it into an offensive war to kill and drive out the natives to satisfy the children of Israel so that they might proceed to enter Canaan without any fear or resistance. Religion was the only tool with which Joshua could spur the expedition, especially since he took charge of the Scrolls, the Torah, after Moses' demise. So perhaps he decided to tamper with some parts of the Torah to incite the Israelites in the name of God. He reasoned that if he could portray God as a God of war and vengeance and make aggressive war a commandment of God, then the Israelites' resistance to war would diminish and he would be able to build an army to attack the Canaanites, which was what many of the tribes were wishing anyway. Hence God's words were used to spur the Israelites by sanctifying a war of aggression to kill and drive out the strong people from Canaan.

Thus what might have been a peaceful re-entry into the Promised Land, or at best a defensive war to gain entry, was turned by Joshua into an offensive war that entailed killing and driving out the natives. Consequently, peace in the Holy Land was ruined forever and the prospects of a peaceful co-existence with the natives have now become impossible to achieve, as we see today in the conflict between the Arabs and Israelis.

In order to support this development historically, it is necessary to consider another view of how the notion of aggressive war came to be incorporated into the Torah. It may make this study rather lengthier than it already is, but in the interest of understanding our world's most profound and volatile topic, a little extra reading may be tolerated.

Most educated liberal Christians believe that all the historical books of the Old Testament down to II Kings were compiled as a continuous history by a Jew living at Babylon about 550 B.C., after the leaders of the nation had been deported there by the Babylonians, and suspect that the Books of Moses were further revised by Ezra in the 5th or 4th century B.C.E. While one can to some extent disentangle the immediate sources, it is extremely difficult to decide how much ultimately depends on sources contemporary with the recorded events, how much reflects songs and other traditions handed down by word of mouth, and how much represents the authors' reconstruction of what people did and said. Both archaeological evidence and the evidence of other parts of the Bible (particularly Judges) have convinced many investigators that the Book of Joshua is largely historical fiction. Of the cities that Joshua is said to have conquered, some are said elsewhere to have been captured by others, notably Caleb and Barak (see Judges 1 & 4); some appear in later books as still in the hands of the Canaanites, which implies that either Joshua never really took them or the Canaanites soon recovered them; Jericho seems to have been rebuilt and refortified by the Moabites soon after Joshua's time (Judges 3.13); and the archaeologists can find no evidence that Ai was inhabited at the time of the Hebrew conquest of Canaan at all, let alone destroyed. (In contrast to this view, as we shall see later from excerpts from Karen Armstrong's book, others believe that Ai was inhabited and the Israelites returned to slaughter all its people.)

The material in the Book of Joshua cannot be precisely dated, but many scholars think it was shaped by the religious revival in the southern Hebrew kingdom of Judah in the 8th and 7th centuries B.C. The northern kingdom of Israel fell to the Assyrians in 722 B.C., and the religious reformers in Judah ascribed its fall to idolatry and apostasy. It seems likely that their interpretation of earlier Hebrew history was coloured by those recent events. They blamed the Hebrews' failure to conquer Canaan completely on unfaithfulness to God, when the real explanation was that the Hebrew tribes became disunited and did not fully co-operate (Judges 5.15b-18 and 23) and the older inhabitants of the land had superior weapons (Judges 4.3, I Samuel 13.19-22). And while it seems likely that Moses had indeed warned the Israelites against mixing with the Canaanites to safeguard them adopting their religion and customs, it also seems likely that his laws were edited at the time of the religious revival to strengthen those prohibitions. Thus in Deuteronomy Israelites are forbidden to marry women of the surrounding nations, but in the Book of Ruth the heroine is a Moabite woman who married Israelite men both times and became an ancestor of David. The author of her story never gives any hint that her husbands broke the law of Moses by marrying her, which argues that there was no Mosaic Law against marrying foreigners in his time and the religious reformers must have added that Law to the Torah later. The same religious reformers seem to have depicted the time of Joshua's leadership as their own idea of a golden age when the Israelites had nothing to do with the Canaanites except to kill or enslave them, but their picture seems to rest on very slender evidence.

Before references may be quoted to further support the argument that Joshua turned the Israelites' entry into an aggressive assault, it is necessary to ponder upon the attributes of God, to consider whether it was really God who was issuing these dictates or His name was being misused. From what we have seen so far, God is not a God of aggressive war. He permits only defensive wars, which are very different in character and purpose from offensive wars. Had aggression or offensive wars been one of His attributes, then He would have already demonstrated it in Iraq and in Egypt. It will be remembered that when His friend, Prophet Abraham, was persecuted in Iraq, God did not call the Iraqis His enemies or start war against them; He simply chose to guide His friend to migrate peacefully to a safer place. Again, when the children of Israel or descendants of Abraham faced brutal and savage oppression in Egypt, God did not wage war against the Pharaohs. He preferred migration once more and appointed Moses to extricate the children of Israel from Egypt. If God were really a God of war of aggression, then the time and place for Him to demonstrate His wrath and warring capabilities would have been against the brutal Pharaohs in Egypt. The Pharaohs had committed every aggression that displeased God, yet He did not wage war against them. The fact that He did not resort to war and chose migration for the Hebrews to avoid confrontation proves the point that God is not the God of war. The Pharaoh brought his fate of drowning on himself because he kept chasing the Israelites; otherwise God simply rescued His chosen people by enabling them to leave the scene of hostilities. Since God had not engaged in any aggressive wars, it is uncharacteristic of Him to suddenly become a God of war at the time of re-entering Canaan and declare the Canaanites His enemies when apparently they had done nothing to harm God or His favourite people. They had provided a safe haven to the children of Israel once and would likely have offered refuge again had Joshua not waged an offensive war. Granted the Canaanites were idol-worshippers and immoral people, but these were no grounds for pronouncing them as enemies of God. Undoubtedly they needed education and reforms but killing them or exterminating them was no solution of their transgression. Declaring a war of aggression was uncharacteristic of God and inconsistent with His conduct as seen in Iraq and Egypt.

Those who claim that God is the God of war and vengeance and spurred the children of Israel to kill the original inhabitants to gain total control of the Promised Land have purposely corrupted God's image, as well as their own faith and scripture, to justify a territorial war. As far as destruction of many nations of the ancient times is concerned, it was not God's war against them; rather it was His anger or wrath brought on by persistent transgression and rebellion by those nations despite God's endeavours to educate and reform them through his messengers. His anger erupting in the form of floods, earthquakes and other natural disasters that destroyed them was an act in the last resort because of their incessant rebellion. Before they were stricken with natural calamities they were, however, given many opportunities to reform their conduct, but they refused, which ultimately brought their destruction. There is a distinction between waging war and being angry because of misdeeds.

Prophet Abraham, who was the first to be sent to the Promised Land by God, never made exclusive claim over this land, nor did he fight against the Canaanites to expel or overpower them to gain control of the territory in his own hands. The Bible clarifies Abraham's position and elucidates that he did make war at least once, when he allied himself with the kings of the Canaanites to attack invading Mesopotamians and rescue his nephew Lot and his household, whom the invaders had carried off. Interestingly, though, he refused to take his own share of the spoils when they had defeated the invaders (Genesis 14). This passage of the Bible is evidence that Prophet Abraham was acting in co-operation with the Canaanites in a spirit of co-existence and helping to defend Canaan against foreign invaders. Had Abraham laid exclusive claim to Canaan, then there would already have been a war or at least a conflict between him and the kings of the Canaanites instead of the co-operation that the Bible clearly depicts. This is convincing biblical evidence that Abraham made Canaan his home in the spirit of co-existence and co-operation with the people and kings of Canaan. It is a totally opposite position to the one supposedly taken later by the Israelites under Joshua's leadership at the time of re-entering Canaan, when they declared an offensive war against the Canaanites to control Canaan and press their exclusive claim over the territory in the name of God. The Bible also demonstrates that Abraham never engaged in any offensive war for territorial gain. His encounter with the Mesopotamians was purely defensive, which is permitted by the Divinity.

As far as Prophet Moses is concerned, it is also irreconcilable to present him as characterising God as a God of war and vengeance: "to me belongeth vengeance and recompence" (Deut. 32.35; also verses 41 and 43); "the LORD is a man of war" (Ex. 15.3; and see the whole song from which the verse comes). Again, if we analyse Moses' position rationally we may ask, if Moses knew that God was a God of war, then why did he not pray to God to deploy His skills in war against the Pharaohs? It would have simplified the matter, instead of taking an arduous journey to escape persecution and asking God to send Aaron to help him out. Obviously, implicating Moses with characterising God as the God of war is irreconcilable. Moses did promote a defensive war in case the Canaanites resisted a peaceful entry of the Hebrews, but that was not akin to promoting war of aggression as attributed to him. Similarly, the narratives in Numbers, Joshua, Judges, and Kings, which clearly represent God as commanding and approving the wars that the Israelites waged against neighbouring peoples, are also irreconcilable. The war proponents also cite King Saul, who is even said to have lost God's favour because he failed to wipe the Amalekites out completely (I Samuel 15).

All these notions of war and similar passages, however irreconcilable they may be, appeal to the modern militant Jews, who freely use them to justify their actions against the Palestinians. Even though one of the Ten Commandments commands the Jews "Thou shalt not kill", the Israelites did not regard either killing their enemies in war or killing unarmed people in obedience to God's command conveyed through a prophet as murder. This shows that when war of aggression is wrongly attributed to God, the corrupted notion impairs the intellect of the believers so that they even forget the meaning of murder.

Having stated this, we now quote some excerpts from Karen Armstrong's book titled *Holy War*. Karen Armstrong is a respected scholar in religion and has written several books about the faiths of Jews, Christians and Muslims. She has also taught religion in Britain and the United States, including the Leo Baeck College for the Study of Judaism and the Training of Rabbis and Teachers. Hence she is a reliable source of information on religion.

She writes on page 5 of her book *Holy War* that:

> The seed of much future strife is found in the original revelation to Abraham. Almost the first words that God spoke when he revealed himself to Abraham were: "To your descendants I will give you this land" (Genesis 12:7). To make this promise good Abraham's descendants had to fight the first of many savage holy wars for this land, which many Jews today still see as essential to the integrity of Judaism. After all, God spent more time promising Abraham that he would give this land to his descendants than making any further theological revelations about himself.

Armstrong further states on page 7 and 8:

> One of the Ten Commandments given to Moses on Mount Sinai was "Thou shalt not kill." Indeed most of these Commandments are concerned with an absolute respect for the inalienable rights of others, and this is one of the greatest legacies of Judaism to the rest of the world. But as they prepared to enter the Promised Land, God told his people that they would have to engage in a ruthless war of extermination. By taking his people back to Canaan, Moses was taking them back to their roots because of God's original promise to their father Abraham. They believed that the land was theirs, but there were other people living there already who had made it their home for centuries, and naturally they were not going to hand over their country without a fight. These people were in the way of the divine plan; they were also enemies of the new Jewish self. Because they opposed values and plans that were "sacred" to the Jews and essential to God's plans for them, they had to be annihilated. The normal human rights that the Jews were commanded to extend to other people did not apply to the Canaanites, who had become the enemies of God. This absolute hostility is a characteristic of the holy war. Because the Canaanites were obstacles to the Jewish fulfilment they had to be exterminated and there

was no possibility of co-existence. "I shall exterminate these," God told his people, "they must not live in your country." (Exodus 23:23,33). It was not simply a territorial matter. The Canaanites had achieved a more advanced culture than the Israelites and their lifestyle would be very attractive to the weary nomads. They could destroy their newly emerging Jewish self and the new religion of monotheism, which was still so revolutionary (evolutionary?) that it was a fragile plant. The Israelites could very easily be seduced by the Canaanites' fertility cults and idolatrous faith. Therefore God gave Moses very clear instructions, frequently repeated in the Bible, about how these new enemies and their religions were to be treated:

> When Yahweh your God had led you into the land you are entering to make your own, many nations will fall before you: Hittites, Girgashites, Amorites, Canaanites, Perizzites, Hivites and Jebusites, seven nations greater and stronger than yourselves. Yahweh your God will deliver them over to you and you will conquer them. You must lay them under a ban. You must make no covenant with them nor show them any pity. You must not marry with them: you must not give a daughter of yours to a son of theirs, nor take a daughter of theirs for a son of your, for this would turn away your son from following me to serving other gods, and the anger of Yahweh would blaze out against you and soon destroy you. Instead deal with them like this: tear down their altars, smash their standing stones, cut down their sacred poles and set fire to their idols. For you are a people consecrated to Yahweh your God. It is you that Yahweh your God has chosen to be the very own people out of all the peoples on earth. (Deuteronomy 7:1-6)

... In a Jewish holy war, there was no question of peaceful co-existence, mutual respect or peace treaties. The little Jewish kingdom was an island of true religion in the ocean of Middle Eastern paganism. There was a religious siege and naturally a deep insecurity. Until the Israelites felt more confident, they could only fight their enemies to the death. When God had saved his people from the Egyptians the ordinary laws of nature had been suspended; so too when the Jews had to establish themselves in the Promised Land, ordinary morality ceased to apply. This is a critical element in the holy wars of both Jews and, later, Christians.

Moses died before reaching the Promised Land. It was Joshua who in about 1200 B.C.E. led the Israelites into Canaan and established the twelve tribes of Israel in the Promised Land by means of a long and utterly ruthless military campaign. He fulfilled the commands of God perfectly. When a town was conquered, it was duly put "under a ban," which meant total destruction and extermination. Men, women, children and even the animals were massacred and the cities reduced to rubble:

480 SHEIKH MOHAMMED NAEEM

When Israel finished killing all the inhabitants of Ai in the open ground
and where they had followed them into the wilderness, and when all to a
man had fallen by the edge of sword, all Israel returned to Ai and
slaughtered all its people. The number of those that fell that day, men and
women together, was twelve thousand, all people of Ai... Then Joshua
burned Ai, making it a ruin for evermore, a desolate place even to this
day. (Joshua 8:24,25,28) Then Joshua came and wiped out the Anakim
from the highlands, from Hebron, from Debir, from Anab, from all the
highlands of Judah and all the inhabitants of Israel; he delivered them
and their towns over to the ban. No more Anakim were left in Israel
territory except at Gaza, Gath and Ashod. (Ibid. 11:21,22)

...The holy war continued for another two hundred years, under the judges
and heroes of Israel like Gideon, Deborah and Samson. As they exterminated
their foes, the Israelites also tried to build up their own faith. As the pagan
towns and shrines were destroyed, temples of Yahweh were built at Shiloh, Dan,
Bethel, Bethlehem and Hebron.

We are grateful to Karen Armstrong and her publishers for producing
the book *Holy War,* which fills in the historical background and highlights
the religious beliefs that thwart peace treaties and resolution of territorial
disputes, which are still going on. As can be seen from these excerpts, the
whole concept of God was drastically changed in the scripture that was
handed over to the Israelites by Joshua after the demise of Moses.

The way Joshua had represented God's commandments gives a grim view
of God. He had been portrayed as a warmonger, hatful, revengeful, brutal,
scornful, unjust and contemptuous of the Canaanites and furiously and
aggressively impatient to exterminate these human beings from their homes,
lands and livelihoods. God has been made to appear as most anxious to
cause every conceivable distress and harm to the Canaanites, so that His
chosen ones could relish happiness and live in the homes and lands that
had once belonged to the Canaanites (Palestinians). The Torah shows
God as a totally unmerciful and un-benevolent, biased and prejudiced
deity who had taken up ruthless war against His own creatures, human
beings. God is quoted as forbidding pity on these people and urging His
chosen people to deny all human rights and privileges to these people,
make no covenant with them, nor show them any pity, and cease to apply
ordinary laws of morality to them. Why would God take such a cruel view
of the Canaanites when they had previously welcomed Prophet Abraham
and done nothing since to harm Him? Surely His words must have been
tampered with.

Joshua's presentation of God's image is blasphemous. It is beyond common sense that the Creator of the human race, including the Canaanites, would harbour such obnoxious thoughts against His own creatures. Humans beings could be disloyal, disbelievers and defiant, but they could never pose a threat to God as His enemies.

Joshua implicated God in warmongering because he wanted to take over Canaan exclusively for the Hebrews at all costs. Hence the Torah appears to have been manipulated to give Joshua the authority he needed to wage ruthless war against the Canaanites. Comparison of words spoken by Moses and Joshua will show that Joshua's words are different from Moses'. As already quoted, one of the Ten Commandments given to Moses on Mount Sinai stated: "Thou shalt not kill." Armstrong tells us that "Indeed most of these commandments are concerned with an absolute respect for the inalienable rights of others, and this is one of the greatest legacies of Judaism to the rest of the world." This was the view of Moses as revealed to him by God. Compare it with the views that Joshua presented in the above excerpts. They are in stark contradiction to Moses. The seeds of hatred and wrongful attributions to God that Joshua appears to have sown have corrupted the faith of the Israelites forever.

Another excerpt from Armstrong's book:

A turning point in the holy campaign was King David's conquest of the Jebusite City of Jerusalem in about 1000 B.C.E. From this point Jerusalem, the "City of David," would be consecrated to the One God, and because of this original Jewish occupation the city would later become holy to Christians and Muslims too… But it is important to note that it did not become "holy" to the Jews until quite late in its own history and in the history of the chosen people, even though the Jews would later see it as essential to the integrity of Judaism. It is also true that its sanctification had certain ironies. David departed from Joshuan practice when he conquered Jerusalem. He did not massacre the Jebusites, though he had shown no squeamishness about massacring *goyim* or the non-Jews in their hundreds elsewhere… David wanted to make Jerusalem the capital of his kingdom and the centre of Judaism, so he had the Ark of the Covenant, a precious relic of the years in wilderness, brought into the city in triumph. He then wondered whether he should build a temple for the Ark, which in some mysterious way localised the Presence of God (the *Shekinah*). But God forbade David to build the temple in Jerusalem and there are two versions of this story. In one version God said that he had always been a nomadic God who had never been associated with one particular shrine. It may be that David, a passionately religious man, realised the danger of identifying the *Shekinah* with one temple, built by human hands. It could lead to idolatry, which lifted an earthly place and a human building to the same level as God himself. In a later version, God forbade David to build the temple because he had shed too

much blood, albeit at the divine command. This shows the first sign of worry
about the morality of the holy war. In this version God tells David that the
building of the temple has been assigned to his son Solomon, the man of
peace. (The name Solomon comes from *shalom* the Hebrew word for peace.)

After nearly two hundred years of war that Joshua had started, a new
prophet of God came to carry on the message of monotheism and refinement and reformation of the children of Israel. He was Prophet David. As
can be seen from above excerpt, he built the city of Jerusalem and ruled
over it as the City of One God. Initially, he wanted to dedicate Jerusalem
exclusively to Judaism, but God forbade him. It is an important point to
note that Jews do not have an exclusive right over Jerusalem, since God had
forbidden it. This is the reason why King David built Jerusalem as the first-
ever centre to worship God on the foundation of monotheism, meaning
that this city is dedicated to all believers in monotheism such as the Jews,
Christians and Muslims. King David was a notable prophet of God, and
through him God was replacing Joshua's warmongering with peace. David
clearly departed from Joshua's practice of wanton killing and destruction of
the fallen cities when he conquered Jerusalem without slaughtering the
inhabitants. All the brutalities that Joshua practised needed to be replaced,
which was what Prophet David did by initiating a peaceful beginning at the
command of God.

This process of transforming war into peace continued as God sent
another prophet after David who was totally committed to peace. As a
matter of fact God gave this prophet the name of peace. He was King
Solomon, the son of King David, who derived his name from the Hebrew
word *Shalom* meaning peace. This shows how urgent it had become for God
to extricate the children of Israel from warmongering and bring peace as a
way of life. It was a great move by God to cast out the abhorrent notion of
war of aggression. The prophethood of Solomon is a further testimony that
God was determined to uproot the Joshuan mentality from the children of
Israel and build the foundation of peace and co-existence. So God placed
"this man of peace in a very different position from his predecessors."
There was no air of militarism in his policies. Armstrong explains how King
Solomon endeavoured to establish peace and took practical measures to
show tolerance to other religious customs by incorporating some of the
characteristics of paganism into his Temple. He took a bold step to impress
upon the Israelites how crucial it was to banish the notion of war of
aggression and embrace tolerance and co-existence with other cultures,
just as Prophet Abraham had done right at the start of his entry into
Canaan or Palestine. King Solomon's message from God was a total rejection of Joshuan teachings of war. Armstrong writes:

Solomon did indeed build a temple. This man of peace was in a very different position than his predecessors... The whole building was designed like a typical Canaanite temple, and instead of expressing the pure monotheism of Moses, the Temple had strongly pagan elements. It seems to have been part of Solomon's policy of assimilation with the surrounding culture. He had established himself as an all powerful despot, like other Middle Eastern kings, although hitherto God and the prophets had insisted that this was an un-Jewish institution, for only God could command his people. Solomon also married foreign wives, which was anathema to the spirit of Judaism and directly opposed to God's specific instructions to Moses. Solomon was a confident monarch and his empire was powerful and secure. He did not feel threatened by the surrounding paganism and felt that a degree of assimilation was acceptable in Yahwism. Violent and absolute rejection was unnecessary to a king who felt that the chosen people had reached a new era of security... The Temple of Solomon was not the only sanctuary in the Promised Land; the older temple continued to function and frequently the priests brought aspects of pagan worship into the rituals and liturgy of Yahwism. They were naturally influenced by the prevailing local religious climate and were not yet ready for the austere monotheism that the prophets and sages were developing. This religious strife in the Holy Land was paralleled by a political division. The northern tribes broke away from the southern kings in Jerusalem and formed their own kingdom which they called the Kingdom of Israel and which opposed the smaller Kingdom of Judah in the south. Never again would the Jews experience the unity and security they had known under Solomon. Further their independence was constantly threatened by powerful neighbours who were building mighty empires in the Middle East. Finally in the year 722 there was a catastrophe. The Kingdom of Israel was conquered by King Tiglath-Pileser III of Assyria. The ten northern tribes of Israel were deported, forced to assimilate and were, in religious terms, annihilated. These ten lost tribes disappeared from history forever.

Karen Armstrong further explains how King Solomon strove to achieve co-existence by assimilating local, rather controversial culture in his Temple.

Thousands of labourers were conscripted into the building force as a form of national service. Like all conscriptions, it was fiercely resented, particularly as it lacked the dignity of military service and seemed to reduce the conscripts to the level of slaves. Was their position very different from the position of their forefathers in Egypt, who had been forced to build Pharaoh's pyramids?

The fact that King Solomon was using the spirit of national service as opposed to military service was not appreciated. Armstrong further ex-

plains King Solomon's peace efforts and the doubts prevailing about him
and goes on to say on the same page:

> There was, therefore, a rather dubious element in the building of the Temple
> from the very beginning. When the Temple was completed there was a further
> irony. When they entered this wonderful new building to pray in the Presence
> of One God, the Israelites would have been inescapably reminded of the
> Canaanite cults that they had been told to destroy. When they entered the
> sanctuary, they would have seen an enormous basin called the "molten sea"
> standing upon the figures of twelve brazen oxen. This was a giant bath for
> purification, but its imagery was identical with the Canaanite myth of Yam, the
> primeval waters. The tall free standing pillars would have reminded them of
> the "standing stones" the fertility symbols of Canaanite cults that they had been
> commanded to tear down. The whole building was designed like a typical
> Canaanite temple and instead of expressing the pure monotheism of Moses,
> the Temple had strongly pagan elements. It seems to have been part of Solo-
> mon's policy of assimilation with the surrounding culture.

This account of history shows that the Temple was designed and built as a
genuine step towards a peaceful co-existence in Palestine. King Solomon
took an outstanding and bold step to depart completely from Joshuan
tradition and embarked on creating a peaceful society that would take the
culture of local cults in its stride. By preserving many of the things in the
Temple that Joshua said God had commanded the Israelites to destroy
among the Canaanites, King Solomon reaffirmed that Joshua was wrong.
King Solomon further broke away from Joshua's commands by marrying
with the natives and others to underscore that co-existence was God's
command, which was why he was paving the way for co-existence to fulfil his
duty to God. Though King David "had shown no squeamishness about
massacring *goyim* or non-Jews in their hundreds elsewhere", later at God's
command he worried about the morality of holy war. King Solomon,
however, never spoke of annihilating or exterminating the non-Jews from
Canaan. King Solomon clearly chose peace and recognised the local culture in the domain of his Temple to establish co-existence. Regrettably, this
great example of King Solomon was lost in the debris of regional history
when the Babylonian King Nebuchadnezzar destroyed his temple in the
year 586 B.C.E.

There is, of course, a great deal more to learn from Karen Armstrong's
book titled *Holy War*. Readers are encouraged to look over her excellent
research to comprehend the Palestinian issue in an historical perspective
and grasp its impact on today's world.

Between the time of the Jews' banishment and their return to Israel in
1948 there is a very long and troublesome history. The most notable

affliction was their persecution in Western Europe, which was recurrent rather than continuous and arose from complex causes, both religious and commercial. As was already discussed, the Jews were subjected to savage treatment and brutal massacres on religious grounds. Many Jews of the time thought that it was the worst they had had faced since their banishment from the Promised Land a very long time ago. They were given two choices, either convert to Christianity or accept death. Many Jews accepted death, but many also chose to convert and became Christians. Based on Karen Armstrong's insights, we learn that anti-Semitism had been growing in Spain since the end of the fourteenth century. The Spanish Inquisition was established in 1483 to hunt down the Jews and convert them to Christianity or punish them by death. The rest of Europe was also intolerant. Few Jews were left in Germany by the end of 1349; they had been expelled from Vienna and Linz in 1421, from Cologne in 1424, Ausburg in 1439, Bavaria in 1422 and again in 1450, Perugia in 1485, Vicenza in 1486, Parma in 1468, Milan and Lucca in 1489 and all Tuscany in 1484. Thus the Jews were being thrown out widely in Europe. They were searching for safer places and pondering on how to convince the Christians to show leniency to them and spare their lives. Thus how to escape the brutality of the Western European Christians became a burning question for Jewish intellectuals and scholars.

Manasseh ben Israel, an intellectual Jew living in Amsterdam, wrote several books pointing out to the Christians that Judaism and Christianity had much in common and the two peoples could live as friends. Apparently, Manasseh was trying to bring an end to the Christian hostility towards the Jews. He was well versed in the grief and misery that persecution had caused to the Jewish people, since his family had been a victim of the Spanish Inquisition and had fled to Amsterdam. So his passion was genuine and his premise was that since the Christian Scripture had been derived from the Old Testament and based on the precepts of Judaism, a realisation of spiritual bond would encourage Christians generally to see their affinity with the Jews, which might then lead to cessation of their hostility towards the Jewish people. Hence the Jewish intellectuals began using scriptural inspirations to change the attitude of the Christians. This seemed the only way to escape the Christian brutality.

The Reformation was another factor that helped the Jews since the Christians were divided between Catholicism and Protestantism and became entangled with each other instead of chasing the Muslims and Jews. The Reformation was profoundly religious, but it did not turn Christianity into a humane and tolerant religion. The Catholics were deeply upset with the Protestants for splitting Christianity and so they started religious wars by persecuting them. From the Protestants' point of view the Pope seemed like Antichrist, and so they organised crusades against the Catholics. Luther and other reformers also saw Muslims as a power that was as evil as the

Papacy. Up to this point in time Luther continued his tirades against the Jews and said that their synagogues and prayer books should be burned. He had already had the Jews expelled from Lutheran cities in 1537. Jews were also thrown out of Calvinist cities, even though Calvin sometimes spoke positively of the Jews. Hence, in spite of the Reformation and the internal rift, both Catholics and Protestants maintained their condemnation of both the Muslims and Jews.

Like Manasseh, there were also other Jewish intellectuals who had been similarly preoccupied with the same question of how to change the Christian attitude through scriptural inspirations to spare the Jews. Thus the Jewish scholars and religious leaders had begun searching for ways and means to convince the oppressive Christians to alter their view of the Jews in the light of their common belief in the Old Testament. One might ask, how did they succeed, or how did the persecution recede, or, so to speak, how did the Jews get off the hook?

The short answer is that friendly contacts between Jews and Christian began because the first leaders of the Reformation wished to read the Bible in their own languages instead of the Roman Catholic version in Latin. Hence they needed Jewish scholars to teach them Hebrew and Aramaic and began developing cordial relations with them. Studying the Bible under Jewish teachers, they naturally adopted many of their teachers' views and interpretations of the text. At the same time, as the Protestant theologians read the Bible for themselves, they came to realise that it provided no foundation for the usual Roman Catholic teaching that the Jewish people as a whole were responsible for Christ's crucifixion and under God's curse for that. From reading the gospels they concluded that only the Jewish ruling clique in Jerusalem had been responsible for arresting Christ and denouncing him to the Roman authorities, and so the Jewish people were not to blame for the crucifixion. They also gave more weight than Roman Catholic theologians had to St. Paul's teaching in Romans 11 that God had allowed the Jews to reject Christ for some mysterious purpose of His own, and He would bring them to the true faith in His own good time; and if God himself had hardened the Jews' hearts against believing in Christ, then they could not be blamed for that, either. This explains why, generally speaking, there is far less violent and open anti-Semitism in Protestant than in Catholic countries and accounts for the difference in points of view between the Protestants and Catholics with regard to the crucifixion of Christ. This was the first success of the Jewish scholars in changing the attitude of the hostile Protestant Christians, who were growing steadily in power and authority.

Then in the course of the three hundred years that followed the Reformation, Protestants became progressively better disposed towards Jews, since many Jews had converted to Christianity and adopted their faith. The transformation of attitude gradually permeated Protestant countries over the next two centuries or so, during which period the Jews were steadily absolved from persecution and allowed to take full part in the social, economic and civic life of Western European countries, which had been forbidden hitherto.

As Christians and Jews began to live in integration, the Christians began to pray to God to put an end to the sufferings of the Jews by gathering them from all parts of the world and resettling them in their own country, Palestine. Many Christians believed that Second Coming of Christ would thus happen and ultimately they would be redeemed. Later in the eighteenth century the Zionists were growing in both Britain and the United States and wishing to see the return of Jews for the same reason. The British Zionists even submitted a petition to Prime Minister William Pitt in 1790 pleading for financial aid to help the return of the Jews to assist the Second Coming.

Keeping up the momentum of the Zionists, a future British prime minister from a Jewish background, Benjamin Disraeli, impressed upon the British people in 1829 that without believing in Judaism their faith in Christianity would be incomplete. They were already practising so many laws and precepts of Judaism that not believing in Judaism would be illogical. He reminded them how much Christians owe to Judaism and the Jewish people. This was the reinforcement of British Zionism. Jewish Zionism would develop in Europe fifty years later.

Once Zionism took root in Britain, the British political and religious leaders inaugurated a drive not only to end hostilities but also to realise the return of the Jews to the Promised Land to hasten the Second Coming. Consequently, the British government established its first consular mission in Jerusalem in 1838 to protect the Jews and at the same time to establish the British government's presence in the Middle East for colonial reasons. A further motive was nevertheless to hasten the Second Coming.

The condition of Jews began improving considerably in the nineteenth century as significant numbers of talented Jews in the Protestant countries converted to Protestant Christianity in order to enter fully into mainstream society. But the real breakthrough for the Jews did not come until Lloyd George, a Liberal British Prime Minister, headed a coalition government of the Liberals and the Conservatives during 1916-1922 and took practical steps to realise what had thus far been the wish of the British Zionists. He arranged for the Balfour Declaration in 1917, which signalled the creation of a Jewish homeland in Palestine for the first time since antiquity. There may have been several influences on Lloyd George, including a religious one, that spurred him to take such a dramatic step..

Briefly, looking into the background of Lloyd George, we may note that he was of Welsh parentage. At the age of two, when his father died, his family were taken to Llanystumdwy, near Criccieth, Wales, the home of his uncle Richard Lloyd, who recognised the latent brilliance in the boy and took responsibility for his education. Lloyd George thus acquired his religion, his industry, his vivid oratory, his radical views and his Welsh nationalism under the supervision of his uncle in a small town in Wales. "His uncle had been a preacher in a fundamentalist Welsh Baptist sect with a tradition of interpreting the Bible quite literally. When Lloyd George listened to preachers talking about Palestine, he could only see Palestine in Jewish terms, as he explained in a speech to the Jewish Historical Society in 1925: I was brought up in a school where I was taught far more about the history of the Jews than about the history of my own land... We absorbed it and made it part of the best of the Gentile character" (quoted from *Holy War*).

Lloyd George reached many positions of distinction during his professional and public careers, including the heights as a social reformer with his Old Age Pension Act (1908), the National Insurance Act (1911) and the momentous "people's budget", the rejection of which by the Lords led to a constitutional crisis and the Parliament Act of 1911, which removed the Lords' power to veto. Although a pacifist, he strongly believed in the national rights of smaller countries and saw the parallel between the Welsh and the Boers. Thus, along with pacifism he was also a man of strong actions based on his social, political and religious convictions. The Balfour Declaration was one such bold action under the influence of his own religious convictions as well as the weight of his war cabinet colleagues.

Lord Balfour was brought up in the Scottish Protestant church and was a typical Zionist in an uneasy anti-Semitism, as he was accused of promoting a Jewish homeland simply to get the Jews out of England. Anyway, he had the support of many Zionist politicians, who included Prime Minister Lloyd George, Mark Sykes, Leopard Amery, Lord Milner, Lord Harlech, Robert Cecil and C.P. Scott. It may be noted that Mark Sykes was Catholic by upbringing and had a strong "distaste for the Jews." Therefore, initially he was opposed to Balfour's idea for this reason. Armstrong pointed out that since he was also an ardent colonialist, a real imperialist, he was later able to see the "Jew" as "our" representative in the Middle East and taking possession of Palestine in "our" name to protect "our" interests. Hence he dropped his opposition to Balfour's proposal for imperialistic reasons.

Lloyd George's support for the Balfour Declaration was probably based on a desire to please two groups of people. One was the large body of British "Dissenting" Protestants (corresponding to the American Evangelicals, but mostly rather less fervid and militant) who sympathised with Zionism and tended to vote Liberal. It was an important political consideration. The other group that Lloyd George also wanted to please were the wealthy Jewish businessmen who had helped float the loans that Britain had needed to fight the war and also contributed substantially to both the Liberal and the Conservative Party (Lord Balfour was a Conservative and former prime minister who had entered the wartime coalition government).

Irfan Husain, a Pakistani columnist writing about the process involved in the creation of Israel in the internet edition of the daily *Dawn* of April 17, 2004 and using some of the insights of Jill Hamilton, a British writer, goes on to talk about the religious strain in George Lloyd's war cabinet. He quotes Jill Hamilton as writing in the prologue of her recently published (October 2003) book entitled *God, Guns and Israel* that:

The motives behind the British decision to create a Jewish homeland have never been fully explained. Nor has a reason been given as to why the discussions leading up to it were never debated in the House of Commons...the final discussions took place behind the closed doors of 10 Downing Street... Because this [Balfour] declaration bears the name of the Foreign Secretary, Balfour, it is usually his name alone which is associated with the formation of the Jewish homeland, yet...he only took up the idea after it was accepted by Lord George's War Cabinet, of which he was not a member...

It turns out that seven out of the ten members of the War Cabinet were Nonconformists who included Baptists, Methodists, Unitarians, Presbyterians and Congregationalists, among others.

This broad strain of Christian belief held the Old Testament very close to its heart. This part of the scripture is far longer than the later, post-Christ New Testament, and is firmly rooted in Judaism.

After the Reformation, a number of sects broke away from both the Catholic Church and the Anglican Church, insisting that they would not accept the intermediary role claimed by the priesthood. This movement was given a huge boost by the invention of the printing press and the translation of the Bible into other languages.

The Evangelical movement is very close to the Nonconformist tradition, and both view Palestine through their deep study of the Old Testament and the events and people it so vividly describes.

For millions, this is the actual history of the period. To believers, the return of the Jews to their ancient homeland is a prophecy that it is their duty to see fulfilled. Indeed the Evangelists firmly believe that the Second Coming of Christ can only occur once the Jews return to the Holy Land.

There is clearly a paradox here: the Jews having been persecuted by Christians for centuries, enduring the worst pogroms at the hands of the British, the Spanish, the Russians and the Poles. This age-old persecution culminated in the holocaust carried out by the Nazis, aided by many of their European collaborators. And yet, a well placed group of powerful politicians who believed firmly in the Bible and its teachings made it possible for the Jews to finally realise their millennia-old dream of their own state.

The paradox can best be understood by the deep affinity between Judaism and Nonconformist Protestantism...

The first call to resettle Jews in Palestine came as long ago as in 1621 when Sir Henry Finch, a member of the Parliament and legal adviser to King James I published 'The World's Greatest Restoration' in which he argued that the English people should support 'Jewish settlement in Palestine'. But James I was angered by Finch's argument that he should pay homage to a Jewish king, and threw both the author and the publisher into jail. However, this book brought the biblical pledge into the consciousness of the increasingly vocal Protestant movement.

Although many took up cudgels for the Jews in subsequent years, it was not until Lloyd George came into power that the Zionist movement acquired its most ardent champion at the highest level of power in the U.K., then the acknowledged superpower. From him, the torch of Zionism was passed on to Woodrow Wilson who put the weight of America behind the enterprise in 1919...

The Balfour Declaration was adopted by the delegates to the Versailles Conference of 1919 in which the post–First World War was carved up. Ironically (and revealingly), the idea was even endorsed by the Arab representative, Prince Faisal, the son of Sharif al-Hussain of Mecca. Faisal was determined to become king of Syria, but had to content himself with being made king of Iraq, a post-Ottoman construct comprising three Turkish provinces. Faisal was advised by T.E. Lawrence (Lawrence of Arabia) who drafted a letter from the Arab prince, which was published in the New York Times in which Faisal 'hoped the Jews and Arabs would work together to reform the Near East'.

Continuing our discussion on how the Jews got off the hook, the above article based on Jill Hamilton's insights into what went on behind the scenes in Lloyd George's war cabinet shows that Jews' return to the Holy Land became a prerequisite to the Second Coming of Christ as long ago as 1621. Furthermore the strongest proponents of this notion were the Nonconformists. The Evangelicals, who are very close to the Nonconformists (and Judaism), took up this idea as their duty and now fulfilling it from the echelons of the American power. However, it remained unexplained how this notion of Second Coming being connected to the return of the Jews came to become part of the Evangelical creed. Did Jesus make this prediction himself? Or was it subsequently added?

Since Western military and political support in resettling the Jews has created an enduring human tragedy in the present-day Palestine, it is crucial to find out what is the real motivation of the Western Christians in helping the Jews even in an unjust manner. It is also necessary to discover the origins of the notion that Second Coming is contingent upon the return of the Jews, so that we may cope with the turmoil that it has created.

As was stated above, after the Reformation a number of sects broke away from both the Catholic and the Anglican churches and leaders of the new Protestantism wanted to read Bible in their own languages. Hence they decided to obtain translations of the text of the original Bible, which was in Hebrew.

It is this writer's assessment that since the Jewish scholars, who helped the reformers learn Hebrew, had been anxious to change Christians' oppressive mentality, as evidenced by Manasseh ben Israel's efforts, they interpreted the Biblical prophecy of Christ's Second Coming to cast an impression that it was contingent upon Jews' return to the Holy Land. This might have been an urgent necessity from their point of view to escape the Christian hostility. Clearly the translation made no attempt to falsify the scripture, since the text used for translation at the time of Reformation is virtually the same as that of the surviving manuscripts. However, the interpretation made outside the scripture has the appearance of influencing the scripture itself. It is particularly true in the case of the new sects that had broken away from both the Catholic and Anglican churches who were not yet mature or sophisticated enough to probe the relevance of this interpretation to the original text before absorbing it as part of their beliefs. They may have been too eager to break away from the old tradition and accept anything new put forward by the scholarly translators even outside the scripture and only as their own interpretation. Thus the interpretation, even though not part of the text, may have profoundly impressed the believers, who then might have taken it as attested in scripture, as seems to be the case with the Evangelicals. Such infiltrations in religious matters are not uncommon. The advent of the printing press may also have helped in the absorption of innovative interpretations into the text, as individual sects were now arranging for printing of their own versions of the Bible independently of the others. Their fervour may have clouded their judgement as they accepted the interpretation that Jesus' Second Coming depended upon the return of the Jews to Palestine. The Puritans, the Nonconformists, and successors the Evangelicals may have been quick to adopt it since they were already heavily tilted towards Judaism and sympathetic to the Jews owing to their own roots in Judaism. Their presence in these sects must have helped easy adoption of this interpretation of the Biblical prophecy. Hence they now regard it as a Christian religious edict and part of the Gospel.

However, there is no real basis for this interpretation in the original text. Had it been so then the Catholic Bible and other Protestant Bibles would also have had at least some reference to this effect and the surviving manuscripts would have borne it out. In that case the Jews would not have been persecuted during the Spanish Inquisition as was outlined earlier. Had the Jewish resettlement been mentioned in the original text or implied in any way as being crucial to the Second Coming, then earlier

Christians would never have treated the Jews so brutally. While the Bible carries prophecies about the Second Coming, it makes no mention that it is contingent upon the return of the Jews to Palestine or how specifically it is going to happen. The general view is that only the "Father in Heavens" knows how it will happen.

Nevertheless the Nonconformists particularly and other breakaway denominations of Protestantism generally began seeing the interpretation about the return of the Jews as their religious duty to hasten the Second Coming. Thus not only did Protestant hostilities against the Jews markedly decline but also a new fervour took birth in these Christian sects for Jewish resettlement in Palestine. These Protestant Christian sects saw the Jews essential for their redemption and also looked at Palestine as a Jewish country according to the Biblical stories.

Amazingly the Christian theologians and scholars did not contest the authenticity of this interpretation within the overall Christian Church. Had they done so, then perhaps it would not have become such a driving factor for the Nonconformists and Evangelicals to impact the Middle Eastern politics so adversely.

As was explained above, the year 1621 is the first time the notion of resettlement took birth into the "consciousness of the increasingly vocal Protestant movement". It is also about the same period of time of Reformation when the Bible was freshly translated. Therefore, it is logical to deduce that the notion of Jews return to the Promised Land came into existence after the Biblical prophecy about the Second Coming was innovatively interpreted outside the scripture without any Biblical support in the original Hebrew text. It also follows that this was about the same time when the Jewish scholars and religious leaders were anxiously looking for ways and means to escape persecution that had haunted them right up to the fifteenth century owing to the Spanish Inquisition. Such an innovative interpretation might have been seen as a dire necessity to convince the Christians by scriptural inspiration to spare the Jews and work to return them to their Promised Land as a precondition of Christ's Second Coming so they might live in peace after all. This was perhaps the only way available to the Jews to induce a change of mind in the oppressive Christians to escape their brutality.

This assessment may provide the explanation of how the notion of Jewish return was connected to the Second Coming. If so, the return of the Jews or their settlement in Palestine as a contingency for Christ's Second Coming may not have any religious significance at all. What the Nonconformists and the Evangelicals have been pursuing as their religious duty, and are still pursuing, may not be truly scriptural, but only a political interpretation presented in the guise of religion. Still, many devotees of Christianity and fervent followers of Jesus Christ have fallen for it, as indeed did political leaders like Lloyd George and, currently, President Bush.

There is another factor in the rise of support for Zionism in Western countries that also needs to be taken into account, which is the revival of anti-Semitism in Europe. If we go back to the Dark Ages after the collapse of Roman civilisation, we find ourselves in an era when very few people in Western Europe had any liquid capital except the Jews, who managed to maintain their commercial links with their own people in countries that remained more civilised, such as the Byzantine Empire and the Caliphate. And whereas Christians were long forbidden to lend money to other Christians for interest, Jews were free to do so. Hence the kings and nobles of Western Europe came to rely on the Jews as their bankers and encouraged them to settle in their dominions to promote trade and commerce. The kings and nobles mostly protected the Jews in return for large loans and gifts of money, but the common people who got in debt to them bitterly resented their sharp business practices and the high interest they had to pay for loans (which was not altogether the Jews' fault, because so many borrowers defaulted that they had to charge high rates to break even). Periodically, in one place or another, the peoples' fury would boil over and they would attack the Jews, robbing and killing them, until the king or lord sent his men in to restore order. In Western European countries from the thirteenth century onwards this syndrome was broken, mainly because of the rise of Italian bankers who lent money at more reasonable rates. Once the kings of England and France no longer needed the Jews as bankers, they expelled them from their dominions. In other countries they continued as moneylenders, but the more settled conditions and the competition of Italian and other non-Jewish bankers led them to lower their rates, and from then on they provoked rather less resentment. But in the less developed societies of central and Eastern Europe the older state of affairs persisted right into modern times, and with it the hatred of Jews and periodic pogroms. Hitler's genocide was only the culmination of a series of killings that began in the Ukraine right after World War I and continued in Poland after World War II. The investigations of the Nuremberg Commission after the war showed that, while Hitler's SS had spearheaded the genocide, large numbers of people in all the countries of eastern and central Europe that the Germans overran had zealously joined in, and even in the Western countries that the Germans had conquered there were people who had helped them hunt out Jews and round them up.

Once that became clear, most educated people in the West came to accept the Zionist argument that the Jews were not safe in Europe, except perhaps in the Western countries with the strongest liberal and democratic traditions; and even those countries, while they had no trouble with accepting educated Jews during the postwar boom, feared that anti-Semitism would break out again among their working classes, as it had in the 1930s, if they took in large numbers of poor unskilled Jews. They concluded that the Zionists were right and the Jews needed a country of their own if they were to survive as a people, and the only practical candidate seemed to be Palestine. Even though other countries in Africa and south America were put forward as alternatives to ward off the traditional tension in the Holy Land, the Zionists insisted on reclaiming Palestine, a demand which the British government was unable to resist.

Thus, Lloyd George's decision to have his foreign secretary, Lord Balfour, a Conservative coalition partner, draft the Balfour Declaration in 1917, asserting that "the British government favoured a national home for the Jews in Palestine, without prejudice to civil and religious rights of the non-Jewish people already living there", which became the forerunner of the policy that would subsequently develop in the West and actively more so in the United States after the Second World War. Although the Balfour Declaration had pointedly promised the Jews a national home, not a national state, effectively Lloyd George became the first British Prime Minister to signal the creation of the State of Israel. From a political standpoint the British government might also have seen an advantage in planting a pro-Western influence in the Middle East, which could be used in some way later to serve the British imperialistic interests such as securing the Suez Canal and controlling natural resources in the region.

While Lloyd George was determined to make good on the Balfour Declaration, he saw the Muslims as an obstacle in his way, since they were ruling over Palestine in accordance with the 1192 A.D. peace treaty with Britain. However, Lloyd George was so preoccupied with the idea of making Palestine a national home for the Jews that he even ignored Britain's oldest peace treaty with the Muslims. As was discussed earlier, this treaty had been violated a few times before by others, but technically the British were still bound by it, since the Muslims, the other party to the treaty, had not infringed any of its terms.

Anyway, what is noticeable is that after the British military action a joint Judeo-Christian effort was born, which slowly became a coalition against Islam with a view to implementing the Balfour Declaration and ultimately creating the State of Israel, so that Jews might be resettled in their ancient homeland. It was expected not only to facilitate the Second Coming of Christ, but also to relieve Western Europe of the burden of the Jews as well as make the Jews vanguard of Western interests in the Islamic world. But the lingering question of what to do with the Palestinians still remained on the minds of the Zionists. They considered many options to dispose of the Palestinians, including a total expulsion to other Arab lands. Besides economic and political considerations, the Christian zeal for the Jewish resettlement also emanates from their belief that Christ would then return to redeem their sins and lead them into paradise. It is an important element of faith of certain Christian sects that needs to be kept in mind, as it would help in assessing the motive of the powerful Western countries in the current Middle Eastern crisis. It would not only explain why there is a Judeo-Christian coalition against Islam, but would also clarify why the Nonconformist or Evangelical Christian West does not make meaningful contributions to, or at least understand, the validity of the Palestinians' or Arabs' point of view or recognise the basis of their concerns. These circumstances would also explain why there is no genuine effort on part of the overall Christian West to solve the explosive situation in the Middle East by recognising the rights of the Palestinians or helping them achieve their lawful territorial claims. It is not so much the intricacies of the issue as a lack of will on part of the Christian West that is holding back resolution of the nasty Palestinian problem.

Thus, not only did the Jews get off the hook, but they also managed to influence the religious faith of the powerful Protestant Christians in such a dramatic way that many Protestant sects now feel obliged to help them in resettlement for the sake of their own religious fulfilment.

While earlier Christian political leaders such as William Pitt, Benjamin Disraeli and Lloyd George had been pushing for Jewish resettlement for religious and colonial reasons, President Bush, a prominently faith-based Western leader, is pursuing the same goal manifestly to fulfil his Evangelical beliefs. He is visibly exploiting the state economic and military power of the United States, despite the constitutional separation of religion and state, to complete the Jewish resettlement that Lloyd George initiated some 90 years ago. President Bush, too, is invading the Islamic world, but his objectives are wholly religious, namely to hasten Christ's Second Coming to redeem the Christians' sins. As a result of his military action, the world is now witnessing human tragedies in Afghanistan and Iraq, where much innocent blood is shed and humanity is savagely treated to defeat the polity of Islam, so that the Jews may resettle completely in Palestine and the Christians may achieve their goal of securing paradise. What a blood-soaked and grisly way to enter paradise!

Prime Minister Tony Blair's support for President Bush is unlikely to have an Evangelical basis, since he is an Anglican with leanings towards Roman Catholicism, which is his wife's religion. Blair's objective in supporting Bush may be an entirely different one, which he has not spelled out except to confound it with the weapons of mass destruction and an imaginary threat from Saddam Hussein. The Spanish Prime Minister Jose Maria Aznar also could not have supported President Bush for Evangelical reasons, since he is a Roman Catholic with a different religious doctrine. However, his thrust against the polity of Islam may stem from the lingering shadows of the

Spanish Inquisition. While both Blair and Aznar may have different religious beliefs from Bush, they do have a great deal of affinity with him in so far as defeating the polity of Islam is concerned. Both leaders supported Bush's policies in the Middle East from their own perspective of defeating the polity of Islam, which would give their countries strategic and economic advantage over the Islamic world.

Looking at the current situation in Palestine, it is painful to see how brutally and inhumanely the Jews are treating the Palestinians. The amount of blood that is being spilled in the East supposedly to pave the way for Jesus' Second Coming could not be by Jesus' own design or the design of the Divinity. "Whatever the future holds for the region and its people...it is the ultimate irony that after centuries of struggle, now that Jews have achieved their goal, they are behaving as the very people who persecuted them. (Quoted from Irfan Hussain's article based on Jill Hamilton's insights)".

After resuming control in Palestine in 1948, the Jews went straight back to the Joshuan tradition of war. They set aside the sanctity of human life or compassion for humanity as they embarked on demolishing the Palestinians' homes and expelling them with brutal force. They quickly drifted away from the path of King David and King Solomon and began treading the path of Joshua. It would seem that all the hard work and efforts made by King David to replace the Joshuan traits and the strides so boldly made by King Solomon to inculcate peaceful co-existence in the tradition of Prophet Abraham have been totally wasted.

Why have the Jews been defying their own prophets and kings? The Jewish defiance of reason and international law and disregard for the current world opinion is both shocking and deplorable. Why do the Jews defy rationality? This question is difficult to answer in simple terms. Nevertheless, it must be analysed in the light of history in order to comprehend the current international trends.

Reflecting on the ancient Jewish history to learn about the origin or the beginning of the habit of defiance in the Hebrew tribes, it can be seen that the notion of chosen people has likely given them an air of arrogance that affected their attitude with regard to other people or their rights. It is highly likely that the Jews have misunderstood the purpose of being chosen. They seem to have construed that the status of chosen has placed them on a higher plateau or in a favourable position with God and so nothing else matters as they have preference over everyone else. This would account for their defiance and arrogance towards rest of the humanity. This is a totally corrupted view because being chosen does not mean that they have preference over the rest of humanity; what it means is that they have greater responsibility to practise a virtuous conduct according to the *Divine Rules* of God and live an exemplary life as light and example for the rest of humanity. They were chosen for this role because of their ancestry in Prophets Abraham and Jacob, who were both very special in the eyes of God. God wanted to demonstrate to the rest of the humanity how beneficial it would be to live by the rules of God and accordingly follow a virtuous conduct that will lead them to a happy, peaceful and prosperous life on the planet earth. He chose the children of Israel for this purpose. This is all that chosen means. There was nothing partisan in God's scheme. God needed to demonstrate some examples to humankind, and so He chose the children of Israel to be that example. Regrettably, the Jews could never grasp the true meaning of God's scheme and interpreted His Grace as a decree giving them some privilege or immunity so they could even mistreat others in the name of God. Their violent re-entry into Canaan and subsequent brutal treatment of the original inhabitants is the greatest infraction of God's scheme of good example.

The origin of their defiance dates back to very early days of their history. The first victim of their defiance and intrigues was their own kith and kin Joseph, who was mistreated in spite of their father's instructions to take good care of him during the trip to Egypt. The story of Prophet Joseph's ordeal is also narrated in the Quran. Their next show of defiance was against Prophet Moses when he went to Mount Sinai to receive the Word of God. Then they contravened the tradition of Prophet Abraham by fighting against the Canaanites instead of fighting in their defence or on their behalf against foreign invaders in a spirit of co-operation and co-existence. It will be remembered that according to the Bible Prophet Abraham fought a defensive war in co-operation with the people and kings of the Canaanites to thwart the invading Mesopotamians. He clearly established a tradition of living in co-operation with the people and kings of his host country rather than engaging in confrontation or belligerency as his progeny have since been doing. Then, again, at the time of re-entry into Canaan, the Jews transgressed and changed the image of God to a God of war and vengeance under Joshua's leadership in contravention of God's attributes of peace and compassion for the human race. In the nearer history, their deliberate defiance of an important clause of the Balfour Declaration is very conspicuous. It will be recalled that while the Balfour Declaration favoured a national home for the Jews, the British government made it conditional upon respecting the civic and religious rights of the non-Jewish people that were already living there. What can be seen from current happenings in Palestine is that the non-Jewish people, the Muslims and Christians, have been denied civic rights in their own country as well as their religious rights in the City of the One God, Jerusalem. This is a stark contravention of the Balfour Declaration, which, incidentally, was indirectly the principal instrument in creating the present day State of Israel. One would have thought that modern Jews would cherish and respect the Balfour Declaration more than any other political pronouncement or instrument, because it laid the foundation for their national home. Regrettably, nothing rational seems to appeal to the Jewish people. But this is not all. The Israelites are also defying the United Nations, the very organisation that created Israel. It is a common knowledge how the State of Israel has been rejecting or dishonouring the U.N. resolutions and ignoring international pleas for Palestinian rights. International law, too, has no value for the Israelis, since they are building illegal settlements on occupied lands and refusing the rights of refugees to return to their homes as provided for in the international law. To top it all the Israelis ignore even the World Court judgements. According to the Mishnah Pirqei Avot 2:12 (Jewish) "By three things is the world sustained; by truth, by judgement and by peace." Judgement means obeying the law, but sadly the Jews do not live up to the teachings of their scripture as they routinely disregard international law and refuse to comply with the World Court judgements. They have not been seen upholding the truth or striving for just peace. They defy all the three great teachings of Mishnah Pirqei.

This is an unacceptable and disgraceful historical record for any religious or cultural community. This has gone on for too long and at too high a human cost. It is now time to stop Jewish defiance of law and infractions of rights of others, so that our world may take a turn for the better and at last long peace may have a chance to prevail.

But that does not look like happening any time soon, because the Jews have gone back to square one and are resorting to Joshuan atrocities as part of their faith, not realising that the Book of Joshua was fiction and that he had corrupted the scripture for his military goals. It seems that the wretched Palestinians are made to pay bitterly for the crimes of King Nimrod and the Pharaohs in ancient history as well as for the crimes and brutality of the Western European Christians and later by Hitler and his Nazis. The Jews, having brought a load of persecution and atrocities from many parts of the world, are now dumping it all on the Palestinians. Had Nimrod not persecuted Prophet Abraham and the Pharaohs and others not persecuted the Children of Israel, the unfortunate Palestinians would not be suffering now or paying for someone else's crime. The Palestinian tragedy was not made by the Palestinian people; rather the people have been made to carry the burden of crimes perpetrated by many others, including Christians, against the Israelites.

Ironically, first religion and then God have been made the root cause of this tragedy. First, the Jews manipulated the tenets of their own faith to justify a territorial claim; then certain Christian sects made matters worse by implicating their religious interest in Jesus' Second Coming and associating it with the Jewish resettlement. No one seems to stop to think that it is ungodly to give somebody's land or property to someone else. It is ungodly to take away the land and livelihood of a people and give it to others for no fault of theirs. God is not a thief who would go around usurping other people's rights or properties for the sake of obliging His favourite ones. God would not be God if He acted in such a partisan way. His attributes are mercy and justice for all humanity, irrespective of whether someone is "chosen" or not. He cannot deviate from His own laws of justice and mercy. To say that God has given this land to the Children of Israel and so the Palestinians should clear out is to say that God is partisan and unjust. But God is not like that. He is Merciful, Beneficent, Loving and Caring and gracious to all humanity. It is indeed beneath any civilised standard of morality to implicate God in such a slanderous way for the sake of making claim on a tract of land. This should be food for thought for modern Jews and Christians.

It seems that everybody wants to fulfil their religious ambitions on the backs of the Palestinians. The Jews want to acquire their Promised Land and the Christians want to secure their entry into Paradise, in both cases on the backs of the Palestinians. Jesus Christ's Second Coming supposedly cannot take place until the Jews are resettled, and the Promised Land also cannot be achieved until the Palestinians are forced out. Hence in both cases the Palestinians are the obstacles in the way of religious fulfilment of both the Jews and the Christians. What a pathetic view of religion!

Anyway, the return of the Jews to Palestine in 1948 was depressingly like their re-entry into Canaan around 1200 B.C.E. At that time it was Joshua who was massacring the Canaanites, razing their cities and towns, destroying their culture and customs, demolishing their temples and homes and reducing them to a sub-human level – all in the name of God and according to the so-called commandments. Today, Ariel Sharon and nearly all the other Israeli leaders are doing exactly the same as Joshua did in the past. There is no change, none at all. As in the past, the Jews are now refusing to make any peace covenants with the Palestinians. Palestinians have been put under the severest ban; their enemies show no restraint, even in killing women and children or destroying their homes, throwing out even the aged and sick. Sharon's army is mercilessly bulldozing their homes just as Joshua razed their cities. The Israelis are bent upon annihilating and exterminating the Palestinians in the tradition of the Torah as revised by Joshua or the later religious reformers. The Jews seem to have abandoned their original path by forsaking Prophet Moses, contravening their own founding father, Prophet Abraham, and ignoring David and Solomon. Joshua is their prime leader, even though he seems to have re-interpreted the Torah for his own military ends and maligned God to make Him look like a God of war and vengeance.

So the Jewish hostilities against the Palestinians continue even to this day. They are waging campaigns of terror and inhumanity in the name of God as part of their religion. The tragedy of Deir Yassin village is a hair-raising reminder of how Jews have used God to massacre humanity. Despite a non-aggression pact with the villagers, Israeli terrorist groups under Irgun and Stern attacked the village to "take revenge when two nearby Jewish settlements were overrun and destroyed during the fighting which had broken out between Arabs and Jews in Palestine." Again we shall quote from Armstrong's book, page 106:

> ...Irgun and Lehi avenged their comrades who had fallen in the battle and began looting and massacring for most of the following day. Two hundred and fifty men, women, children and old people were massacred and their bodies mutilated... Begin (Menachem who later became Israel's prime minister) sent his congratulations "on this splendid act of conquest ... As at Deir Yassin, so everywhere, we will attack and smite the enemy. God, God, thou hast chosen us for conquest." (p. 68; originally taken from Johnson, *A History of the Jews*, p. 29.)

Note how Menachem Begin revelled in massacring human beings and mutilating their bodies and praised God for choosing Irgun and Lehi to commit this kind of crime and inflict this inhumane treatment. It did not end at Deir Yassin; Arab Jaffa was the next victim of "Looting, pillaging and destruction. Begin himself has commented that the story of Deir Yassin did a great service to the Jewish state: it got rid of the Arabs." (p. 69; originally taken from Brenner, *The Iron Wall*, p. 143.)

Harping on divine authority for exclusive rights and grabbing Palestinian land on the false pretexts of religion or God's command or security has outlived its purpose. It is now time to emerge from the clouds of passion and emotions and from under the cloak of falsehood to think realistically and consider rationally that a just and loving God could never have commanded even His chosen people to annihilate or exterminate the original inhabitants of Palestine. That was certainly not the intent of the Balfour Declaration, which specifically protected the civic and religious rights of the non-Jewish people already living in Palestine. From all that we can see, God as well as the earthly people wanted to rehabilitate the afflicted Jewish community in Canaan or Palestine so that they might live in peace and harmony with other inhabitants of this land. This was God's delight, as practised and demonstrated by Prophet Abraham, as well as the intent of the international community. Alas, the Jews have defied them all.

Someone has to get up and remind the Jews of the true spirit of the Divinity and the historical facts about the Holy Land, to redress a most ominous condition that has gripped our world. The Christians would have done better to accept this challenge. However, they seem mostly to have surrendered under the weight of their bigoted faith for securing paradise through Jewish channels, and the Westerners also seem to have been disabled or silenced by Jewish economic power. Consequently, the powerful Jewish lobby has subdued the Western front by the powerful Jewish economic constraints. Evangelical America is also restricted by its economic self-interest and faulty religious beliefs; so it, too, has precluded itself from rendering any objective or useful service to end the international crisis. In fact, the United States has aligned itself with the wrongheaded policies of the Israelis and thus become part of a scheme that has assumed authority to define freedom fight or terrorism however it may wish. Hence the definition of terrorism has fallen into the hands of those who turn truth into falsehood and vice versa to achieve their territorial goals and perpetuate economic domination over the region. They paint all their atrocities as *bona fide* self-defence and brand even the most genuine freedom fighting by their opponents as acts of violence and terrorism. How ironic and pathetic! There is no measure of truth left any more, and worst of all, there is no sign of improvement in the international climate under Christian or Western ascendancy. It is most regrettable that peace does not seem achievable under Western ascendancy, because the West profoundly lacks the fundamentals of peace.

Thus Muslims are the only ones left to carry the burden of arousing worldwide public opinion and reminding the Israelites that living with other religions and cultures is far more precious than killing helpless Palestinians for the sake of a tract of land, which ultimately belongs to no one. As weak as they are, the Muslims will have to rise to the occasion and meet this challenge with their spiritual and moral force. They also need to engage the Jewish scholars in technical religious debates to thrash out the veracity of the land claims, as well as to remind the Jews how they have flouted so many divine laws, treaties, international laws and U.N. resolutions – how they have disregarded even the spirit of the Balfour Declaration when they ignored the religious and civic rights of the other inhabitants of Palestine.

Taking no action or doing nothing to redress the woes of our world is to admit that the powers of transgression, falsehood, bigotry and injustice have defeated us all. Can we live with this, or should we not try to redress transgression?

While the older generation may be too hidebound, the new generation of our New World must confront the Israelites on the philosophical or literary fields and drive home to the Jews that ideologically and conceptually they have been wrong for too long. Not only have they harmed themselves but they have also harmed others, especially the Muslims in the present-day context.

Things must now change, not only for their sake but also for the sake of the rest of humanity, so that we may see peace and tranquillity in our world. The Jews must be either persuaded academically or impelled politically to take note how a military leader (Joshua) in the name of God fabricated a false claim over Palestine, how God has since been implicated and abused by the Israelites, and how the children of Israel have been twisting and turning facts to defy many precepts of the Divinity, just to press a dubious territorial claim. This state of affairs is no longer acceptable in our modern world. The Jews' inhumanity to the Palestinians has surpassed all limits of patience. Already it has taken countless innocent lives and ruined the peace of our world. It is no longer a matter of territorial dispute or religious or ethnic quarrel; it is a crime against humanity. This is an urgent situation that requires the immediate attention of all peace-loving citizens right across the world, to take a stand to guard truth and speak out on behalf of peace.

We shall close our presentation on Palestine with another quotation from Karen Armstrong's book, *Holy War*, page 75, which reads:

> Since the Crusaders such peaceful co-existence has been impossible and the long history of tragic violence between the people of the three faiths began in a vicious Western initiative. It will be one of the arguments of this book that it is not enough to condemn the behaviour of either the Israelis or the Arabs in today's conflict; the West must also bear a good deal of responsibility for what has happened... Arabs and Jews were still inspired by passions that were not wholly rational but which were fired by old religious myths. Ultimately and tragically, the conflict would lead to a revival of the old habit of the holy war.

Karen Armstrong's reminder to the West (the Christians) is very significant. What she seems to be saying is that, since the West (Christians) contributed to the making of the present-day Palestinian tragedy, the West or Christians are now morally bound to right their wrongs. Will her words of wisdom be of any avail or will they fall on deaf ears, like those of Nelson Mandela?

The Kashmir Dispute

The Kashmir dispute is the next source of bitterness in the Muslim world. British officials left behind this tragedy by making an unjust and unfair division of India. It led to three bloody wars between India and Pakistan, who were at the brink of a nuclear showdown in 2003. The Kashmir dispute has taken the lives of tens of thousands of innocent civilians and become the most dangerous and explosive issue in the subcontinent.

The tale of Kashmir is another example of the disregard for Muslim causes and suppression of Muslim rights that had become almost a fashion during the entire period of Western domination of the world scene. It began when the British finally decided to divide India as the only way to absolve themselves from the responsibility of ruling it, which had been made difficult by native demands for freedom. The United States made matters worse by pressurising Britain to speed up India's liberation, which forced the British officials to appease the Congress Party leader Jawaharlal Nehru, who was designated to be the first Prime Minister of India, by acquiescing in an unfair partition that left behind the problem of Kashmir.

Lord Mountbatten, the British Viceroy, is largely to blame for the inequitable partition. He was working under a plan to develop an alternative to the British Empire so that Britain's economic interests and its world domination might continue in a new form. To achieve this, the British government came up with the idea of a new and vastly extended British Commonwealth comprising all the colonies that would be getting freedom from Britain. The object was to maintain Britain's influence over its former colonies, so that it might continue to benefit from their natural resources and also have the use of military bases in case of another world war or a war against the Communists. India was the first non-white British possession to become independent, so it was extremely important to bring independent India into the fold of the new British Commonwealth. Accordingly, Mountbatten's main concern in working out the partition plan was not to ensure a fair deal for both Hindus and Muslims but to make sure that it did not go against the wishes or interests of the future Indian Prime Minister. Nehru was aware of the British government's long-term objectives, so he effectively blackmailed Mountbatten to obtain improper, even illegal, concessions. How the original territorial allocations in the Punjab were changed to give strategic Gurdaspur and Ferozepur to India despite their Muslim majorities gives one example of territorial manipulation by the British viceroy. Obscuring the future of princely states such as Jammu and Kashmir was another of his unjust decisions, which were heavily tilted towards Nehru to win him over so that he would bring India into the Commonwealth.

While Pakistan was unable to do anything about the Punjab partition, it decided to contest the Kashmir issue not only because Kashmir abutted Pakistani territory but also because its population was over 80% Muslim. According to the rules of the division, this territory ought to have been allocated to Pakistan. Nehru wanted Kashmir not because the population was mainly Hindu but simply because his ancestral roots were in the Kashmir valley. He effectively blackmailed Mountbatten into leaving the resolution of the question open until after the formal declaration of independence, despite opposition within Mountbatten's administration from his deputy, General Ismay. Once India became independent as a dominion, Mountbatten became a governor-general rather than a viceroy and was constitutionally obliged to act as Nehru, his Prime Minister, advised him. Thus an unfair and unjust decision was made knowingly by the representative of the British Crown, which has since become a nasty problem and taken tens of thousands of innocent lives.

When the dispute between India and Pakistan escalated into an armed conflict and India began to lose, Nehru took the matter to the United Nations, requesting an immediate ceasefire. The Security Council acted on his request and ordered a ceasefire, but at the same time passed a resolution that this dispute should be resolved by a fair and impartial plebiscite according to the wishes of the people of Kashmir. India accepted this resolution, and so did Pakistan, but India afterwards put obstacles in the way of implementing it. Another resolution was then passed to get things moving, but India never co-operated with that one, because it had never intended to give up Kashmir. The fact that after going to the U.N. in the first place India then consistently refused to comply with its directives shows that it only wanted to circumvent the world organisation to obtain a crucial ceasefire, because it was losing ground; otherwise it had no intention of resolving the dispute. Prime Minister Nehru then used his personal connections with the Soviet Union and got it to use its veto in the Security Council to thwart any further U.N. proceedings on the Kashmir issue. From then on the Soviets, following their own global interests, obliged India and consistently blocked implementation of the U.N. resolutions, even though the Soviet Union had originally approved them.

There are more intricate details of how the U.N. efforts were thwarted and how the Graham and later the Dixon Commission failed. The United States also cooled in its enthusiasm to get this dispute resolved peacefully, due to its own global interests. After the assassinations of King Faisal of Iraq and his prime minister had led to the collapse of the anti-Communist Baghdad Pact, to which Pakistan had adhered, President Kennedy decided that strategically it was no longer in the global interest of the United States to antagonise India over Kashmir, and so American support for a peaceful and just resolution withered away. It was a sad breach of friendship with Pakistan, which had done so much for America in the fight against Communism.

Although the Soviet Union was the prime culprit in thwarting the U.N. proceedings, in the end it seems that the Kashmir tragedy has become a product of triangular suppression of the Muslim rights. The British started this problem, India refused to abide by the ground rules of the partition and finally the United Nations (thanks to the Soviets) betrayed the people of Kashmir. It is not that the United Nations is powerless in such cases; it has power to enforce its will, as it did when it pressurised Muslim Indonesia to secure the right of self-determination for the Christian population of East Timor. It is not a question of lacking capability or power; it is a matter of not using the power to serve justice to the Muslims. This is perhaps why there is no effort at the world centre to press Hindu India to secure the same rights of self-determination for the Muslim Kashmiris that were secured for the Christian population of East Timor. The Muslims view this discrimination as a blatant suppression of Muslim rights on religious grounds, which fuels emotions and produces radicalism.

It would not be out of place to say that the United Nations has failed as a world organisation for all the people of the world. It is perhaps because the creators of this world body were staunch imperialists who, despite the changing times, did not give up their imperialist mindsets. Britain, France, the United States and Soviet Russia were the main architects of this organisation. Britain's former Prime Minister Churchill, who was a devout and unflinching imperialist, chiefly drafted the framework of the United Nations constitution and instituted the mechanism of the veto for the five great powers, to keep world control in their hands so that they could steer the whole world according to their own global objectives and to serve their own interests even at the cost of fairness and justice. Consequently, this world organisation is seriously hampered. No matter how strongly the rest of the world may try to achieve certain objectives and have the General Assembly pass resolution after resolution, nothing can be done until the five veto-holding powers agree to it. It is the same situation as when change can happen only when the King gives his royal assent; otherwise, no matter how much the subjects may struggle, they will not get their wish. The General Assembly has been reduced to the same level of helpless subjects, subservient and subordinate to the imperial masters who control the Security Council and continue to do business in the old tradition of imperialism.

Sadly, our world has made no progress, in spite of so much talk about advancement in the realms of justice and rights of all citizens of the world in a true democratic atmosphere of freedom and human rights. It has been demonstrated on many other occasions, besides the Kashmir issue, how the veto privilege is abused and how obstacles are placed in the way of fair and just resolutions of explosive issues involving the Muslims. This world organisation has failed many times owing to its flawed constitution and showed convincingly that it has become irrelevant and impotent at fulfilling its principal duty of preventing wars. Perhaps it is now time to revisit the constitution of the United Nations with a view to stamping out the evil tool of imperialism, the veto power of the five, which hampers its unimpeded function in serving the interests of all citizens of the world. The Muslim world is utterly disappointed with the way the U.N. works and sees no hope that it can ever function fairly for them. A change in the Charter of the United Nations is now due and essential to restore world confidence in this organisation. There can be several alternatives to safeguard the world organisation from making irresponsible decisions, but veto power of the five is not one of them.

It is also deplorable that Britain has washed its hands of the problem that it left behind in the subcontinent. It never came back to clean up the mess that Mountbatten created between India and Pakistan. It could have played a positive and constructive role to get a fair resolution of this problem, but it never felt morally responsible to intervene in the Kashmir dispute. In today's world, British Prime Minister Tony Blair talks a great deal about moral reasons for attacking Iraq and cites moral grounds to support the war on Iraq in spite of rebuttal by the Archbishop of Canterbury. However, one does not see any enthusiasm in Prime Minister Blair to work for peace in the Indian subcontinent, or at least help in sorting out the problem that British officials created in the first place in Kashmir. One gets the impression that Blair is using moral arguments over Iraq for convenience' sake rather than as a principle.

Thus, Pakistan along with the people of Kashmir is caught in a three-way tug-of-war that has closed the doors on a just resolution of a Muslim problem. Bilateral dialogue can be a good thing, providing there is also a will to succeed. So much dialogue has already taken place over the last fifty years, but India has never budged from denying Kashmiris their rights. No matter how much dialogue may take place between India and Pakistan, India is not going to concede the Kashmiris their full and complete right to self-determination. A full and complete service of justice will not happen unless international pressure is brought to bear upon India in the same way as it was on Muslim Indonesia over Christian East Timor. The current dialogue is also likely to fail unless it is backed by international pressure on India.

Muslims' disappointment and frustration with the world's apathetic attitude over more than fifty years has made them resort to armed struggle as the only avenue left for them to seek justice for their cause and freedom for the people of Kashmir from a brutal Indian military occupation. What is even sadder is that when the Muslims resort to struggle to secure what the world has failed to deliver to them, their struggle quickly gets branded as an act of terrorism. No distinction is drawn between armed struggle for freedom and terrorism for the sake of violence. What has gone on in Kashmir is not creating violence for the sake of violence; rather it is the Kashmiris' exercise of their inherent right to appeal to arms to secure their freedom. Kashmiris are not terrorists or especially violent people; they are a prey to the Indian aggression and victims of the Western indifference to Muslim rights.

The Chechen Saga

Chechnya is another sore episode where Muslims are denied sovereign rights and subjected to social and economic oppression because of their religion.

Today the world is rejoicing and greeting the European Christian countries newly freed from the yoke of Communist oppression, but little is said about the Muslim states that are still caught in the old Communist grip. Such is the double set of values in our world.

Historically, Chechnya is not part of Russia. The fact that Tsarist Russia seized this country in a brutal military action, forcibly annexed it in 1818 and has exercised administrative control ever since does not make Chechnya a historical part of Russia. Before the Russian invasion Chechnya had always been an independent country with its own history and culture. It still has the whole infrastructure to survive independently and live in the community of nations peacefully and productively as a sovereign nation.

The tragedy of Chechnya does not get its due publicity in the Western press, owing to either its remoteness or the usual media lack of interest in Muslim issues. So, this author decided to read the war account by a Russian correspondent named Anna Politkovskaya to learn about Chechnya from a Russian writer. Politkovskaya specialises in social issues and has written an enlightening book entitled *A Dirty War* about the North Caucasus region in which she brings out background of the intricacies and brutalities of the Chechen war. John Crowfoot's translation of her work into English and Thomas de Waal's excellent introduction should also be acknowledged. This book has added to our insight on Chechnya, so we have made use of some of its information in our commentary and added our own assessment to complete this presentation.

Regrettably, the Tsars usurped the Chechen's freedom and seized this small Islamic territory in the North Caucasus in 1818 after a terrible military action. The Communists continued the brutal suppression and took extremely harsh measures to undermine Islam in this region. Stalin even expelled the entire Muslim population in 1944 – officially for collaborating with the Germans when they invaded the Caucasus in September 1942, but he had another motive, too, behind this expulsion, which was to break the national spirit of the Chechens and their desire for self-rule. The Chechens' co-operation with the Germans was natural, because they, like the Balts and Ukrainians, saw the Germans as liberators from Stalin's tyranny. However, as with the other military people, Stalin's aims went deeper than just punishing the Chechens for collaborating with the Germans. He was aiming to destroy the Islamic character of this territory by driving out the Germans, expelling the Muslims and colonizing Chechnya with ethnic Russians in the expectation that the population mix of Chechnya would change so drastically that it could never revert to being an Islamic State independent of Russia.

Stalin's colonization program has indeed affected the population mix and made independence difficult, just as it has for the Latvians; but it could not eradicate the Chechens' passion to retain their Islamic character and their enthusiasm for freedom and sovereignty. Their exile to Kazakhstan caused them "mass trauma". "Tens of thousands died on the way and

Chechnya was abolished and erased from the map." The Ukrainians and the ethnic Germans of Soviet Russia were treated in the same way when Stalin also exiled them. The Chechens were devastated as a people and as a nation. While in Kazakhstan the Chechens were continually discriminated against and denied access to education or jobs, not to speak of any respectable positions in the government. As a result, the younger generation of Chechens took to crime and other shady practices to find livelihoods. "The Chechens were allowed to return home only in 1957 after Nikita Khrushchev's Secret Speech denouncing Stalin, but even then the Chechens remained second-class citizens in their own republic, subordinate to the ethnic Russians." Despite the passage of time and changing circumstances in Russian society, the Russian attitude towards the Chechens had not changed because of their affiliation with Islam.

The Chechens are proud and practising Muslims, so they follow their religion devoutly. They had to put up with their hardships at the hands of the brutal Soviet dictator Stalin, but they did not therefore give up their religious and cultural heritage, any more than the European peoples who suffered the same kind of persecution. They are still not prepared to do that, in spite of the repression imposed upon them by the Putin régime. They have never been receptive to Communism. They have remained committed to their own social and religious culture and resisted the changes that the Soviets brutally tried to impose upon them. The younger generation of Chechens was extremely resentful for having been exiled from their own country and neglected in social and economic progress by the hardline Communists. When after 1957 they resettled in Chechnya they began taking out their frustration on the ethnic Russians and asserted their rights as a Muslim nation. Hence a growing ethnic and religious tension developed between the Muslims and the Russians. When the Soviet Union fell apart in the 1980s, both Muslim Chechnya and Daghestan hoped that they would also gain full independence like the other republics; but since they had been annexed and were administratively parts of Russia, not separate Soviet republics, that did not happen. In spite of the administrative complexities created by the Russians, the people of these two Muslim states had not given up their ambition for independence and continued to aspire for freedom from Russia. Equally, Russia was determined to deny them freedom, which resulted in greater suppression, by military force. Consequently, even more tension developed between the ethnic Russians and Muslim Chechens.

Amidst Russia's chaotic transformation from Communism to a free-market economy, General Dudayev became president of the republic and gave a new spin to Chechnya, seeking to pull its people out of frustration and unrest by proclaiming independence unilaterally in September 1991. As might have been expected, Moscow was not at all pleased; so an angry exchange of words occurred but neither party immediately started hostilities. General Dudayev was a patriotic Soviet, spoke better Russian than Chechen and was married to a Russian woman. His connections with Russia were real, so he was prone to agree to some reasonable terms of settlement that would address Chechen grievances without tearing apart the Russian Federation. His unilateral declaration of independence was basically a ploy; in fact he "sometimes offered very favourable terms for re-joining Russia." His was a militant way to settle the differences, but Boris Yeltsin did not make any peaceful approach either, perhaps because he was not yet experienced enough in the art of negotiating and settling disputes through peaceful means or recognising the rights of other communities. So he reacted fiercely and issued an ultimatum to Dudayev instead of opening a dialogue with him. Had Yeltsin been more subtle, he could have neutralised Dudayev by some concessions short of secession, and in return for genuine autonomy, Dudayev would likely have agreed to make Chechnya an integral and permanent part of the Russian Federation. What the Chechens really wanted was fair social and economic treatment, greater autonomy and control over their natural resources and economic and industrial policy and above all complete freedom to practise Islam, even institute Islamic laws in their family and daily lives. It should not have been difficult to make these concessions, but Yeltsin had not yet totally given up the Communist mentality or acquired the habit of respecting other people's wishes. His response was negative, and thus the best opportunity of settling the Chechen grievances was lost. Under pressure from his former hardline Communists in his politburo, Yeltsin decided to wage a war on Chechnya in 1994. This became a brutal war fiercely fought by both sides. The Chechens surprised the Russians by inflicting heavy losses of lives on the Russian army, but they themselves also suffered grievous losses and damage to their country. Dudayev lost his life in this war.

Yeltsin's expectation was that he would be able to finish the job swiftly and decisively, but the Chechens surprised him. A prolonged internal war would have been both costly and risky, because it could have affected the new Russia's future. The country was going through a very delicate phase of transformation, and Yeltsin worried that the hardline Communists might capitalise on this war to take over the country and revert back to Communism. So he decided that ending the dragging hostilities was urgently in new Russia's own interest. On the other hand, he did not want to give up the Chechen republic either. So in August 1996 he suggested to Chechnya's new president, Aslan Maskhadov, a "five-year moratorium on the republic's disputed status", in return for which Yeltsin would remove the Russian army from Chechnya and give the Chechens full authority to run their own internal affairs.. The question of Chechnya's independence would be postponed for five years and then settled peacefully between the parties.

Maskhadov naturally found this offer attractive, so a peace agreement was signed between the two and the war was ended. The Chechens went back to rebuilding their cities and economy and looked forward to a peaceful settlement of their grievances with Russia in a foreseeable future. Proceeding with his efforts to rebuild Chechnya, Maskhadov held elections in January 1997, which were overseen by international monitors, who acknowledged that they were fair and Maskhadov's victory as president was authentic. This was a healthy sign. Yeltsin invited Maskhadov to Moscow officially to reaffirm the agreement that they had signed before Maskhadov was constitutionally elected. Ratification by a new agreement in May 1997 was a reaffirmation of commitment from both sides to abide by the peaceful course. This was great news for Chechnya, too, because now the republic could devote its full attention to social and economic development and to creating a healthy religious environment for its overwhelmingly Muslim population. Chechnya was at peace and so was Russia. This was a success for Yeltsin because he had shown that he was able to control the hardline Communists who still occupied important posts in the military, the intelligence services and other government departments.

It will be remembered that when Russia switched over to a free-market economy the people and the state faced many hardships. The country was not accustomed to free-market practices, nor was it experienced enough in social and political freedom. Consequently there was mismanagement of the economy, which opened the doors for corruption as shady elements became openly active. There were currency and financial frauds of all kinds and acute shortages of food supplies, because the traders did not yet understand demand and supply and the black martketeers deliberately manipulated them, leaving grocery shelves in many stores empty and thereby creating hardships for consumers. The Ruble had taken a nosedive, and the people were having to sell their valuables just to buy food. Public complaints became common, and many citizens began yearning for a return to the old system, which had at least given them food on the table. The opponents of change were quick to capitalise and blamed the free-market economy for the hardships. They demanded that strong men should take over the reins to control the situation and deal with the criminals and the rampant corruption. Everyone feared, including the United States that conditions might be ripe for the hardliners to seize control and revert back to Communism. The hardliners were already making strong bids for the prime minister's post, but so far Yeltsin had kept them at bay.

Finally, the hardliners lost patience. They saw a window of opportunity because in addition to the administrative and economic chaos, Yeltsin also had a personal drinking problem, which affected his health and made him vulnerable. Thus the hardliners went back to their old tricks. They seem to have hatched a scheme to re-ignite war in the North Caucasus region in order to unsettle Yeltsin and demonstrate to the nation that he was incapable of managing the country's affairs. His successive prime ministers not only failed in economic management but also at keeping peace in the Federation. The hardliners' threat was that, if Yeltsin did not replace them with a strong man from their own ranks, then he could face an internal revolt. Though Yeltsin was physically almost incapacitated, he still resisted the hardliners, fearing that they would undo everything that he had done to create a new Russia. Yeltsin's resolve against the hardliners left them with no choice but to undertake a drastic and dramatic measure that would force him to yield to their demands and appoint a hardliner as prime minister, or else quit office himself.

How it was done is shocking but consistent with the KGB practices and counterintelligence operations in which the Communists were well trained. They had grown accustomed to toppling régimes in foreign countries by acts of violence and terrorism to install pro-Communist dictators in the days of Soviet rule. Now they faced a similar challenge at home, but toppling Russia's own government ran the risk of a civil war, which could destroy Russia totally. Therefore the scheme had to be one with limited consequences. Hence they selected Chechnya as their catalyst for dissolving Yeltsin's regime, knowing that the Chechens already had an unfavourable reputation and if somehow they could be implicated in violence, that would reflect badly on Yeltsin's ability to maintain law and order. The conspirators also knew that the Chechens had the willingness to fight for their independence as well as religion; so if somehow they could be involved in violence, that would create the required upheaval and arouse public disapproval of Yeltsin. The idea was to grab power and at the same time keep the public on the conspirators' side. The Chechens were to be cast as the bad guys to win the support of the Russian public.

But the Chechens had absolutely no reason to provoke hostilities. They were busy rebuilding their republic from the ruins of the first war and optimistically looking forward to a peaceful resolution as stipulated in their agreement with Russia. Aslan Maskhadov was a skilful negotiator and was working with Yeltsin prudently towards a peaceful settlement. Consequently, there was no chance that the Chechens would resort to hostilities against Russia under Maskhadov's leadership.

But disturbing the peace was not difficult for these veterans of the KGB and counterintelligence services. They realised that even if the Chechens would not enkindle violence, their name could still be used if someone else would commit the crime, which could then be blamed on them owing to their bad reputation. Hence the diehard Communists went back to their old technique of hiring saboteurs and using criminals to instigate violence that could then be attributed to the Chechens. Finding saboteurs and criminals was not difficult. Certain criminal Daghestanis were good candidates, owing to their close links with the insiders in Moscow as well as their rivalry with the Chechens. They were chosen to carry out acts of violence and terrorism and make it look like as if the Chechens had committed them. Since their role is crucial to understanding the true nature of the Chechen saga, it is important at this stage to know more about Daghestan.

Daghestan is the second largest Muslim-populated republic in the North Caucasus region and was also forcibly seized by the Tsars in 1818. Though they came from the same region and practised the same religion, the Daghestanis are temperamentally different from the Chechens, in that they do not fervently aspire to freeing themselves from Russian domination as the Chechens do. Consequently, they have mixed feelings about independence as well as Islamisation of the republic. While there are some strong pockets of Daghestanis who are devout Muslims and yearn for an Islamic state, there are others who prefer for social and economic reasons to maintain the status quo and carry on as part of the Russian Federation. The latter group certainly did not want any union with Chechens in an Islamic state. In contrast, some Chechens were enthusiastic to forge an Islamic union of Daghestan and Chechnya in the North Caucasus region; Chechnya's radical leaders Shamil Basayev and Emir Khattab had been dreaming and planning to realise this goal ever since Chechnya signed its peace agreement with Russia. All the peacetime energies of these two leaders were concentrated on laying greater Islamic foundations in Chechnya while also working on Daghestan to bring it into the Islamic fold. Insiders in Moscow were fully aware of these trends and maintained contacts with these two leaders in roundabout ways. One was through Daghestan's "criminalised politician brothers, the Khachilayevs, who had shadowy connections in Moscow" and another was through a "prominent Kremlin insider and business tycoon Boris Berezovsky – a man with long-standing business links in Chechnya and a murky political agenda in Moscow." "It was also an open secret in Chechnya that the telephones and the radical Islamic website used by the invaders [a later undertaking by the Chechens against Daghestan] had been paid for" by Berezovsky. Thomas de Waal goes on to explain in the introduction that "inevitably, this being the Caucasus, there are also suggestions of conspiracy. Some suspect that the Chechen incursion [into Daghestan] was deliberately provoked by someone in Moscow to justify a strong military response" against Chechnya. "The two men [Basayev and Khattab] were invited into Daghestan by two criminalized politician brothers, the Khachilayevs." "What needs no proof is that Basayev and Khattab's incursion into Daghestan was the cue for a momentous shift of power in Moscow; the entry on to the Russian political stage of a new strong man, the then head of the counterintelligence service or FSB, Vladimir Putin."

Apart from inviting the Chechen incursion into Daghestan by the Khachilayev brothers under sinister influences from Moscow, there were two other significant developments that need to be kept in mind. "The first tremor, on 4 September, came with the slaughter of Russian soldiers and their families in Buinaksk in Daghestan. Shocking as it was, this made little impact outside the North Caucasus. But then the whole country was traumatized. Two apartment blocks, seemingly chosen at random, were blown up in Moscow within a week. More than 200 people were killed in their beds. A fourth and final blast in the southern city of Volgodonsk killed 17 more people. The explosions were terrifying acts of murder, all the more so because no warnings had been given and no responsibility claimed. The Russian authorities laid the blame on 'Chechen terrorists' – only to get a stout denial from Shamil Basayev that he was involved."

The conspiracy theorists have again posed some challenging questions: How come Basayev was accused of randomly killing civilians in Moscow, when he had never targeted civilians before? And was it not true that the main beneficiary of the bombings was the new administration of Vladimir Putin? It is indeed strange, to say the least, that the explosions happened out of the blue when Chechnya was at peace – and then stopped again so suddenly. Fighting only broke out in Chechnya after the chain of explosions had ended.

We have quoted these excerpts so that our readers may keep this information in mind when we come to discuss the intricacies of the Chechen war.

Reverting to the main story, we see that Shamil Basayev and his partner Emir Khattab, a Saudi Mujahid, were prominent proponents of the Islamic ideology. Khattab had come to participate in the 1994-96 war along with thousands of other Mujahideens from Arabia and decided to stay permanently in Chechnya to help build *Madrasas* and *Masjids*. Both these men aspired to develop an Islamic state in the North Caucasus that would include neighbouring Muslim Daghestan. The insiders in Moscow knew about their role in the 1994 war and were also aware how zealous these two men were to spread Islam in the region. The collaborators of the Moscow insiders pretended to be supporters of the Islamic movement and convinced Basayev and Khattab that, while most Daghestanis would like to come into the Islamic fold, some did not favour such a union. So it was necessary for them to come to Daghestan to iron out this opposition before the Islamic union could take shape. The argument was convincing enough to lure these two men into Daghestan on the pretext that some levelling of the ground was needed to quell local opposition. They were told that some limited use of force might be necessary to pave the way for the envisaged Daghestan-Chechnya Islamic union. Both Basayev and Khattab fell into the trap, believing that the majority of Daghestanis was on their side and only a small operation would remove the obstacle. They had no inkling of what underlay the invitation, because those who had extended it were acting in a pre-planned conspiracy to implicate the Chechens in criminal activity.

Consequently, Basayev and Khattab collected an army of nearly two thousand warriors and marched into Daghestan on August 7, 1999. They anticipated that Daghestanis favouring Islamic state would welcome them and support their mission. They were utterly surprised when no local support came forward to welcome them and the subject villages, which they had gone to chastise, put up a stiff resistance. Hence, what was supposed to be a quick and small operation developed into a large-scale war. Basayev and Khattab were veterans of the 1994 war; so fighting back fiercely came to them naturally and they were quickly sucked into hostilities, killing Daghestani villagers, destroying their homes and bringing upon them the misery of war. The Daghestanis then made urgent appeals to Russia for help, and the whole country was in shock and uproar at what the Chechens had done. The hardline Moscow insiders, with military backing, surrounded Yeltsin with threatening complaints that his administration was weak and leading the federation towards disintegration. Yeltsin was put under enormous pressure to allow the strong men to take over power and suppress the disruptive and terrorist acts of the Chechens. Two days after the hostilities began, on August 9, 1999, Yeltsin yielded to their pressure and appointed Vladimir Putin, the then head of the counterintelligence service or FSB, as Russia's new prime minister. Putin was the chosen strong man of the hardliners, and it is conceivable that he was the mastermind who hatched this entire scheme as head of the counterintelligence service. Putin immediately flew to Daghestan, assessed the situation and ordered the Russian army to move in. Soon Basayev and Khattab realised that the conflict was out of their hands and once the Russians got involved, they took a step back and hostilities subsided. The Russian army had also arrived on the scene. The Daghestani victims expected the Russians to round up the criminals and punish them severely for the atrocities they had committed against the pro-Russian villages. Basayev gathered his men in one place, expecting to be surrounded by the Russian army and apprehended.

But to the horror and dismay of the villagers, it did not happen. Instead the Russian army stood quietly by and allowed Basayev and Khattab, along with their remaining men, to escape to Chechnya. The villagers complained to the Russians and asked why they would not apprehend these criminals and nip the evil in the bud. But the Chechens were not let go without a reason. Putin and his ring of hardliners had bigger plans in store and wanted to use these warriors, or at least their names, to carry through the remaining part of their larger scheme. The Daghestan operation was only the first step; other things were to follow from it and these men were again needed to provide the background and excuse for launching the next phase. If they were apprehended and locked up, then there would be no one to blame for the next stage of operation against Chechnya. Basayev and Khattab led the only active band of warriors, so it was crucial to keep them intact for later use, which was why they were allowed to escape without any resistance.

Putin's objective was not just to come to power. He had an agenda: namely, to control the corruption and criminal activities that had become rampant during the transformation. He was determined to bring stability to the eroding Ruble and secure adequate supplies of food and other essentials in the marketplace, and most of all to preserve the integrity of the Russian Federation by quelling secessionist movements such as the one in Chechnya. The hardliners viewed Yeltsin's truce with Chechnya and his agreement to settle the dispute peacefully with disapproval, fearing that it might lead to Chechnya's separation and also open doors for other autonomous republics, such as Daghestan, to demand separation. Putin did not want to give the North Caucasus region any right to separate, now or later; so he had to create conditions that would give him a chance to destroy the Chechen leadership and all other activists completely. This could only be done by an act of war, but Chechnya was at peace with Russia. So now Putin and the ring of hardliners went to work on their next phase, which was to create war conditions that would allow them to attack Chechnya and accomplish their mission of destroying the Chechen separatist movement and cutting the roots of all aspirations for Islamic states.

But Putin had a hurdle in his way, the peace between Chechnya and Russia; so several other steps were taken to disrupt the peace. Again the Daghestanis were used, and on September 4, 1999 an attack was launched on Russian soldiers and their families in Buinaksk, in which they were slaughtered and their quarters destroyed. Suspicion was quickly cast on the Chechen warriors, some of whom might have remained in the vicinity, but everything else pointed to Daghestanis as the perpetrators of this crime. The impact was local in the North Caucasus region, and it did not stir the Russian public effectively, since they were all too accustomed to hearing of these kinds of atrocities in the Caucasus. Trauma and tragedy had to be brought closer to the Russian people to arouse the anger and revulsion that would give the hardliners a signal to attack Chechnya. So the final component of the scheme had to be extremely provocative and deadly. One week after Basayev and Khattab were allowed to escape Daghestan, two apartment blocks were blown up in Moscow, killing over 200 people immediately and 17 more shortly after. This was a terrible thing to happen to the Russians. Fingers inevitably pointed at the Chechens, because only a few days before they had been involved in hostilities in Daghestan and it was conveniently assumed that they were now turning their viciousness on Russian civilians. The outburst of anger and cries for revenge were resounding. Putin was already looking for this to happen, so he wasted no time in launching a brutal and ruthless military operation against Chechnya. He had the full support of Yeltsin and the Russian people, because they were inflamed with anger and athirst for revenge after having been hurt right in their homes. The attack on Moscow brought tragedy home and the hysteria and government propaganda held the Chechens responsible for this horrible crime. Cries for revenge and war on Chechnya were inevitable, which was what Putin was looking for to carry out his plan against the Chechens. The rest of the world was also outraged and accepted the premise that Putin had a reason to go to war against the nationalists in Chechnya, but they pleaded on behalf of the innocent Chechen people and asked Putin to be discreet. But Putin did not care. He proved himself to be a ruthless and cold-blooded murderer of peaceful Chechens.

The hysteria and anger, fuelled by propaganda, grew so overwhelming that no one had a chance to evaluate the circumstances or even check the veracity of the allegations. Maskhadov desperately pleaded with Putin that Chechnya had no reason or motive to bomb Moscow, as it had no outstanding issue or dispute with Russia. He cited his two agreements formally concluded with Yeltsin and assured Putin that he was fully abiding by them. Basayev and Khattab also swore that they had had nothing to do with the crime of Moscow; they had just returned from Daghestan and had not yet recovered from their shock at how they had been tricked into their hostilities there, which they now regretted. They had had no reason or motive or even opportunity to carry out Moscow bombings. There was absolutely no benefit for the Chechens in attacking Russians at all. They pointed to the Daghestanis, who had tricked them and now were also tricking the Russians by carrying out this horrible crime so that Russia would unleash its military might against the Chechens. The Daghestanis had played into the hands of the Russians before luring Basayev and Khattab into Daghestan, and now they were again playing into the hands of the Russians, so that Putin could unleash Russian wrath on Chechnya. But Putin was not interested in listening to reason or logic or learning about the facts; indeed the evidence suggests that he must have known about the plot and may well have masterminded it himself. He had been the chief of the counterintelligence service, so he should have known all about this operation.

The enigma of the bombing has not yet been solved. In September 2000 the Russian authorities said they had arrested 63 people in connection with the attacks. Interestingly they said that most were of North Caucasus origin, but there were very few Chechens among them. These lines are taken from Thomas de Waal's introduction to Anna Politkovskaya's book *A Dirty War.*

The point to note here is that when at last an inquiry was made into the matter, the Chechen participants turned out to be "very few." The others were mostly Daghestanis.

It should be noted that Daghestan was not as volatile as Chechnya had been. It had no grudge against Russia, as many Daghestanis were pro-Russian and were quite contented to be part of Russia. They had no reason to blow up the Russian military camp in Buinaksk on September 4, 1999 or the two apartment blocks in Moscow one week later. But the fact that the Buinaksk operation occurred in Daghestan and most of those arrested in connection with the Moscow job were Daghestanis implicates Daghestan in violence against Russia. Why did the Daghestanis do it and help to create turmoil against the Russians? The answer lies in the two criminalised Daghestani brothers, the Khachilayevs, who had shadowy connections in Moscow. It has been demonstrated that they were acting under influence of Moscow insiders, and it is reasonable and logical to infer that they were also the instigators of the two operations against the Russians with the blessing and help in planning of the Russian secret service. Otherwise, it is hard to see why Daghestanis would act against Russia. The real beneficiary of the Daghestani operations was Vladimir Putin, who not only became prime minister and later took over the presidency from Yeltsin but also succeeded in crippling the Chechen separation drive and the Islamic movement. The loss of Muscovites' life and property was "unavoidable collateral damage" of the kind that self-centred and brutal leaders are accustomed to accepting as the price for their misguided missions.

Chechnya and the Chechens were brutalised, massacred and obliterated for a crime they did not commit. If one reads Politkovskaya's book about the details of Putin's war on Chechnya, one will know how brutal, ruthless and inhuman his actions have been: how homes and cities and the entire infrastructure of Chechen civilisation have been destroyed on the pretext of a totally unfounded allegation of crimes against the Russian people. The Chechens did indeed fight back and inflict heavy casualties on the Russian army, but inevitably the Russian army prevailed in the end because of its size and might.

It may be reiterated and emphasised once again that Chechnya had two peace agreements with Russia, which were signed by their heads of state. There is no evidence that Chechnya in any way contravened these agreements. Even the incursion of Basayev and Khattab into Daghestan was not against Russia, and since the Chechen government was not responsible for that, it could not be construed as a violation of the agreements with Russia. In any case the pro-Russian Daghestani brothers, on whatever pretext, had lured these two men into Daghestan as part of a larger conspiracy. The Chechens did not violate their undertakings to Russia, nor did they commit any aggression against the Russian people.

Anna Politkovskaya also tells us that one of the Khachilayev brothers has since been murdered, but she did not elucidate the reason or who might have been behind this murder when these brothers were so well connected with the Moscow insiders and most likely had their backing and protection. The murder of one of the brothers is significant. Though Politkovskaya had not explained, the suspicion is that while both brothers were working for Russia, one of them may have been the principal architect of all the Daghestani operations under Moscow's supervision and planning. He may have known too much about the Moscow insiders, their names and identities and the full nature of their plans, which seems to have made it necessary to eliminate him to obscure the insiders' conspiracy about the Moscow bombings. There seems to be no other explanation of why such a well-connected Daghestani would be left without protection by the secret agents to be murdered. Politkovskaya also does not tell us whether there was ever a police investigation into his murder or whether any suspects were held for interrogation or found guilty of this crime. If not, that too seems odd, especially when the victim had such good connections in Moscow.

The people of Chechnya now find themselves under the same yoke of despair and hopelessness that other Muslims suffer from the occupation of their lands and the usurpation of their sovereignty. They, too, have no international support or even active sympathy in the international community, since they have been made look like terrorists and placed in the overall category of Islamic terrorists that the West has contrived. The brutal oppression of the Russians has left the Chechens with no option but to resort to armed struggle to gain their freedom. No one seems to recognise the legitimacy of the Chechen struggle or how hard-pressed the people of Chechnya are to regain their rights. The outside world easily falls for Russian propaganda and blames the Chechen armed struggle as an act of terrorism.

The Chechens are devout Muslims who have suffered long spells of atrocities and brutalities at the hands of the tsarist Russians and Soviet Communists. The tribesmen of the North Caucasus "are a proud race, not easy to coerce." They have seen wars before and survived. They have the mettle to survive wars again, but the price will be too high in terms of human lives and damage to property.

The difference between a freedom fight and acts of terrorism could be subtle if it is aimed at the servicemen and military establishments of the enemy. The best way to illustrate this phenomenon to the American public is to remind them their own war of independence and struggle for freedom (1775-83) against British domination. Although Britain was not brutalizing the population, the Americans nevertheless considered their rule an outside occupation of their country.

A reflection on America's history would show that American independence was not achieved without a rebellion or resorting to acts of violence, including terrorism, against the British and the Loyalist colonists who supported them. The American freedom fighters, bravely as they fought, were compelled by circumstances to take up arms against the British, since the British were not going to grant them freedom without a fight. This is a regrettable attitude of all occupiers, as we can see in Palestine, Kashmir and Chechnya. The occupiers use the full force at their disposal to suppress freedom movements and stubbornly refuse to vacate their occupations unless they are forced out by armed insurrection. Hence the oppressed captives are left with no recourse to gain freedom except by taking up armed struggle. The British put the Americans in this constraint; so the Americans, too, were left with no recourse other than an armed insurrection or rebellion to gain their freedom from the occupying British.

It would be well if occupiers would concede to the pleas and plight of their captives and voluntarily vacate their occupation. But, as much as one may wish it, that does not happen in the real world. So, then, what do you do or what did the Americans do when caught in the same situation? Emulating the American War of Independence does not mean that armed struggle or violence is preferable; no, certainly not. What it means is that, failing an alternative to war, armed insurrection is the only recourse available for the captives or oppressed subjects of aggression. Therefore, finding alternatives is crucial to avoiding wars. However, the initiative for an alternative must come from the occupiers rather than the captives, since they alone have the power and authority to make decisions.

However, it does not happen, because the occupiers are so drunk on military power that they know no other way to behave. Many intellectuals have pondered on finding a nonbelligerent way to escape oppression, but they have failed owing to the stubbornness of the occupiers. To get over this enduring hurdle, an American intellectual produced an interesting concept of dealing with oppressive situations. It is not only pertinent, but also worthwhile to remember that honour, liberty and freedom were so precious for the American intelligentsia that they even concluded that defying law or mounting resistance to escape tyranny was honourable for the sake of freedom.

A renowned American essayist, Henry David Thoreau (1817-66), who wrote a book entitled *Civil Disobedience,* promoted the notion "that it was more honourable to be right than to be law-abiding; that every individual ought to resist a tyrannical government." Thoreau wrote his book many years after the American War of Independence. Although Thoreau advocated resistance to a tyrannical government, he did not encourage armed resistance.

Nevertheless freedom is so precious and indispensable for the development of free societies and political liberty of nations that sometimes it is acceptable though regrettable to go through insurrection even at the cost of war and destruction. Sometimes there is no other way left to rid oneself of the oppression except to defy the law and resist tyrannical government. Hence, it would appear that if a nation's honour were at stake or its rights are usurped then it can break the law to rectify the unjust situation. This is the underlying principle of freedom fight. Similarly, if a country is taken over by a tyrannical régime, whether internal or external, then it is also justifiable to resist such a régime, even by taking up arms.

Looking at the current Muslim plight in the light of America's own war of independence, we can see that the Muslims in Palestine, Kashmir and Chechnya are not doing anything different from what the Americans themselves did over 200 years ago. We can surely also see that freedom is precious and indispensable for the Muslims, too, for their political liberty and the development of free societies. Defying the law of the occupiers to secure right and resisting tyrannical government to escape oppression would also be justifiable in their case.

What is needed to deal with the Muslims' strife is a little more understanding of their predicaments. Muslims are not inherently warmongers or terrorists. Oppression and tyranny by the occupiers of their lands have made them so. If their case is viewed without prejudice, then we can appreciate that their struggle is no different from any that of any other nation that has had to fight for its freedom.

Besides having to struggle against outside occupiers, the Muslims also have internal difficulties with their own rulers, whether they are political despots or religious fanatics. Thus external and internal forces have compounded their struggle for freedom and liberty, which needs to be recognised and supported by the rest of the international community for the sake of the freedom and liberty of Muslim societies. But freedom does not mean freeing a people on the one hand and then subjugating them in other ways.

The difficulties facing the Muslims are many, but the greatest of all is the Western bias against Islam emanating from a twisted faith. It is owing to this bias that the West is reluctant to extend a helping hand to the Muslims. Most of the oppressive and despotic kings and rulers in the Islamic world have been appointees of the West, who brutalised the Muslim societies for their own purposes as well as to serve the interests of their masters. This patronage has not been disbanded. These vassals are usually called "our friends", but in reality they are the long arms of the West, which is engaged in exploiting the natural resources of the Islamic world by aiding and abetting the despotic régimes.

Whenever Muslim nationalists and other activists try to dislodge these despotic régimes by agitation or any other means, the secret services from the West come to thwart their efforts and rescue their oppressive clients. The example of the1953 Iranian revolution proves the point. The Algerian effort through a democratic process was also thwarted. Indonesia was doing well under Dr Sukarno until General Suharto appeared on the scene and so on. The Egyptians have a similar grudge that a despot has been anchored in their country by the same forces, and the list goes on. Granted, their national armies take the actions, but the controlling generals are often on the payroll of the Western powers. Hence it might appear as an internal operation, but in reality the directive comes from outside.

When Muslims try to resolve their external problems, they face a particular resistance. When they try to correct their internal situations, they face the same resistance in a different form. The persistent resistance to their efforts, both external and internal, aggravates their resentment and directs their anger towards the same centre of gravity. This explains why there is such intense hatred, especially against the United States. Not only do these Western acts hamper Muslim efforts for freedom, but they also end up provoking hatred, inflaming the Muslims' emotions and destroying any chance of long- term goodwill and peace.

8

September 11 – The Untold Story

There are so many unanswered questions and unproven allegations that doubt on the official version of the 9/11 episode inevitably stands out. It gets even more distrustful when President Bush willfully avoided judicial inquiry to establish Al-Qaeda's or bin Laden's involvement in the 9/11 attacks. His reluctance to institute the 9/11 Commission and shunning the judicial process create the impression that there might be another side to the 9/11 story that President Bush is consciously trying to suppress. Later his profusely availing himself of the political benefits and capitalising on the phenomenon of terrorism to bolster his leadership and justify a wider military operation against the Muslim world makes many analysts uneasy as if there was a purpose in not thwarting the 9/11 attacks.

If we review how President Bush conducted himself before and after the 9/11 attacks, and also take into account the aggressive or intimidating utterances of Israeli leaders and match them with the bent of mind of Paul Wolfowitz, then we can see that 9/11 was a kind of perfect occurrence that people like Nathan Yahu and Wolfowitz had been yearning to use as a pretext for war against the Islamic world to ultimately benefit Israel as well as gratify the Evangelicals who passionately wish for Jewish resettlement in Palestine to hasten Jesus' Second Coming. This is the backdrop of the untold story.

While the nineteen Arabs were undoubtedly in those planes, the enigma is who put them in there and who was directing them. To unravel this enigma we shall channel our study in three broad avenues to reach a plausible conclusion about the untold story:

1. The lack of conclusive or concrete evidence of linkage between the hijackers and Al-Qaeda or bin Laden and CIA's inability to penetrate the 9/11 plot;
2. The theory of motivation and the question of beneficiary;
3. President Bush's inert posture against bin Laden and his less than diligent response to the PDB of August 6, 2001.

The admission by George Tenet, the Director of the Central Intelligence

Agency, that it simply failed to penetrate the 9/11 plot raises a host of questions. For example, how could a vagabond terrorist operating from a cave somewhere in Afghanistan succeed in outwitting the world's most sophisticated and vastly resourceful intelligence agency? Secondly, it is not enough for the agency merely to say that it failed. It owes to the American public to explain how it actually failed in such a disastrous way, when it is designed to succeed owing to its resourcefulness and its close network of surveillance and agents around the globe.

The agency's failure could be explained in two ways. One way is to say that the agency just badly failed. One could think of various reasons to account for this failure or find enough compassion to overlook the agency's inadequacy given the number of limitations, which may be cited as beyond its control. This would be an easy way to let the CIA off the hook. The other way to discern the cause of its misadventure is to say that the CIA failed because it was not looking in the right direction. These two ways of evaluating the agency's performance could spark an animated debate about the conclusions. While the first approach would be more sympathetic, the second, implying that the agency might have been barking up the wrong tree, could become contentious. Regardless of the controversy, this writer wishes to explore the probability of barking up the wrong tree, to be sure that nothing is left to chance in determining the facts about the 9/11 case.

There is no doubt in this writer's mind that the CIA did its best to pursue bin Laden and Al-Qaeda to find out what they were thinking and how they were planning to hurt the United States. The CIA may have found many pieces of information and a host of leads about bin Laden's activities or plans during its intense investigation of the terrorist network, but surprisingly it found nothing relating to the 9/11 plot. This is shocking. George Tenet described during his testimony all the measures that the CIA had put in place in 1999 to keep diligent surveillance over Al-Qaeda and bin Laden. These elaborate measures totalled 74 operations of which 25 were inside Afghanistan, including co-operation, presumably through cash handouts, with some tribal chiefs to keep track on bin Laden's activities from within. This was a remarkable effort, and it would appear that the agency did everything that it deemed necessary to watch bin Laden's activities, especially after the attack on the two embassies in 1998.

However, when the scenario of barking up the wrong tree is considered, it is not a reflection on the CIA but rather an indication that its focus may have been too single-tracked. Is it not possible that the agency was unaware of the 9/11 plot because it was hatched elsewhere by a third party that the CIA was not watching as closely as it was watching Al-Qaeda? The premise is that had the agency's focus been broadened to encompass other suspect centres with Arab concentration, it would have spotted activities of other perpetrators, too, who might have been engaged in grinding their own axe. Such adversaries may have found it opportune to exploit the international anti-Islam climate and decided to fabricate acts of terrorism only to assign the blame to the Muslim radicals, knowing that it would come naturally to everybody's mind that Muslims must have been the culprits. That would then put Muslims in deeper trouble from which they (the adversaries of Islam) could benefit in the long run. Logically, it fits the motives of other adversaries of the Muslim world. This may be a remote possibility, but it cannot be ignored, because there are other interested parties who would like to see Islam and the Arab world get into deeper trouble. The existence of exploiters and copycats is all too familiar to the investigative community to be ignored.

In fact a very rare occurrence took place in India when its parliament was attacked, for the first time ever, in a bizarre and unusual way soon after the 9/11 tragedy. India was quick off the mark to blame Islamic terrorists based in or at least linked with Pakistan for this attack, saying that its sacred institution of democracy had been assaulted with Pakistan's complicity. The hysteria attracted international sympathy. Thus India was able to turn this tragic event into an excuse to attack Pakistan, hoping that the international community would support the action in the same way as it supported the United States in attacking Afghanistan. The animosity between India and Pakistan is well known and this seemed an opportune time for India to put down Pakistan in a formidable way. Pakistan was already in deep trouble, and it was perhaps India's best chance to settle the score with Pakistan once for all. International opinion was also inflamed; so the moment appeared ripe for India to do something, even fabricate terrorism, to create grounds for attacking Pakistan while international emotions were still inflamed against the Muslims, especially suspecting Pakistan as a safe haven for the terrorist network. Everything seemed perfect; so India made a bizarre move and came to the brink of war against Pakistan. In the midst of the hysteria and propaganda, the need to produce evidence or proof was ignored in the same way as the United States had done earlier. It was a perfect demonstration of how to exploit a tragedy for political and territorial benefits. Those who closely followed this case will remember that it was India's copycat attempt to grind its own axe against Pakistan. In the end, the case never went anywhere, because it had no grounds. In fact, when Pakistan openly took a position against terrorism and it became clear that it could not have been part of the attack on the Indian parliament, the State Department warned India in a friendly tone to abstain from taking advantage of the deteriorating situation in the region.

The surprising thing is that even after the Indian copycat attempt became known, it still did not dawn on the CIA that there could be some other perpetrators who might also want to take advantage of the tension between the West and the Islamic world. Although a look around was warranted to eliminate all other possibilities, the CIA seemingly remained fixed on its single-channel focus on bin Laden even though it had found no concrete grounds for implicating him beyond his bad reputation and its own assumptions and presumptions. There were sufficient reasons for the agency to look around for other probable perpetrators even after the fact of 9/11, but it apparently did not explore other contingencies, since it has not mentioned anything about them.

The agency apparently felt no need to look around, even when it became evident that neither it nor the FBI had any conclusive or concrete evidence to link 9/11 with bin Laden or Al-Qaeda. The FBI admitted during the 9/11 investigations that it had found no contacts between the hijackers and the known Al-Qaeda cells in the United States, which it had been watching closely. The CIA also produced no evidence of any links, saying it was totally unaware of the 9/11 plot. Neither intelligence agency could produce any clear or conclusive proof of a link between the hijackers and bin Laden.

Frankly, bells ought to have rung in the CIA headquarters to find out why that was so and whether there might be other elements on the international scene that would wish to exploit the situation for any other purpose. The missing links and lack of enthusiasm in both the CIA and the FBI to look for other probabilities are the real crux of the 9/11 mystery.

Looking back at George Tenet's statements, we do not remember him giving any specifics of the CIA failure abroad in detecting the 9/11 plot comparable to the mishaps in communications that the FBI admitted to on the home front. One would have to ask how it is possible, after such an extensive operation and elaborate surveillance network as the DCI described in his statement, that the agency would return empty-handed.

The 9/11 plot seems to have been in the works for nearly two and half years, if not three or more, of which fifteen months were spent in preparation in the United States and at least a similar time must have been spent in preparation in Germany or elsewhere. This is a long enough time for the CIA to have bumped into this plot somewhere abroad if it were looking in every direction. The fact that Mohammed Ata travelled from the United States to Prague and Spain and returned shows that his plot had international connections, which the CIA ought to have picked up from its international network. Furthermore, there also ought to have been some communications between Afghanistan and Germany, which the CIA would have picked up from either its own surveillance operation or being tipped by the Germans. These missing detections are indicators that Afghanistan might not have been involved in the Germany plot. Lack of funds or manpower could be cited as a handicap, but given what the agency had, there were no security lapses or slackening in intensity in the surveillance work in Afghanistan that would explain why bin Laden's link with his Germany cell was not detected. George Tenet did not mention any mishaps in the agency's operations, nor did he explain why he did not keep an eye on other international centres such as Germany. What he said was that the agency failed to penetrate the 9/11 plot. It is not that they were not looking, it is only that they could not find any clues. The CIA's apparent inability to discover anything about this plot thickens the mystery and prompted this writer to pay attention to the possibility of a third party. It has now become a reason for him to contemplate and probe further to explore what other explanation there may be for the 9/11 tragedy.

Before analysing the third-party contingency it is necessary to reflect briefly on the following questions:

a) Was the security lapse incidental or intentional?
b) What is the proof of a link between Al-Qaeda and bin Laden with the nineteen hijackers who lived and operated from Germany?
c) Is it technically possible that ill trained and unqualified flyers, who had only rudimentary training on single-engine aeroplanes of the type of Cessna and were licensed to fly only single-engine planes, could take command of a wide-body 767 Boeing Jet aircraft? Could they fly this aircraft so perfectly, chalk out the flight path and hit the target in the bullseye merely on the basis of training on simulators?

Taking up these questions, it will be seen that the lapse in security is not in question, since it has been acknowledged and accepted by all inquiries thus far made. What is in question is whether this lapse was incidental or intentional. Had the lapse been incidental or due to negligence, then the delinquent officials would have been taken to task and disciplined at least departmentally. Since no such action was taken, it gives the feeling that perhaps there is more behind these lapses that has not been divulged or taken up for investigation. To complain about the lapses and yet not take action against the persons who were responsible for these lapses is very unusual.

As far as a link of bin Laden with the nineteen hijackers is concerned, there is no conclusive evidence to show that Mohammed Ata or any member of his gang ever went to Afghanistan for training or instructions about the 9/11 attacks. Only two members of this group had previous contact with Afghanistan, but none of the ringleaders ever went there or met with bin Laden for any briefings. Apparently, the burden of proof that bin Laden controlled these hijackers or induced or instigated Mohammed Ata and his gang to perpetrate 9/11 attack has not been specifically carried out.

Lastly, it has also not been established by expert inquiry whether Mohammed Ata and his co-conspirators had sufficient technical hands-on training and knowledge to take over the 767 wide-body Boeing jet planes, slow down the engine speed without stalling the engines, descend from nearly 30,000 or 40,000 ft to a level of approximately 1400 ft without nose-diving, find the exact location of the Twin Towers, make a perfect loop to turnaround the planes, and locate the target to hit it in the centre piercing the planes inside the building. These are tricky manoeuvres that only hands-on training on jet aircraft could perfect. The outside condition of the planes was stable, as seen on the two videotapes, which indicated that there was no commotion or agitation inside the cockpit. There was no wavering or erratic flying, no tipping of the wings or any unsteadiness in the flight, and the pilot did not appear to be struggling to locate the target since the planes made no zigzag moves. Everything went smoothly. The hit was too perfect to believe. How did Mohammed Ata and his partners figure out the flight path to bring the planes accurately over the Twin Towers, or is it possible that this path was already fed into the computer, which was then operated by a remote control to accomplish a perfect hit? These points ought to have been considered by technical aviation experts of international standing to determine whether or not the Ata gang had the capability to accomplish all those sophisticated technical moves in the air. Are simulators alternative to hands-on training or are they only accessory to training? Since there has been no independent technical inquiry, all these doubts linger on, making the 9/11 plot even more suspicious.

It is also important to note that such a complicated operation could not have been carried out without ground co-ordination or support? The U.S. officials have not addressed the question of ground support or the people managing the co-ordination.

As we write US officials have informed the 9/11 Commission that a Pakistani national named Khalid Shaikh Mohammed (KSM) has confessed to being the mastermind of the 9/11 plot. Scanty details of the plot were narrated and attributed to him alleging that he hatched the plot, recruited the nineteen hijackers and kept bin Laden informed of the whole operation. This is a bizarre story. First, the supposed confession was obtained while KSM was in captivity where he might have been subjected to extreme torture for which the Guantanamo Bay prisoners' camp has become infamous. Second, KSM might have made this statement only to escape the brutality and torture of the interrogation. Captives commonly make even false confessions in such circumstances just to escape torture or obtain respite from the interrogators. Seeing the brutality at the Abu Gharib prison in Iraq it is not difficult to imagine that KSM might also have been subjected to similar or greater brutal treatment that "softened him up" to co-operate and say the things that the captors wanted to hear. Third, if his statement was so reliable and credible, then why was KSM not presented to the 9/11 Commission in person as prime witness to prove bin Laden's involvement in the 9/11 plot? He is currently in U.S. custody and could have been brought before the 9/11 Commission to make direct testimony instead of a statement through the interrogators. It was crucial to produce KSM in an open hearing to make his confession credible; otherwise whatever has been attributed to him lacks credibility, especially when his confession was obtained in dubious and torturous circumstances that surrounded his captivity.

Moreover, if a Pakistani national were to be the mastermind and chief recruiter, then it would have been natural for him to pick up at least some volunteers for this mission from his own Pakistani sphere of influence to ensure that he had reliable and confidant accomplices who were experienced and proficient terrorists as well as loyal to him so he could manage the operation successfully. The fact that no Pakistani was included and all the ringleaders were unknown Arab students drawn from institutions of a foreign country proves the point that a Pakistani could not have been their recruiter. Thus the insinuation that KSM was the mastermind loses even more credibility. The implication that bin Laden was connected with the 9/11 attackers through KSM is equally devoid of credibility. Propping up KSM as the mastermind seems to be a desperate attempt by the true conspirators to shield the real mastermind(s) of the 9/11 attacks.

KSM has proven himself to be a sloppy and tactless person who could not have kept this massive operation secret for several years before it was finally carried out. His demeanour showed that he could not be careful enough even to protect himself since he did not know how to make a safe phone call, so how could he be credited for keeping the world's most sophisticated act of terrorism a secret for several years? He does not appear to have the calibre to mastermind such an extraordinary operation, nor does he have the intellectual makeup to keep it a secret. If we look back at the circumstances in which he was arrested in Pakistan we will see how tactless he was when he made an unsafe phone call knowing that the authorities were pursuing him. He not only exposed himself to arrest, but he also got a few of his colleagues into trouble simply because he was not careful enough. Furthermore, he was a known Al-Qaeda member, so the CIA must have been on his trail, too, and would have detected something about the 9/11 plot from his demeanour or sloppy communications. Since there has been no evidence from either the CIA or the FBI to corroborate KSM's statements by other means, it is conceivable that his story could have been invented at the Guantanamo Bay prison. As well, if he were the recruiter of the hijackers, then he ought to have visited Germany several times and also met with Mohammed Ata and others, possibly at the Islamic centre, which was frequented by Mohammed Ata, Al-Jarrah and others. In that case the German intelligence service would have noticed it since they were watching the comings and goings from Afghanistan. Nothing has been said about KSM's visits to Germany or accounts of his meetings with Mohammed Ata.

Although bin Laden was pleased to see that the United States was hurt, which may have been his psychological outburst owing to deep resentment against America, he in fact categorically denied involvement in the 9/11 attacks. Millions of other angry Muslims might also have drawn similar perverse gratification from America's ordeal, but that cannot be construed as a proof of their involvement in this crime. Conclusive evidence is required before a person may be implicated in a crime. Since there has been no conclusive evidence to link bin Laden with the nineteen hijackers, it is reasonable to assume that he may have been telling the truth about his non-involvement in the 9/11 attacks. A judicial inquiry would have clarified this controversy, but President Bush purposely refused to hold any judicial inquiry and thereby blocked the judicial process from finding out the truth. Why he did not favour inquiry right away is mystifying and thickens the clouds of suspicion about the real perpetrators of the 9/11 attacks.

Undoubtedly, Osama bin Laden had been active against the United States, so he would be a logical suspect of the 9/11 attacks. Accordingly, he is viewed and branded as the world's biggest terrorist and criminal. However, the dictates of jurisprudence still require evidence to augment the accusation. Saddam Hussein was also once called a liar and accused of the crime of hiding the WMD, but he denied having them. No one believed him until Dr Kay finally said that we were all wrong. Thus the American Chief Investigator effectively vindicated Saddam Hussein's position that he was telling the truth all along that Iraq had no WMD, which were seemingly destroyed as far back as 1994. It was not Saddam Hussein's lie but rather President Bush's lack of willingness to accept the truth that led to the Iraqi war.

Is Osama bin Laden's another case where President Bush does not have the will to accept the truth? Bin Laden may have spoken the truth, but President Bush might not have had the will to accept it.

All eyes are now fixed on the 9/11 Commission to lay out facts of this case to demonstrate bin Laden's link with the 9/11 plot. It would clarify who had been telling the truth all along and who may be suppressing the truth or not showing willingness to accept the truth.

Without seeing concrete evidence against bin Laden, it is reasonable to surmise that a third party may have had a hand in effecting the 9/11 tragedy to take advantage of the opportune time and serve its own purposes. Thus the possibility of a third-party involvement may be real. It warrants thorough consideration and evaluation.

As much as one would like to believe in the American version of 9/11, the question of credibility of the officials, including those in the presidential office, hampers an unequivocal acceptance of the official version.

If we look back on the track record of several American presidents, especially the ones of the last fifty years or so, we find, regrettably, that many were found not speaking the truth or being forthright, owing to political considerations.

Those who are familiar with the history of recent American presidents would know how President Roosevelt lacked proper information on how and why the Pearl Harbor attack was not thwarted, and President Johnson's administration was unclear about the Kennedy assassination. He is also reproached for not being forthright with the American people about the true extent of the Vietnam War. President Nixon was openly exposed as a liar. President Reagan simply forgot his misdeed, but his officials were caught lying. Reagan was also dubbed a terrorist president since the International Court of Justice ruled that he used unlawful force (terrorism) in South America and ordered him to pay compensation to the victims, which Reagan defied and the United States still refuses to do. President Bush Senior remains silent about Saddam Hussein's invasion of Kuwait. Did Saddam Hussein do it on his own, or was he somehow induced by the American intelligence services to provide a pretext so that the elder Bush could overpower the oil-rich Middle East? Saddam Hussein's own idiocy may be a factor, but Ambassador Madam Gillespie's response to his query on how America would react if he were to seize Kuwait implied a go-ahead from the administration. Gillespie's dubious gesture or body language creates a suspicious impression that perhaps President Bush Senior had something to do with Saddam's notion of invading Kuwait. As a former Director General of the CIA, he must have known how to organize covert operations and keep quiet about them. His motives of overpowering the Middle East primarily for the sake of "our raw materials" are clear from the ways he frightened the Islamic world by sheer American military power and established U.S. military bases on Islam's sacred soil. He, too, may have had a covert plan, but he managed to keep it a secret owing to his expertise from his CIA days.

American presidents have been consistently determined to secure their "raw materials" from as early as the 1940s, but more vigorously since the 1973 oil embargo. So it is conceivable that President Bush Senior was aiming to control the oil-rich Middle East and needed a pretext to overpower the region militarily. There has been no inquiry to clarify this probability, or whether Saddam Hussein will ever be asked or given the chance in a court trial to explain why and under what circumstances he decided to invade Kuwait or what prompted him to take that action.

The case of President Clinton was the most pathetic of all. Even though he is a lawyer by training, he lied under oath.

Now President Bush Junior is also trapped in questionable circumstances about the existence of the weapons of mass destruction and his reason for invading Iraq. Whether he knowingly misinformed the American lawmakers and the public about his intentions in attacking Iraq is now a matter of congressional investigation. The American intelligence community is also suspect over the WMD report and is undergoing unusual scrutiny into the ways it collects or creates intelligence information. President Bush is under a further cloud over whether his obviously lax or less than urgent handling of the Al-Qaeda threat was in any way connected with the preconceived war plan.

This poor track record in credibility makes it difficult for an outsider to accept American versions of events without question, especially where intricate political affairs are at issue. Consequently, from an outsider's standpoint it becomes necessary to treat the incidents of 9/11 with a premise of doubt. The question then becomes, Who else would have the capability, both materially and creatively, or the experience in staging terrorism? Who else would fit the bill, and what could their motive be? Historically, one has to inquire who else may be experienced in terrorism and who may also have an axe to grind, or who might wish to see the Islamic world plunge into greater turmoil, in order to reap benefit from its misery.

History has been our guide throughout this presentation, so history will again be our guide in discovering who might be the third party in the 9/11 riddle. Looking for reliable sources in international affairs from a historical perspective, our eyes turn to the eminent American intellectual and researcher of history Professor Noam Chomsky. He does not need any introduction about his competence in research in international affairs and knowledge in history. Professor Chomsky has dealt with acts of terrorism quite extensively and has also commented when acts of terrorism were self-inflicted for political advantage. He brings into light the name of another party, other than Al-Qaeda and bin Laden, that has actually harmed American facilities, killing scores of Americans and damaging American property with the specific motive of inciting American rage against its own enemies so that ultimately it might benefit. Professor Chomsky has actually made our task easier in discovering who else might have had a motive and capability to hurt the United States, or the experience of killing American servicemen and damaging American facilities to create an explosive situation so that it might benefit from the fallout. We refer to his book *Fateful Triangle: The Origin of the "Special Relationship"* and quote what he said on pages 31 and 32:

> the Israeli terrorists' attacks on US facilities and other public places in Egypt (the Lavon affair), and the attack on the unmistakably identified *U.S. Liberty* with rockets, aircraft cannon, napalm, torpedoes and machine guns, clearly premeditated, leaving 34 crewmen dead and 75 wounded in "the Navy's bloodiest 'peacetime' international incident of the 20th century." In both cases, the general reaction of the press and scholarship has been silence or misrepresentation. Neither has entered history as a deplorable act of terrorism and violence, either at the time or in retrospect. In the case of the bombings in Egypt, the Israeli novelist Amos Oz, writing in the *New York Times*, refers to the terrorist acts obliquely as "certain adventurist Israeli intelligence operations"... The

nature of the attack on the *Liberty* was also evaded not only by the press fairly generally but by the government and by a U.S. Naval Board of Inquiry, though highranking figures had no doubt that the official report was a whitewash; former chairman of the Joint Chief of Staff Admiral Thomas H. Moore, for example, states that the attack "could not possibly have been a case of mistaken identity," as officially claimed.

Two points stand out from Chomsky's research. First, the Israelis have committed terrorist attacks on U.S. facilities in order to exploit the fallout. Second, the Israelis have staged terrorism in a third country (the Lavon affair in Egypt), which was not only acknowledged but also characterised as "certain adventurist Israeli intelligence operations". It is clear from this research that the Israelis have a history of committing terrorist attacks on the U.S. facilities. Their intelligence services are not only accustomed but also experienced in planting acts of violence and terrorism specifically in order to derive benefit from the fallout and so advance their greater objectives. Harming American lives or damaging American property did not deter them from staging acts of terrorism for their own ends. The attacks on the *USS Liberty* and the Lavon affair are two glaring examples in which the Israelis targeted the United States to lay blame on Egypt.

This is an eye-opening piece of history that can untangle the mystery of the 9/11 plot and fill in the gaps where both the CIA and FBI may have been lacking. For the sake of self-interest the Israelis would not hesitate even to hurt their own best friend and benefactor, provided they could find a way to shift the blame onto the common enemy and then watch the power of the American military destroy them.

There was a time when America did not want to upset the Arabs, for obvious reasons of oil, by openly taking side with Israel in the Arab-Israeli conflict. But the Israelis not only needed America to be on their side openly but also wanted America to weaken Egyptian military power by a retaliatory attack, so that whenever a military engagement between Israel and Egypt would occur, Egypt would already have been weakened. Hence the Israelis committed two acts of terrorism against America, making it seem as if the Egyptians had done them, to incite American fury and anger against Egypt, as well as to divert America from siding with the Arabs.

These two examples clearly show how American facilities (properties) were damaged and American lives wasted (34 crewmen) for the sake of inciting American fury and inflaming the U.S. against Egypt. In the case of attack on the *Liberty* when Israeli's involvement became clear, it used the excuse of mistaken identity to tone down the American reaction. Had Israel's role in this attack not been detected on time, the blame would most certainly have fallen on the Egyptians, inciting the Americans to take military action against Egypt, destroying its military establishments. We might say that the bell saved the Egyptians. The Israelis were then put on the carpet, but they defended their action on grounds of mistaken identity.

Professor Chomsky describes in the above passage how these incidents were whitewashed and erased from history. The Israeli sympathisers within the American government system and media must have helped to silence this issue and whitewash the inquiry. Even though Israel may have been excused, the fact remains that it has a track record of staging terrorism against the United States for political advantage. The fact also remains that the Israeli intelligence services are accustomed to planning and staging acts of terrorism in third countries to help the greater cause of Israel by implicating its enemies in explosive situations. The Lavon affair in Egypt must have involved the work of impostors, Israeli intelligence agents who disguised themselves as Egyptians to attack a U.S. facility so that Muslims might be seen visibly as attacking the United States. This is an example of how Israeli agents have the ability to disguise themselves successfully.

If this knowledge is applied in today's context, then it will become evident that what happened in New York on September 11, 2001 could have been the replay of previously tried and tested methods by the Israeli secret service. The only noteworthy difference is that 9/11 was an overwhelmingly huge operation compared to the previous ones, because more intense and unflinching retaliation by the United States was required at this time.

In the case of the *Liberty* incident there was no American complicity; so the facts about the Israeli involvement quickly came to light without any obstacles from the administration to their discovery. However, in the case of 9/11 no U.S. effort has been made to probe whether there is any possibility of Israeli involvement in this incident. Had there been any U.S. inquiry from the standpoint of discovering Israeli involvement, then perhaps corroborating evidence involving Israel might have come to light. Nevertheless, it cannot be overlooked, because, besides bin Laden's bad reputation, Israel also has a bad reputation for hurting the United States, as can be seen from the two examples quoted above. Israelis have material resources and intellectual capability to hatch and carry out such a bizarre scheme. Israelis have more than sufficient motive to work on such lines. Their track record would show their experience in acts of terrorism, and for this reason they may well be the third party in the 9/11 plot. It could be another adventure of the Israeli intelligence to serve Israeli interests in the same way as was attempted in both the *Liberty* attack and the Lavon affair.

History provides more examples to show how other countries, including the United States, have used acts of violence and terrorism to their advantage. At the risk of repeating, it may be reiterated that the strategists of the Pearl Harbor era were anxious to jump into the European war, but the America First Committee in the House would not let them do it. Even though American intelligence is aileged to have known that Japan was planning to attack the naval base, they either overlooked or ignored the warnings and let the attack proceed, causing the loss of many American lives. The ensuing tragedy was then at once used as a reason for entering the Second World War. Critics suggest that the attack on Pearl Harbor was controllable, even avoidable, but the strategists deliberately ignored the warnings, since they wanted the tragedy to happen so they could exploit it for their war objectives. The considerations of loss of American lives or damage to American property played no part in preventing the attack. A political objective became more important, and so American lives were sacrificed. Whether the critics are right or not, it becomes a valid question to ask whether 9/11 allows of the same explanation. Only the 9/11 Commission can dig into this question deeply and throw light on it.

In another instance Professor Chomsky lectured on the 9/11 occurrence and made several educated observations about this tragedy. He made an important comment about bin Laden's calibre in his book entitled *9-11*, on pages 59-60, and said:

> One has to be cautious about this. According to Robert Fisk, who has inter-viewed him [bin Laden] repeatedly and at length, Osama bin Laden shares the anger felt throughout the region at the US military presence in Saudi Arabia, support for atrocities against Palestinians, along with US-led devastation of the Iraqi civilian society. That feeling of anger is shared by rich and poor and across the political and other spectrums. Many who know the conditions well are also dubious about bin Laden's capacity to plan that incredibly sophisticated opera-tion from a cave somewhere in Afghanistan. But that his network was involved is highly plausible, and that he is an inspiration to them, also. These are decentralised, non-hierarchic structures, probably with quite limited commu-nication links among them. It's entirely possible that bin Laden's telling the truth when he says he did not know about this operation.

Professor Chomsky and Robert Fisk, a renowned British journalist, are both well-informed and knowledgeable persons in political and interna-tional affairs. Their educated observations carry considerable weight. Thus it becomes believable when both these gentlemen say that bin Laden could not have had the capability to pull off such a sophisticated operation from a cave somewhere in Afghanistan.

It is also believable, based on Chomsky's analysis, that bin Laden's net-work (or the disgruntled Muslims) may have been used to effect 9/11. Who might have used them is not difficult to discern, in view of the motives and expertise in masquerading displayed by the Israeli intelligence agents. The Israelis can be great impostors. They demonstrated in Egypt what they could accomplish by posing as Islamic terrorists. If they adopt Islamic attire and appearance they could easily pass as Muslim Arabs. They can be fluent in Arabic and well versed in the Quran and Sunnah to get by among Muslims. How an Israeli spy penetrated Hafiz Assad's government posing as a Muslim Arab, and how an Israeli disguised as Idi Amin fooled the Ugandan army at the Entebbe airport in 1976 to end the hijacking of an Israeli plane, show their proficiency in the art of imposture.

Knowing their capabilities and experience, it is not difficult to surmise that the Israeli intelligence services were quick to exploit the anti-Islamic international climate that had been created by bin Laden's operations against the two U.S. embassies. The temptation was to stage bigger and more damaging acts of terrorism to spark off greater American fury against the Muslim world. Recruiting disgruntled young Muslims for the scheme to make it a bin Laden or Islamic act of terrorism was not difficult since there are many angry and frustrated young Muslims who are anxious to wage a war against the United States.

There is no shortage of disgruntled Muslims who have been sliding into deep despair and acute desperation over a long period of time and are now so frustrated that they would do almost anything or listen to almost anyone who would help strike back at the enemies of Islam. Such frustrated Muslims are assets that could be easily exploited by a third party such as the Israelis. They could be used to stir the United States in such a drastic way that America's anger and its resulting retaliation would bring about a colossal instability in the Arab and Muslim world that would ultimately benefit Israel. The objective would have been to provoke the United States on its home ground in a massive way that would unleash the full thrust of its military might against the Muslim world. The Israelis could then benefit from the ruin that American military action would bring upon the Muslim world, such as we are now witnessing in Iraq. Such a chaos and devastation would create ideal conditions for the Israelis, who would then deploy their own modern methods of psychological warfare to overpower the defeated Arabs and the Islamic world. The polity of Islam would be eroded by then, and the Muslims would have lost will and hope to stand up against American might. The Islamic world would be so devastated and destabilised by the American military power that the very survival of the Muslims would become precarious. They would succumb or capitulate before the Judeo-Christian military might just as Colonel Gaddafi has recently done. Thus the expectation was that the Muslim world would be so cornered that it would have no way out except to yield to Israeli demands, which are, of course, territorial gains. Israel would then commit the Arabs to a non-aggression pact so that it could accomplish its ultimate territorial goals and hopefully live in peace in a commanding position in the region. This is the ultimate motive that Israelis have been pursuing for a very long time.

Israel's objectives are obvious. Israel has deeply charged religious goals of seizing further Arab territories. The Zionists also have an enduring ambi-

tion of expelling the Palestinians from the whole territory of a greater
Israel to establish a totally Jewish state. Israel does not want to see stable or
strong Arab neighbours for fear that they would interfere or thwart its
territorial ambitions. Accordingly, its covert agencies had been active in
generating internal disturbances by misguiding unthinking Muslim radicals
to take actions in the name of Islam. It is not difficult for the Israelis to
disguise themselves as Muslims and freely penetrate into the Muslim groups,
posing as their brothers and showing them ways to hurt the enemies of
Islam, including the Arab despotic régimes.

Thus, equipped with the skills in disguising and a clear motive and
mandate, the Israeli intelligence experts could have found Germany a
fertile ground for recruiting desperate young Arabs and training them in
the name of Islam and under bin Laden's umbrella to attack the enemy.
Young men like Mohammed Ata, Zaid Jarrah and Al-Shehi, who had never
been involved in terrorism before and never been part of any organisation
until something happened in Germany, somehow became determined
terrorists. This must have been the most sophisticated operation of skilful
intelligence agents who took advantage of the international climate and
incited these students in the name of Islam to act against the enemy of
Islam. There is no record that they ever went to Afghanistan or met with bin
Laden or KSM, the supposed mastermind of 9/11, yet they were filled with
hatred for America. Theirs was an extraordinary transformation and an
equally extraordinary success, which could not have happened without the
covert help and planning of people better versed in subversion, such as the
Israeli secret service. Had 9/11 been the plot of people like KSM, who are
demonstrably sloppy, the CIA would have bumped into their operation
somewhere and in some way, since it was closely watching the activities of
the Al-Qaeda network. However, if the 9/11 plot were not developed by Al-
Qaeda then understandably the CIA would have had no clue about it, as
indeed was the case.

If the 9/11 plot were hatched by the impostors outside the network of
bin Laden and away from Afghanistan, that would explain why the CIA
failed to detect it. The agency was tightly focusing on bin Laden and
Afghanistan, but nothing was happening there, which is why the agency
failed to detect any clues about 9/11.

The implication of a third party is a serious matter, and now it is the
responsibility of the 9/11 Commission to probe it further, either to accept
this theory or to find credible grounds to reject it. George Tenet might be
asked to clarify further and give a definitive explanation of why his agency
failed to detect any clues about 9/11 when he had put Al-Qaeda under such
a tight surveillance. Is it because he may have been barking up the wrong
tree and not looking at what the Israelis were doing? Or did it never occur
to him that the Israelis might re-enact the USS Liberty and Lavon incidents

in some way to reap benefit from the tragedy of 9/11? Did he know about the track record of the Israelis in trying to exploit American rage by staging acts of terrorism against the United States, and how much was he concerned about that? Did he never take any precautionary measures against possible Israeli acts of terrorism against the United States?

As was outlined above, the last avenue for exploring the third-party theory is President George W. Bush himself. A merely cursory look into his presidency will not bring the whole picture into focus; rather an extensive study is required using knowledge of the influences and type of both political and religious advisers that surround him. We shall also need to develop some sense of how the president works and how his policies are formulated. A short sojourn into the workings of the White House could clarify how President Bush is running his administration.

Broadly speaking, it is the officials, the bureaucrats, the assistant secretaries and the deputy secretaries and advisers in the State and Defence departments who conceive long-term objectives and fashion policies to achieve whatever goals the president may set. Owing to their political environment and sometimes inadequate academic backgrounds, many presidents lack the broad vision or depth of knowledge of intricate matters. Hence in approving policies they usually depend upon the expertise and professional advice of their officials. These officials are usually highly knowledgeable academics, scholars and trained psychologists who know how to make favourable impressions on presidents. Consequently, presidents whose political careers may be driven by personal ego or business interests usually do not match the high degree of intellectual and academic flair of their advisers and are mostly prone to accept their theories or theses. Usually, the opinions of these advisers are reinforced by the so-called think-tanks that exist in various institutes, which are mostly dominated by academic and scholarly talents who peddle particular points of views or the points of view of certain lobbies from the American forum. They succeed in shaping American public opinion by their plausible assessments. In times of controversy the American public relies upon their analysis, and so these institutes play an important role in shaping public opinion. How these institutes are funded and who their corporate sponsors are is not always disclosed, but sometimes the intensity of their focus suggests that they may be toeing the line of some vested interest, whatever it might be. .

To elucidate this point, we would quote a knowledgeable American journalist who had access to sensitive information and has written about it in his article of October 26, 2001 in the *Executive Intelligence Review*. Michele Steinberg actually named the officials who may have propelled the present-day concept of war against Islam. Paul Wolfowitz, the Assistant Secretary of Defence, is mentioned emphatically, along with Richard Perle, a former Assistant Secretary of Defence in the Reagan era, also known as the "Prince of Darkness." Professor Zbigniew Brzezinski, the former National Security Adviser to President Jimmy Carter, and his protégés, including Harvard Professor Samuel Huntington, are also named. Steinberg categorised Wolfowitz's coterie as the "Wolfowitz Cabal", which he described as an "Enemy within the U.S." These officials, many of them staunchly pro-Israeli, have been at the heart of U.S. foreign policy for decades.

The pro-Israeli activists play important parts in promoting Israeli interests within the American forum. Besides U.S. official and private channels, they also have access to other international resources, such as Conrad Black's Hollinger International, to propagate their ideas. This organisation "owns the British Tory Party-linked Telegraph PLC, whose International Advisory Board is headed by former British Prime Minister, now Lady Margaret Thatcher. Hollinger also owns the *Jerusalem Post*, another war-mongering press outlet." Then there are media outlets owned by the top British-Israeli propagandist Rupert Murdoch, who owns newspapers like the London *Times*. Thus the scope for carrying through the Israeli agenda by means of American policies and shaping public opinion in America and Europe by manipulating the public forum and media is wide open to these pro-Israel activists.

Steinberg wrote in a piece published in the *New York Times* of October 12, 2001 "the grouping [the Wolfowitz Cabal] wants an immediate war with Iraq, believing that the targeting of Afghanistan, already an impoverished wasteland, falls far short of the global war that they are hoping for. But Iraq is just another stepping stone to turning the anti-terrorist 'war' into a full-blown "Clash of Civilizations", where the Islamic religion would become the "enemy image" in a 'new Cold War.'" These extremely important and meaningful words of Steinberg expressed on October 12, 2001 actually unravel the entire war policy that President George W. Bush had been following from the very early days of his presidency. Steinberg clearly shows that just attacking Afghanistan did not satiate the appetite of the war advisers. Their sights were set on Iraq as a stepping stone to a larger war against Islamic civilisation, which was what President Bush had been pursuing under different pretexts, many of them false.

The "Clash of Civilization" theory, developed by Zbigniew Brzezinski and his protégés, including Harvard Professor Samuel Huntington, used geopolitical theory to define the Arab and Islamic lands as an "arc of crisis" stretching from the Middle East to the Islamic countries of Central Asia in the then Soviet Union. In his article of "Clash of Civilizations", Huntington highlights the religious differences and predicts that a clash between the Western and Islamic civilisations is inevitable. The idea that civilisations would clash over modernity is inappropriate and unrealistic, because different cultures have previously co-existed in the human history by adopting tolerance. If modernity meant creating uniformity or universality, then civilisations would indeed clash as the powerful ones tried to eliminate the weaker ones. In the present context, the Western civilisation based on supposed Christian values and the precept of Holy War is dominant and would seemingly try to replace Islamic values by imposing those values on the vulnerable Islamic populations. Such an attempt in the name of modernity would undermine the beauty of diversity in human society. Uniformity tends to be bland, whereas diversity is not only appealing but also colourful. Hence it would have been prudent, from the point of view of a diverse human society, if the Harvard professor, instead of predicting that civilisations would clash because of religious and cultural differences, had promoted the idea of co-existence of civilisations by appreciating other cultures and practising tolerance.

The history of the past several centuries reveals that the driving force of the West has been imperial domination through clashes and the elimination of vulnerable cultures. Extermination of the First Nation cultures in the American hemisphere, suppression of the Aboriginals in Australia and transformation of the culture of the African Americans are fruits of clashes with other cultures. If the clash with the Islamic civilisation is meant to impose a similar fate upon the Muslims, then it will not serve the ends of peace, because the Islamic world will vehemently resist such an attempt. Our modern world does not need a Huntington-style thesis predicting clashes of civilisations; what is needed is to cure the disease of imperial domination and exploitation of the weaker cultures and civilisations, so that we may see an era of live and let others live. Regrettably, that does not seem to be a priority for the dominant school of American or Western intellectuals or academics and scholars, which perhaps explains why they are predicting clashes instead of pleading for co-existence. They may have an ulterior motive against Islam, which is why they are focusing on clashes and peddling this idea from the echelons of American power, so that ultimately they may realise their goal of helping Israeli territorial ambitions.

Brzezinski and Huntington are reputable intellectuals who greatly influence United States government policies as well as American public opinion. It is disappointing that Professor Huntington did not put forward a thesis on how to live and let others live, so we might see a harmonious and diversified human society. Instead, this eminent scholar harped on the religious differences and predicted that clash was inevitable or imminent, as if he knew that such a clash was in store or even planned.

As for Brzezinski's role, we have seen from Steinberg's comments that "he wanted to use the 'Islamic card' against the Soviet Union, and in doing so, began the policy of promoting Islamic fundamentalists who, however, turned against the moderate and pro-Western Arab and Islamic governments. After the end of the Cold War, the Brzezinski/Huntington crowd updated their 'arc of crisis', declaring that the Islamic religion is the enemy in a new war in which religions, rather than political systems, inevitably battle each other. However, trained by British and U.S. special intelligence services and the CIA, and armed by the Israeli military networks, the very terrorist drug-runners in the Islamic world who were launched by Brzezinski and 'adopted' by the Iran-Contra networks run by Lt. Col. Oliver North, under the elder Bush's Executive Order 12333, have become the main suspects in terrorist attacks against the United States."

What we learn from Steinberg's quotations is that Paul Wolfowitz, who is an intensely pro-Israel American Jew and whose coterie was characterised as the infamous Wolfowitz Cabal, appears to be able to spin American policies from an Israeli perspective. We have already shown that Zbigniew Brzezinski, another pro-Israel American Jew, was instrumental in building the Mujahideen force against the Soviets in Afghanistan and creating terrorists like Osama bin Laden and his Al-Qaeda associates. As Steinberg mentioned, these Mujahideen were trained by the American and British intelligence services and armed by Israeli military networks; so these individuals had intimate connections with intelligence agents and were well known to the US and British secret services as well as the Israeli intelligence. They were the "Islamic card" that Brzezinski would use in America's war against Communists. Later the "Islamic card" may also have been used by the Israeli intelligence service to effect the 9/11 tragedy. Note that the "Islamic card" is readily available for whoever wants to play it in the name of Islam.

Thus Brzezinski, Huntington, Wolfowitz and Perle, who are supposed to make up the Wolfowitz Cabal, apparently laid the ground for a clash of civilisations, which would later be turned into a full-blown war against Islam of which the principal beneficiary would be Israel. The Islamic card was in their hands to play by implicating the Muslims and Islam. Subsequently, hawks like Donald Rumsfeld and Dick Cheney would join hands with the war proponents against the Islamic civilisation.

Thanks to Michele Steinberg's insight and quotation, we are now able to understand why the Reagan administration would subsequently declare Islam an enemy. Since the same group of advisers would also join other administrations, this notion of enmity would be carried forward as an integral part of American policy.

Since many advisers surrounding President George W. Bush date from the Reagan and Bush Senior era, his policies appear to have the same general characteristics as those of the two former presidents. Therefore, it is pertinent to reflect upon the policies of both Presidents Reagan and Bush Senior to see how President Bush Junior is influenced in shaping his own policies towards the Islamic world.

Taking the case of President Reagan first, we see that he was a man of mixed character owing to his career in film acting. Politically, he was a man of strong convictions and ambitions backed by an imaginative mind. Personally, he was affable, though strictly partisan, and extended courtesy even to his adversaries, who would often mollify their positions due to his effusive and charming personality and compromise with him despite their differences of opinion. Immediately after taking the office, President Reagan announced "our crusade now begins." This was a clear indication that President Reagan had a profound vision to turn around America in many ways. His manifesto was varied but not fully spelled out. In any case he was now ready to pursue his ideals resolutely and forcefully from the office that he had just assumed. Owing to his age and experience his plans were well thought out and he was well positioned to accomplish his goals. Thus, he initiated many programs to turn America around in a defining manner.

On the home front he was committed to revolutionising the economy by drastic tax cuts, deregulating the economy and resorting to deficit financing, which brought about a rapid economic upturn between 1983 and 1986. His economic success is dubbed "Reaganomics." He also went ahead to build and modernise the USA's defences to enable the country to negotiate abroad "from a position of strength." His space-based military defence was known as "Star Wars."

Politically, while President Nixon had made the White voters a mainstay of southern politics as compared to President Lynden Johnson who mobilised the Blacks in the south, President Reagan made religion the defining force of the south. Therefore, he encouraged the participation of religiously minded persons in national politics. Consequently, mostly Evangelical zealots from the south (about 100 or so in total) have now become the ultra-conservative backbone of the Republican Party. Thus religion overwhelmed American politics for the first time during President Reagan's term of office and has since become a dominant factor rising from the southern horizon of the United States.

Apart from all the other things that President Reagan did on the home front, his foreign policies involved much action, thrills of wars, aggression and a belligerent posture, just as an actor would like to play the hero in films. When he announced that our "crusade now begins", everyone interpreted him as aiming at the Communists, which he did and eventually succeeded in defeating them in Afghanistan thanks to the *Jihad* and sacrifices of the Muslim Mujahideen. However, no one was able to discern at that time that Reagan's second tier of crusade was, in fact, religiously motivated and aimed at Islam until he announced it after the fall of the Berlin Wall in the late 1980s.

President Reagan's declaration that Islam was America's next enemy was sensational and came out of nowhere since all the Muslim states were close friends of the United States and there was absolutely no reason to brand Islam as an enemy in those days. The Muslim intelligentsia and political leaders were America's friends. They had just helped Reagan win the war against Communism, which, by the way, would have been hard, if not impossible, to win without their support. Today, he is receiving much credit for winning war against Communism without even firing a shot, but back then he was pleading with the Muslims to come to join him and start the firing in his war against Communism. He was loudly beating the drums of *Jihad*, luring Muslims in the name of Islam and calling them dedicated Mujahideen to fight against godless Communism. Though the outgoing National Security Adviser Zbigniew Brzezinski set this line of action in motion, President Reagan meticulously followed all his schemes in organising the war against Communism. He poured American tax dollars behind the Mujahideen and profusely armed them to defeat the "evil empire." Later he took all the credit for defeating Communism, or he is given full credit, without recognising that it was the Muslims who fought and defeated the Communists on the battleground of Afghanistan. Thousands of Muslims laid down their lives in this war and Afghanistan was devastated, from which its people are unable to recover, yet the Muslims are not given credit for being an important ally or partner in defeating Communism. All the credit is given to President Reagan as he is now hailed as the champion who saved the world from the evil of Communism and made America a safer place. The part played by the "Islamic Card" is totally ignored, not even mentioned just to give the devil his due. Such antipathy is the result of religious aversion against Muslims. This is how Reagan's America had been ungenerous to the Muslims and biased against Islam.

Not only did President Reagan not give due credit to the Muslims, but also, soon after the victory, he went on to say that Islam was America's next enemy. It made absolutely no sense. Islam was America's best friend, as it had helped it win its greatest ideological war. How could Islam become America's enemy so quickly and dramatically without a cause? Instead of being appreciative or even grateful, Reagan went on to denounce Islam. What President Reagan actually did was to show the world a deep sense of aversion for Islam that had been building in the minds and hearts of many American fundamentalists or resurging crusaders due to their own bigoted religious beliefs. There was no Osama bin Laden and Muslim terrorism, or Islamic terrorism as the West likes to call it, had not been born yet. There was absolutely no cause for declaring war against Islam in the 1980s. All the terrorism and turmoil that we see today actually sprang from Reagan's declaration of war, so he could be held responsible for disturbing world peace by declaring an unfounded and unnecessary war against Islam. But, then again, it might also have been the excitement and thrill of war from his flair for acting and showmanship that set him on a war footing against Islam without rhyme or reason. His advisers, such as Dick Cheney, Donald Rumsfeld, Richard Perle and a host of others, must have been delighted by

Reagan's war declaration because it would have given them a chance to work on their own ambitions of waging war against Islam. So, they must have taken up his lead and gone on a spree constructing a long-range war plan against Islam, which is now showing its ugly face in Iraq and elsewhere in the Middle East.

Very little was known about the full extent of Reagan's mindset as many people were unsure of some of his policies, especially against Islam, and thought that he might have been just grandstanding. However, when he passed away in June 2004 a great deal was spoken about his private thoughts and philosophy that had not been explicitly spelled out thus far in public. One of the things that his close confidants came forward to tell was how passionately religious he was. While the Bushes are manifestly committed to religion, Reagan was pursuing his ambitions for his faith quietly from the office of his presidency. How he had been paraphrasing biblical messages in his quotations and speeches to project his policies, and how he had been patronising religious resurgence from the south, has only been acknowledged recently.

It was also revealed that his second wife, Nancy, had quite an influence over him and some close friends thought that she was actually a partner in Reagan's presidency and may have had considerable influence over his attitude of mind, affecting at least some of the state policies. She strongly believed in conservatism and one of the first things that she is said to have done after her marriage in 1947 was to convert Ronald Reagan from a social and liberal democrat to a conservative and persuaded him to quit the Democratic Party and join the Republican Party. Before her influence Reagan was an active Democrat and admired the Democratic Party leadership under Franklin D. Roosevelt. Nancy Reagan's political influence, or perhaps interference in state affairs, came to the forefront when she disagreed with the performance of Secretary Gerald Regan and pressed for his dismissal, which in the end happened, showing how overbearing she was.

Religiously, Nancy is a devout Presbyterian. Thus, her religious proclivity may also have altered or greatly influenced the religious sentiments of her husband. President Reagan's own persuasion, combined with his wife's devoutness, produced the religious fervour that figured so prominently in the Reagan era. Their combined faith-based zeal may have been the reason or religious grounds upon which President Reagan declared Islam as America's next enemy even without a cause. Otherwise, there was no rhyme or reason to make such an irrational pronouncement on such an unnecessary basis. Anyhow, this whimsical casting of Islam became a legacy for both the Bushes, who took the matter further and inaugurated the war that had been conceived in the Reagan era. This war has since become the cause of enormous international unrest and taken tens of thousands of lives of Muslims as well as many American lives.

Besides targeting Communism and Islam, Reagan was also aggressive in South America and used unlawful force (terrorism), which earned him the reputation of being a terrorist president. His concurrence with Israeli Prime Minister Menachem Begin for hostilities in Lebanon against the Palestinians showed his aversion for the Arab or Muslim points of view. Anyway, President Reagan was too old and senile to undertake the second tier of his crusade, the war on Islam, himself. He nevertheless laid the foundation for an enduring conflict and left behind a legacy for the similarly faith-based Bushes to carry on his unfinished crusade against Islam. To ensure continuity of his crusade, he brought the Bush family into the presidential arena, knowing that they were also averse to Islam just as he was.

True to Reagan's expectations, Bush Senior retained many of the same advisers; so he, too, took a stern posture against the Islamic world. He found an excuse (the Kuwait pretext), however it happened, to overpower the Arab world and frighten the Muslim countries with American military might and by establishing military bases on Islam's Sacred Soil, as the world saw during the first Gulf War.

Was not the first Gulf War avoidable? It is interesting to note that Soviet President Mikhail Gorbachev obtained Saddam Hussein's commitment to withdraw from Kuwait, which was delivered by Tariq Aziz during his visit to Moscow and later communicated to President Bush Senior by Gorbachev. However, President Bush Senior rejected Gorbachev's mediation and took the option of war instead of trying to use peaceful means to resolve the Kuwait crisis. Probably it will never be known who prompted Saddam Hussein to invade Kuwait, but it is obvious that his action benefited President Bush Senior and gave him a huge opportunity to overpower the Middle East despite Gorbachev's mediation to end the crisis by peaceful means. Obviously, President Bush Senior's conduct was as unreasonable as President Reagan's declaration of war against Islam had been. But, then again, they were both pursuing an unreasonable objective of waging war against Islam.

President Bush Senior was so incensed against Islam that he even ignored the prudence of showing sensitivity or respect to the Muslims' religious feelings when he went ahead to establish American military bases on Islam's sacred soil. Later this insensitivity would become the main problem for world peace, because President Bush Senior's action gave birth to a violent bin Laden, who became an open enemy of America in 1995 principally on account of America's military bases in Saudi Arabia. President Bush Senior's disregard for the religious sentiments of the Muslims showed how averse he was to the religious sentiments of Muslims or Islam itself. He had embarked on an expedition to carry out the anti-Islamic policy left behind by President Reagan, and the first Gulf War was his initial step in that direction. However, he lost the momentum when he was defeated in the presidential election unexpectedly, so the task of waging a wider war against Islam remained unfulfilled.

Although President Reagan's momentum against Islam was interrupted with the defeat of President Bush Senior, his planners of the war against Islam and strategists in the establishment maintained the thrust on Islam. They continued to push the anti-Islamic policy on other administrations. Hence these strategists must have carried their war policy into the Clinton administration, too, since the President Bush Junior later disclosed that President Clinton had also been contemplating taking military action against Saddam Hussein. Meanwhile in 1996-1998, Osama bin Laden had started his armed operation against overseas establishments of the United States, demanding withdrawal of the American army from Islam's sacred soil in Saudi Arabia. Consequently, President Clinton took action against bin Laden and Al-Qaeda, but he made no move against Iraq, even though he might have conceded to the strategist's argument that such an action was also required. Their expectation was that this action could then be spread to other Islamic states, such as Syria and Iran, on the pretext that they were providing safe havens to the terrorists. Still, President Clinton did not move against Iraq, presumably because he lacked a credible excuse. This was a clear message to the hawks that President Clinton would not engage in their proposed war plan unless there were convincing reasons to do so, and also an indication that no other president would entertain the idea of war against Islam as America's next enemy without first seeing convincing grounds to initiate the attack.

The war planners, having vast resources and immense brainpower, could have masterminded a massive tragedy on American soil to create a traumatic urgency that would spur the American public in a profound way. This would give them a cause to muster public support and an excuse for initiating their pre-planned global war against Islam in the wake of the war against terrorism.

American history shows that the American public is accustomed to seeing its government act on pretexts, without which support for war is hard to come by. This is an old habit and an important part of the American psyche, because the Americans like to believe that they are the good guys of the world and even undertake wars and sacrifice their lives for the sake of goodness in human society. It may be their good-natured weakness, but the politicians and policymakers see it as an opportunity to exploit public opinion for their own ends. There is a long trail of incidents starting as early as 1898, when the U.S. battleship *Maine* was mysteriously blown up in Havana harbour, giving a reason for declaring war against Spain, and so on.

Besides needing an obvious cause, another reason why the American public is usually reluctant to support wars is because moms and dads do not like to lose their loved ones. The war strategists have always faced this problem. Mere verbal pleas and war rhetoric do not work, so the strategists create or exploit emergencies to show the American public a real need to come on side for the war. It has been the pattern of all warring presidents. Roosevelt did it with Pearl Harbor, Kennedy and Johnson did it in Vietnam War, Carter and then Reagan did it in Afghanistan when Brzezinski manipulated the Russian invasion, and the elder Bush did it in the wake of the Kuwait crisis.

Given President Clinton's evident reluctance to undertake a global war against Islam, it is conceivable that the Wolfowitz Cabal developed a scheme to incite America against the Muslim world by fabricating a disaster in the United States and then assigning the blame to the Muslims, so that they might be targeted globally. Paul Wolfowitz has been described as a man of great talent, imagination and academic backing, quite capable of constructing elaborate war plans and executing them meticulously to achieve the desired results.

"Wolfowitz came to national prominence in early 1992 as the author of a secret Pentagon memorandum that was leaked to the *New York Times.*" In this composition Wolfowitz displays wild imagination for war plans to crush a perceived enemy, Russia. He also advocates deterring "potential competitors from even aspiring to a larger or global role" (quoted from Steinberg). He showed in 1992 that he had intellectual capacity to conceive a plan, however vicious it might be. As an American Jew of Polish descent, he is likely to have admired another such academic, Professor Brzezinski, and known him quite closely, learning from him about his plan for using terrorism to defeat Communism. Brzezinski had successfully exploited the fact that that terrorism creates tragedy, which in turn arouses all-round anger as well as sympathy that can be capitalised on for mounting retaliatory military action. Wolfowitz saw how successful Brzezinski's plan had been in Afghanistan, not only in drawing out the enemy into the open but also in defeating it decisively. Given their probable relationship, Brzezinski could have been his mentor in utilising terrorism and devising a war plan against Islam based on self-generated terrorism. Constructing a war plan based on terrorism is quite within the intellectual capabilities of Paul Wolfowitz.

Hence the war proponents have recognised that to engage the American public sufficiently to start a global war against Islam, they needed an act of terrorism on the American soil that they could portray as an Islamic act. This writer's educated guess is that sometime between 1998 and 1999, after the bombing of the embassies, the Wolfowitz Cabal must have turned to the Israelis to capitalise on bin Laden's terrorist reputation and stage a trauma on American soil to enrage the American public against the Islamic world. The strategists had been looking for an excuse to start global war against

Islam and Israel was about the only outside power that could help them achieve this goal. Wolfowitz must have known that bin Laden's reputation would instantly attract international attention to him and Israel would manage to escape unscathed. He must also have known that Israel had the capacity to engage in covert operations and implant terrorism if the fallout would further its own long-term territorial objectives. The benefits for Israel from a defeated Arab or Islamic world were obviously enormous; so its willingness to oblige Wolfowitz would not have been difficult to explain.

The fact that Yitzhak Shamir and Ariel Sharon had come to power between 1995 and 1998 must have made it more tempting for Wolfowitz to seek co-operation from Israel's hawks. If the Israelis could re-enact their past performance in the *USS Liberty* and Lavon affair in some innovative way against the United States, then the resulting blame from such terrorism could be assigned to bin Laden, especially when he had such a bad reputation all over the world. The Cabal knew that if anyone could do it from the Israeli side, then a collaboration of Shamir and Sharon was the best bet, because any other modern Israeli leader might not have agreed to do it. Shamir and Begin had been seasoned terrorists, members of two militant Jewish underground organisations that had committed violence and terrorism against the British and the Arabs before the establishment of the state of Israel. Sharon's close association with Begin and Shamir and his own direct or indirect terrorist activities in the Sabra and Shatila refugee camps made him, too, an accomplished terrorist. Although Begin and Shamir faded away from death and old age, Sharon remained active in Israeli government circles. He was minister of national infrastructure in 1996 and again foreign minister in 1998. He was elected chairman of the Likud Party in 1999 and also served as a member of the Foreign Affairs and Defence Committee of the Knesset. Thus his aptitude in terrorism and influence in Israeli government circles made him a suitable candidate, the third party, to implant an act of terrorism on U.S. soil so that the blame might fall on the Muslims and give the United States an excuse to unleash its military might. It should also be borne in mind that there are two underground Zionist terrorist organisations that have never been fully disbanded, nor have they changed their tactics of planting terrorism for the greater cause of Israel. The Likud Party is well acquainted with those hardliners, who may now have fallen under the overall leadership of Ariel Sharon.

It seems quite possible that the nucleus of war proponents led by the chief architect Wolfowitz might have touched base with the Zionist terrorists to solicit their expertise to enact a grotesque and despicable act of terrorism that could be spun by propaganda and hysteria to implicate the Muslims, and which could then be used against the Islamic countries on a worldwide scale. Brzezinski had shown that, given the right incentives, Muslims could be enticed to carry out acts of violence and terrorism in the belief that they were serving the cause of Islam, which might be then used against their own selves. Hence the objective could have been to find disgruntled young Muslims, the Islamic Card, as well as help them to perpetrate a vicious act of terrorism against the United States in the name of Islam. Finding the disgruntled Muslims could not have been difficult for the sophisticated intelligence services. This is what seems to have taken place in Germany. The idea was to lure the angry young Muslims and somehow implicate them in a horrific crime, so that the American public could see them attacking America. Once the Muslims were implicated, then the task of initiating the war would become easy. Then, at the end of the day, this crime would open door for lashing out at the Islamic world to accomplish the anti-Islamic objectives that had occupied the minds of the planners ever since President Reagan had declared Islam America's next enemy in the late 1980s. The finer details would have been completed by the Israeli intelligence.

If the Israelis did not have the experience and capacity for terrorism, including against the United States, then this line of thinking might seem farfetched. However, the *USS Liberty* and Lavon affair, coupled with the history of Zionist underground terrorist activities, make it plausible that the Israeli terrorists could have come into action once again to serve the cause of Israel. 9/11 would not have been the first time the Israelis staged a terror-based plan involving loss of American lives and damage to the United States property to serve their own interests. They have done it before to arouse American anger and incite American military action against the Arabs (Egyptians). They have the capacity to do it again for the same purpose.

Using tragedy is an extraordinary and cruel way to achieve political goals. Regrettably, the Israelis show a particular flair for deriving advantage from tragedies. They see so many benefits from tragedies that they do not seem to hesitate even to create them with a view to extracting benefits from them.

Causing huge loss of lives and colossal property damage does not pose any moral constraint on the Israelis. They are quite accustomed to wasting human lives to obtain their territorial and political goals. Remember how the King David Hotel was blown up in Jerusalem in the 1940s killing scores of British servicemen. The perpetrators of this heinous crime were none other than Israel's prominent leaders, two of whom, Begin and Shamir, later became Israel's prime ministers. Britain shamefully unrolled a red carpet to welcome Israeli Prime Minister Menachem Begin, who had personally massacred many Britons, including the ones in the King David Hotel. This is a perfect example of how politics make strange bedfellows. Then there is the tragedy of Dir Yassin. How Begin revelled in massacring human beings is a clear indication that killing innocent human beings for the greater cause of Israel is no barrier to the Israeli leadership.

The loss of lives entailed in such a horrific scheme would not have been a deterrent, since these highly motivated policymakers would have been making a grand scheme, supposedly in their greater national interest. Achieving success had a price, and they might have seen paying that price, even at the cost of some American lives as a cost of the national objective. The views expressed by former Secretary of State Madeleine Albright elucidate how American officials view tough situations when they face hard choices. In a statement over national television, as narrated by Professor Chomsky, when asked about the estimates of a half million deaths of Iraqi children as a result of sanctions under her régime, Madam Albright admitted that such choices were a "hard choice" for her administration, but said, "we think the price is worth it." Madam Albright was knowledgeable about American short-term and long-term policies, so her comment that paying a price even in terms of human lives is worth the goal would suggest that sacrificing human being for the sake of a policy is acceptable to the policymakers. Loss of human lives is regarded as the cost of the policy.

Granted that human lives would be sacrificed for the sake of pursuing a policy, the next point to consider must have been, Where should this price be paid? If a traumatic event took place somewhere far away, that would not incite the sentiments of the American public as much as a tragedy at home. Thus the Wolfowitz Cabal could have chosen America as the venue for a tragedy, because that would infuriate the American public and help create an environment of hatred of the Muslims. It could then be used as a valid excuse for waging the preconceived worldwide war against Islam in the name of war against terrorism. Life becomes meaningless for strategists when they are obsessed with achieving political or religious goals.

Knowing the background of the hawks and their affiliations with Israel, an Israeli hand in effecting the 9/11 tragedy cannot be discounted. As can be seen from the above-cited incidents, Israeli prime ministers have been involved personally in planning and carrying out acts of terrorism. What was there to stop Ariel Sharon from staging a similar act of terrorism to the ones that former Prime Minister Menachem Begin and others had committed against Britain and the United States? In the course of his career, Ariel Sharon has amply demonstrated a terrorist bent of mind. Efforts have been made at the international level to indict him for war crimes, but that is still pending. He does not appear to have given up on violence or acts of terrorism, as can be seen from his current policies and actions against the Palestinians. So, what is there to stop him from carrying on the tradition of Begin and Shamir and staging terrorism even against the United States, if it can serve the greater cause of Israel?

It is not a farfetched idea given that Israel has a track record in staging acts of terrorism against the United States, killing Americans and damaging American property; it is a plausible theory supported by the examples cited above. Bin Laden is not the only terrorist in our world. The Israelis have demonstrated their skill in staging terrorism and they have the capacity to do it again if the blame would damage the Islamic world and so benefit them. Given the position and influence of officials like Perle and Wolfowitz, the Israelis may have found ways to mobilise the wrath of the American military to suit their purposes. If they could somehow unleash American might against the Islamic world, then at the end of the day they would be the winners.

As president, one of the first things that George W. Bush did was to appoint his team of advisers. On the political side he retained many of the old advisers, and so his presidency has many characteristics of those of both Reagan and Bush Senior, particularly in relation to Islam and the Muslim world. Men like Donald Rumsfeld, Dick Cheney and Paul Wolfowitz formed the core of the war advocates. Richard Perle wielded direct influence during his tenure as chairman of the Defence Board and later continued to peddle his views through his friendship with Wolfowitz. Condoleezza Rice also joined this inner circle, owing to her own predictions for war against the Islamic world. The majority of these key policymakers had formulated Reagan's policy that pronounced Islam as America's next enemy and they seem to have brought the same policy into the present Bush administration. Hence President George W. Bush was exposed to a preconceived idea of war against the Islamic world, which may have coincided with his own Evangelical pursuits to make it the topmost priority of his administration. Thus, a combined effort of the Evangelical President Bush and the war proponents went into constructing an extremely aggressive policy against Islam. The premise was that all Islamic countries were pathetically weak and could be annihilated militarily one by one. So the essential part of the policy was to engage Muslim countries in wars, so that they might be defeated and effectively exterminated as a military or religious force. The Muslim countries were neither willing to engage in war with the United States nor in a position to do so. Hence it was necessary to drag them into a war situation. Through intense intelligence reports and arms inspections it was also ascertained that Muslim countries were no match for American military power. The plan was to attack them while they were still vulnerable, so that once they were overpowered militarily, changing their religious or cultural traditions would follow as a natural course. When an intellectually lacking President Bush Junior appeared at the helm of America, the hawks seem to have seized the moment to fulfil their previously conceived plan.

Besides Wolfowitz, Perle and others, the younger President Bush's key advisers included people like Richard Armitage, Robert Blackwell, Stephen Hadley and Dov Zakheim, who had been associated with the administrations of Reagan and the elder Bush and would have had influence over their policies, which included waging wars in South America and the first

Gulf War. They are now also members of the younger President Bush's administration, making his policies similar in character to the previous ones. These advisers could also draw on the advice of veterans like Brzezinski and Perle, who are both acquainted with Wolfowitz, who in turn had been a pivotal war adviser in several administrations. These individuals had the intellectual capacity to mastermind any scheme that would be bizarre and yet convincing. They have enormous American resources and media power to work with to achieve their goals.

Besides his hawkish political advisers, President Bush also has several fundamentalist religious advisers who whet his religious ambitions and keep his faith-based policies in motion. Besides Rumsfeld and Ashcroft, who have been described as staunch fundamentalist Christians, people like Karl Rove and Don Evans, emerging from Evangelical movement in the South, have profound influence on Bush's religious shaping. As was mentioned earlier, Dick Cheney and Dr Condoleezza Rice are two other influential persons close to President Bush. The choice of Dick Cheney as vice-president was surprising. For one thing, he had a heart ailment, and for another, he seemed to have passed his active days. To bring him on indicates that there must have been a special bond between them or a special purpose that Cheney could still fulfil. Cheney's passion for war against Islam unravels the mystery of his appointment as vice-president. It has now become clear that he was the most powerful proponent of war against Iraq, just as he had been the dominant hawk in the first Gulf War. This would explain why President Bush needed him despite his heart ailment. The choice of Dr Rice was a mixed bag. In addition to being a competent and articulate executive, she is also the daughter of a Methodist preacher, as was stated in an earlier chapter. Hence, Dr Rice also comes from an Evangelical background and has an affinity with President Bush's own religious bent of mind. So she, too, would have been staunchly in favour of war against Iraq (Islam). Her concurrence and support for war is very valuable for the president. It would explain why she enjoys a special relationship with him, as was previously stated. She may have been privy to many matters that President Bush conceives and executes from his office. It has now come to light that she was his strong supporter in the war against Iraq, even though there was no justifiable cause for war. To cap it all, President Bush and his family have been under the influence of other Evangelical preachers who do not hide their aversion from Islam.

Thus, while he had the benefit of the war strategists to plan war against Islam, the President also had input from Evangelical religious advisers who fanned antipathy to Islam on religious grounds. The combination of hawks and fundamentalists in the White House has now produced deadly war machinery against Islam. President Bush denies targeting Islam, but his actions and conduct belie his statements. Many Muslims see him in the image of a new crusader, determined to conquer the East by defeating Islam to spread Evangelical Christianity and force the Second Coming of Christ to redeem the sins of the Evangelicals. So it appears from the claims of President Bush that God has now intervened in human affairs and is guiding his chosen man to wage war against the infidels. This may explain why President Bush justifies his policies in the name of God and on the basis of "calls." These are the characteristics of a crusader that our world thought it had left behind many centuries ago.

The 18-member Defence Policy Board is another important vehicle in formulating America's military plans and developing strategy for implementing American policies abroad. This is another official arm of the government of the United States that could be used both by the president and the hawks to develop war plans. Members of this board have capability to translate the president's ideas or the notions of his "calls", as well as their own ambitions, into forceful military action. If the majority happen to lean one particular way, then the American military plans will also lean the same way. It is public knowledge that until recently Richard Perle, a staunch pro-Israeli hawk, was chairman of this board. Other members have included Secretary of State Dr Henry Kissinger, House Speaker Newt Gingrich, Director General of Central Intelligence Agency R. James Woolsey, Deputy Chairman of the Joint Chiefs of Staff Admiral David E. Jeremiah, Vice-President Dan Qualye, Defence and Energy Secretary James R. Schlesinger and President Carter's Defence Secretary Harold Brown. These are highly influential men in America's political setup, and whatever decisions they make are usually approved by the president. As was said earlier, if they were to tilt against Islam, then America would tilt with them.

When President George W. Bush assumed the office, the hawks must have given him the same advice as they gave to the two earlier Republican presidents. Hence war against Islam also became the centrepiece of his policy. Seeing his enthusiasm for war, war architects like Paul Wolfowitz must have gone immediately to the drawing board to hatch a broader scheme of war against Islam. This is why Michele Steinberg pointed out as early as October 2001 that "the grouping [meaning the Wolfowitz Cabal] wants an immediate war with Iraq, believing that the targeting of Afghanistan, already an impoverished wasteland, falls far short of the global war that they are hoping for."

What seems to have happened is that when Wolfowitz noticed that war against Islam was also on the president's mind, he then enlarged the president's concept and perhaps dropped the hint that the Israelis were working on a project that would create a formidable excuse to initiate global war against Islam. This exchange of ideas may have taken place at the very start of the Bush presidency. Defence Secretary Donald Rumsfeld could have been the link between the president and Wolfowitz, which is why Rumsfeld enjoys a special relationship with the president. A quick visit to Washington by Ariel Sharon in March 2001 may have been designed to reinforce the apparent planned Israeli role that would help the president achieve his Evangelical goals as well as facilitate the war ambitions of the hawks. Needless to say, ultimately it would also pave the way for realising Israel's territorial goals. If so, President Bush contemplated waging war against the Islamic world right from the early days of his presidency. As was stated earlier, former Treasury Secretary Paul O' Neil threw some light on war talk against Iraq as early as January 2001.

How President Bush positioned himself from then onwards, and how he attended to urgent matters, would reveal what was going on in his mind. His conduct in office would become the keynote of the thesis that he may have been aware of what was going to happen in the coming months. So much was documented against bin Laden and Al-Qaeda, yet he made no move at all against them. Dick Clarke, a former head of counter-terrorism in the White House, and others have attested that the president was duly advised through his national security adviser about the dangers posed by bin Laden and Al-Qaeda and the need to counter them. These matters are now on public record and have sparked intense debate in the United States over why the president did not act promptly despite warnings from his advisers.

His excuses are unconvincing. This writer's assessment is that the hawks, perhaps including Dr Rice, must have advised him that taking action against bin Laden prematurely would limit the war only to Al-Qaeda and perhaps only to Afghanistan. This would fall short of the wider war they were hoping for, as was pointed out by Michele Steinberg and stated earlier. From the hawks' point of view it was expedient to wait till the Israelis had accomplished their terror-based operation on the United States soil, because then the president would have a justifiable reason to start a global war against Islam in the wake of the war against terrorism. There is no other logical or practical explanation for not acting earlier, when both the outgoing administration and some of the current advisers had given so many warnings about the threats that bin Laden posed to the United States. If America had acted sooner against bin Laden, then he and his outfit Al-Qaeda would have been devastated and put out of business in no time, but there would have been no excuse left for the wider war that the hawks had been hoping for. Thus, it was necessary to leave bin Laden intact and let Al-Qaeda live on, so that when the big bang occurred, they would be held responsible and the door would open for a global war against Islam. Otherwise, there is absolutely no justification for an inert policy, especially in the light of the PDB of August 6, 2001.

When 9/11 did happen, the president came down like thunder, as if he had been building up his wrath and waiting for the moment to arrive to unleash military force in a most devastating way that would frighten the whole of the Islamic world. Every Muslim country was put on notice that if they did not co-operate with the United States, then they would be considered as harbouring the terrorists and subjected to military action. His pronouncement that "either you are with us or with them" made every Muslim country suspect and an enemy. Critics ask why he did not take a similar sort of action in the spring of 2001, which would have avoided 9/11 and its resulting tragedy. There were enough valid reasons on the table to take action forthwith. There can be no logical explanation for this inert posture except that the hawks advised him to wait for the big bang. This alone can account for President Bush's less than urgent posture against Al-Qaeda or his failure to nip the 9/11 plot in the bud.

The war on Iraq, how absurdly it was launched and how undefined it was, is the ultimate clue that untangles President Bush's entire game plan. It needs to be reviewed step by step, not only to reinforce the thesis set out above but also to comprehend what President Bush is all about.

Briefly going over the history, it will be seen that the Bush administration tried to coin excuses, one after the other, to convince both the American public as well the international community that war against Iraq was necessary. Regrettably, the American officials used even unsavoury tactics of falsifying the situation just to persuade the American public to back their stand on war. The president led the campaign of citing excuses, and then more vocally his Defence Secretary Donald Rumsfeld stated before the American people that the administration had left no stone unturned to avoid the war and that Saddam Hussein had left them with no option but to resort to war. The unsuspecting American public naively believed in these statements. However, it has now come to light that real options were available to avoid the war, but the Bush administration intentionally ignored them because they had pre-planned to use Iraq as the stepping stone for starting a global war against Islam. Hence the option of avoiding war was disregarded. The administration unnecessarily ignored an option as reports in the America media indicated that genuine effort was made by the Iraqi régime to accept all demands for disarmament through verification by the Americans to avoid the war. The offer from the Iraqis was addressed to the Deputy Defence Secretary Paul Wolfowitz and handed over by reliable sources to the American officials for consideration, but it was not pursued. The Defence Department does not deny having received the offer, but the administration refused to consider it as a basis for negotiating with Saddam Hussein. That was hardly a matter of leaving no stone unturned as Rumsfeld claimed; a very real stone was left unturned, and the possibility of avoiding war was purposely missed. This is an example of how the Bush officials have not been forthright with the American public.

It is important to note that there were opportunities to avoid wars in both Bushes' terms of office. The first one came through Gorbachev and now the second one was communicated through the auspices of Paul Wolfowitz. In both cases efforts for peace were purposely overlooked in favour of war. It goes to show that war was a prior commitment for both the father and the son, which they inherited from President Reagan. The fact that the elder Bush could easily have removed Saddam Hussein during the first Gulf War, but decided to leave him in power, might suggest that it was pre-planned to use the pretext of Saddam Hussein successively to inaugurate the war against Islam that had been initiated during the Reagan era.

As far as the veracity of the claims for war is concerned, it has now been accepted both in the United States and internationally that they were false and misleading. This situation has put the President and his intelligence apparatus on the spot, so much so that a congressional inquiry has been started to investigate how the false information emanated in the first place. The role of the CIA is now under intense investigation, whether it knowingly contributed to fabricating false information or was simply too incompetent to ascertain the facts.

Since the foregoing paragraphs were written, the congressional report has now been made public, as well as the British government's own inquiry, the Butler report. By a strange coincidence the intelligence services of both the United States and Britain failed simultaneously and mysteriously under similar circumstances. It strikes one as odd that the world's two greatest intelligence services would fail at the same time and in similar circumstances. The CIA works with a budget of over forty billion dollars and has a network of thousands of sophisticated personnel who are highly trained and proficient in assessing information to take appropriate actions. The network sifts information to eliminate or reduce the probability of misinformation. They have the manpower and resources to check and recheck and countercheck the information, especially when it might plunge the country into a war. The British have similar sophistication in their intelligence services. Why did they not complement each other's work to cover each other's mistakes when their top leaders were co-operating with each other so closely? How could both intelligence services fail simultaneously?

The document prepared by the CIA, which became pivotal in spurring the United States to war, was extremely tactfully constructed. As the Acting Director of the CIA explained in a recent television interview, the first five pages or so of this document contained material that may be seen as supporting the existence of the WMDs. This was enough for the war proponents to go ahead with the invasion. However, the acting director pointed out that the subsequent pages contained qualifiers, which would have cautioned the readers that there were dissents to this assessment, so it may not make an outright case for war. His argument to defend the CIA was that nobody seems to have read their report from cover to cover. It seemed as if the administration and the lawmakers only read the portions that suited the purpose of their war plan and did not pay attention to other parts of the same report that might have prevented them from deciding for war. He mentioned that there was flawed information in the document but there were also dissents and qualifiers that needed to be taken into account. The CIA may try to defend itself on the grounds that nobody seems to have read its report in full but the question is, Why did the CIA present a crucial report in such a misleading manner? Why was the yes for war presented in the first five pages and the no for war buried in the subsequent pages? This raises suspicion about the integrity of this document. Collecting flawed information and then presenting it in a misleading manner badly reflects on the CIA and gives reasons to believe that it could have been intentional to meet the demands of the war proponents.

Anyhow, in both the United States and Britain the intelligence communities have been severely criticised for sloppy intelligence that led both governments to war on false or insufficient grounds. While both reports acknowledge a large-scale failure and point out a fundamentally flawed approach or breakdown in the culture of the intelligence communities, surprisingly they do not hold any individual or group of individuals responsible for this deadly misinformation. Both reports lay blame on collective failure of the secret services but neither pinpoints who that collectivity might be and what could have been its motive in producing such a blatantly flawed intelligence report. Both reports are very emphatic in pointing out that there was no interference at all nor any pressure from top-level officials to fashion the reports in any particular manner to meet any demands of the American president or the British prime minister.

The visits of Dick Cheney, Rumsfeld and Wolfowitz among others to the CIA headquarters while it was still building a case against Iraq are serious infractions of the agency's independence. Although the CIA's acting director dismissed these as routine client visits, their implication is that the White House influence was applied while the CIA was still working on the Iraq report, which may explain why the report was fashioned in a misleading manner. The CIA would never admit yielding to outside pressure, nor would any government official allude to it, but the circumstances cast a thick cloud of doubt over the purpose of Rumsfeld's visit.

Hence we have two reports that tell us nothing new but only what the general public already knew – that the WMD information was false. Nothing is said about how precisely the fiasco of misinformation happened, who initiated the falsification or who was specifically responsible for building the case for war on flawed and even nonexistent intelligence. The general public in both the United States and Britain understandably remain confused and unsure about the real truth that lies behind both the 9/11 and the invasion of Iraq.

Under the existing government systems in the United States and Britain, where top officials often cover backs of each other or whitewash an inquiry, it is impossible for the public to know the truth, especially when the top leadership might be involved in unsavoury acts. Seemingly this is currently the case with 9/11 as well as the invasion of Iraq. Nevertheless there are still possibilities for digging out the truth or at least arriving at plausible conclusions that would make it emerge under its own force of truthfulness.

Despite all the misleading and mitigating confusion, President Bush is not out of the woods. Seeing his friend in trouble over the fiasco of misleading information, Israeli Prime Minister Ariel Sharon came to his rescue, as Israeli sources publicly accepted blame for circulating this flawed intelligence and claimed that they had been misled by their own Iraqi contacts. The American electronic media recently carried this piece of news. It was a shocker, but it was also the beginning of the end of the game.

Is the Israeli explanation trustworthy? It will remain questionable whether they were really misled or there was a motive for fabricating false intelligence to mislead the Americans deliberately, so that President Bush might wage war against the Islamic world and carry out President Reagan's mandate. Anyhow, it would fit in the general framework of the thesis that the Wolfowitz Cabal and the Israeli Prime Minister Ariel Sharon were engaged in fabricating a situation that would turn public opinion in America against the Islamic world. If they could do it over war on Iraq, then why could they not have done it for the sake of a larger war against Islam in the wake of the 9/11 tragedy?

What then emerges is that the agency was exchanging information and working closely with the Israelis. If so, then there are reasonable grounds for believing that the agency would also have been aware of other operations that the Israelis were engaged in, such as the possible 9/11 plot. The probability of this collusion gains credence when the agency claims that it had been closely watching bin Laden and Al-Qaeda but could not detect any clues or penetrate the 9/11 plot at that end. That may be so because the agency had not applied its attention to the Israelis, perhaps because it might have already known what the Israelis were engaged in. Lack of a widely focussed attention seems uncharacteristic of a worldwide intelligence agency. It brings back the question: Was the lapse incidental or intentional? Many critics are now wondering why the FBI and the CIA missed so many clues or potential leads.

George Tenet, the Director of Central Intelligence, has an enormous burden of responsibility to explain how and why he failed to detect any clues of the 9/11 plot from his surveillance of bin Laden. He must also explain why he did not keep an eye on other centres, such as Germany, where Arabs were living in large numbers and which accordingly were available to be used by bin Laden as he had been using other outside centres in Africa, the Philippines and Indonesia. Since bin Laden was obviously using international centres to carry out his anti-American plans, it ought to have been a routine matter for the CIA to keep an eye on all probable international centres with large Arab populations. Why was Europe not brought into the focus to see whether bin Laden was also doing something there? Director Tenet must also explain how much he knew about the Israelis' capabilities in terrorism and whether he had any grounds for suspecting that they might capitalise on terrorism against the United States for their own purposes.

Tens of thousands of people have died in Afghanistan and many more are dying daily in Iraq because George Tenet failed to detect the 9/11 plot or thwart it. The American loss of lives amounts to only three thousand and damage to a couple of skyscrapers, but the loss that Muslims are having to bear runs into tens of thousands of lives and colossal damage to their homes, businesses and livelihoods in Afghanistan and Iraq. All this could have been avoided had George Tenet carried out his responsibilities judiciously and succeeded in instituting surveillance operations properly.

George Tenet could still help to stop the killing and the massacre of the innocents and the bombardment of their homes and cities by revealing what he may know about the real perpetrators of this crime. If he could not find any clues against bin Laden, then where did the clue lie? George Tenet is the only man who may have this knowledge, or at least the resources, to find out the facts that could help defuse the deadly war that President Bush is waging on the back of his failure. George Tenet owes it to America to dig out the truth about 9/11.

Finally, the last support for this writer's thesis is President Bush's own conduct in his relations with Israel's Prime Minister Ariel Sharon. It is customary for every American president to have cordial relations with Israeli prime ministers, so what is the difference?

The difference is very noticeable. Although President Bush's general posture on the Middle East had displayed the characteristic American support for or bias in favour of Israel, his unwarranted praise for Ariel Sharon and endorsement of his extremist policies bespeaks some deeper understanding or commitment between the two leaders. It started right at the beginning. While President Bush discarded Yasser Arafat from the Middle East talks on grounds of his association with violence and terrorism, he did not apply the same standard to Ariel Sharon, despite his conspicuous record in violence and crimes against humanity. On the contrary, President Bush went even further to elevate Sharon's image by lauding him as a man of peace. This was a bizarre pronouncement. It is one thing to favour Sharon, but to call him a man of peace despite his record of atrocities is an affront to the intelligence of the international community. There must have been some pressing reason for President Bush to make such a laudatory and outrageously inappropriate statement. One may favour a friend, but not by mocking the intelligence of the international community. No one else has called Sharon a man of peace. Where did President Bush get this idea, when the rest of the world is denouncing Sharon for his atrocious conduct and militant policies? Ariel Sharon must have been cashing in dividends for some service that he had rendered to President Bush personally; otherwise the president had no reason to take such an unprecedented and controversial a step.

President Bush continued his unjustifiable praise of Sharon when he approved all the conditions of Sharon's terms for the Middle East settlement during his visit to Washington in April 2004. It was stunning how President Bush surrendered to Sharon's dictates when he departed from the norms of international law and the Security Council resolutions to approve Sharon's illegal and immoral terms for ending the Palestinian dispute.

Why would a president already mired in so many controversies create more controversy in an election year by approving such controversial terms from such a dubious Israeli leader? Building settlements on occupied lands is illegal according to international law. It is also against international law to deny refugees the right to return to their homes after hostilities have ceased. How could a president in an election year be so insensitive to international law and upset the international community as well as attract criticism at home? By taking a unilateral stand President Bush has thwarted the development of amicable conditions and killed all prospects of a mutually agreed solution. He may have approved Sharon's terms, but they will not go anywhere because they are not just, nor are they acceptable to the Palestinians. So what was the motive for President Bush to engage in something like that at such a critical moment in his political life? Was it a payback time or a case of quid pro quo? It needs expounding.

This writer's assessment is that the Israeli involvement in the 9/11 plot was based on Israel's deriving territorial benefit at the end of the day. President Bush must have known about it and seemingly made the deal. Accordingly, having completed his part – i.e. creating an excuse for President Bush to wage holy war against the infidels – Sharon came to town looking for his *baksheesh* (reward), and by golly he got a pocketful of it!

There is no sense or logic for President Bush, either in the text or in the timing, in putting up such a controversial show at such a critical time. The only explanation of this illogical move is that President Bush must have been bound by commitment over a deal with Sharon that after he had created the pretexts for war, he would be rewarded in an unprecedented way. President Bush seems to have agreed even to contravene America's own entrenched policy, which sent waves of shock and surprise everywhere and ignited the entire Muslim world. Why did he have to make such an unpopular move and take a risk that endangered his presidential candidacy as well as foreign relations and world peace? Or did he simply think that the American people are so unconcerned about outside world affairs that it would not matter to them what he does on the international scene?

Sharon may have become anxious that President Bush might not win a second term, so he came rushing to cash in his part of the deal, since there is no assurance that the next man in the White House would go as far to accommodate the Israelis. And President Bush could not possibly say no, not even plead that this is not the right time, nor were these the right circumstances to create one more headache. Sharon is a hard man; he was after his pound of flesh, so he would not give President Bush the leeway, regardless of his troubles. Had there been no prior commitment or pressure from Ariel Sharon, President Bush would not have made such a controversial move at this time.

In all probity this absurdity ought to have been postponed till after the election. Why did President Bush not try to postpone it as an electioneering tactic? What was his weakness, and why did he succumb to Sharon at such a critical point in time? What could be the explanation except that he was bound by a deal? Sharon, having done his part of the deal, pushed President Bush to do his part by granting territorial benefit to Israel. Sharon knew that once the terms of settlement of the Palestinian issue were cast in agreement with the president, then they would become part of American policy, since there is no precedent that one president would rescind an agreement with Israel that another president had made. So the job has been completed and the payoff has taken place. The world has to live with the tragedy of 9/11 without knowing whodunit.

One might say that President Bush yielded to Sharon in such a dramatic way to appease the Jewish voters and get Jewish funds for his campaign and favourable exposure in the Jewish-owned media. This may be true, especially in the case of the 'swing' states but President Bush is also committed to appease the Evangelical voters in the south who were thrilled by President Reagan and supported his policy of war on Islam. Since Sharon could have been an accessory in ultimately appeasing the south, President Bush was obliged to reward him in such an unprecedented way.

Anyhow, President Bush's concessions have the semblance of a second Balfour Declaration in that they seal the fate of the Arabs and open door for the Israelis to take over effectively the whole of Palestine. Like Britain, the United States is also using military power to finalise the goal for which the Balfour Declaration had laid a foundation in 1917.

President Bush is consistently showing a pattern of rewarding those who helped him wage war against the Islamic world in the wake of the war against terrorism. The latest example is how he is protecting Rumsfeld, who, as was said earlier, could have been the link between the president and

Wolfowitz with regard to the 9/11 plot. Despite Rumsfeld's failure to manage the Department of Defence properly as was seen in the case of the abuse of the detainees, the president described his services as a "superb job." While the nation was suffering indignation and embarrassment over the abuse of the prisoners, the president was saying that it was in debt to Rumsfeld for his superb services in combating terrorism. Where is the superbity? But this is usual for President Bush, to reward or protect those who may have helped him wage war on Islam with absurd commendations and appeasements. Both Sharon and Rumsfeld are cases in point.

In closing, this author has assiduously ventured to search for the truth about the 9/11 plot. This tragedy has taken thousands of American lives and tens of thousands in the Islamic world and ignited a wildfire of terrorism globally. The insanity of killing innocents must stop. Only truth can do it, but, regrettably, truth is the most suppressed factor in the entire episode of 9/11. The 9/11 Commission has accomplished merely part of the task since it was given mandate only to investigate the intelligence failure and prescribe recipe to avoid it happening again. Therefore the 9/11 Commission did not touch upon the crucial question of whodunit and totally relied on the presumptuous position of the administration that bin Laden and Al-Qaeda were the perpetrators of this crime. Hence the whodunit aspect was effectively left out of the probe and the 9/11 plot remains unproven as to who might have schemed it and in whose interest was it to inaugurate war between the West and Islam.

A systematic way to understand the whodunit aspect of the 9/11 plot is to go back to the history of the United States to discern how its identity was shaped and who were the domineering or pushing group of people who took over leadership of this developing country and now control its power and dictate its policies. A look back will unfold how the American conscious self was developed and how various strains, including the aversion for Islam, were made part of this consciousness. These considerations will also unravel the basis upon which present-day American policies are founded and also help in comprehending the complicated matter like the 9/11 plot.

Since the overall thrust of the current United States policies is aimed at Islam and the Islamic countries, it is important to trace the background of this enmity. As was already discussed, the enmity of Islam started in Europe at the beginning of Christendom's crusades in the eleventh century. Islam was considered a wicked religion and Muslims were always regarded as evil people. This impression was cast so deeply into the Western psyche that subconsciously it still influences the attitude of majority of the Western citizenry. Originally both the Jews and Muslims were considered the "other side" or the enemies of Christianity. However, as was discussed in previous chapters, the Jews managed to get out of the cycle of hatred, but the Muslims remained trapped because they neither converted nor influenced the Christian faith in any way. Consequently, they remained, as they indeed do today, the subject of Western hatred.

When Christianity split after the Reformation, the hateful attitude against Muslims continued as the Protestants were describing Muslims as 'Mohammedan Catholics' as a show of their hatred for Catholicism by equating Catholics with the evil Muslims. The Catholics were doing the same by calling the Protestants as the 'Mohammedan Protestants.' In both cases the Mohammedans, or more accurately the Muslims, were shown as the evil people and any one linked with them was considered equally evil. This state of mind was widespread in all branches of Christianity, and when a group of Puritans decided to move from England to the New World in 1620 it brought this hateful mindset with it to America.

The influence of the Puritans on America is profound and defining as it laid foundations of how this New World would develop, shape its identity and what its territorial, economic and religious objectives would be. Hatred of Islam was an integral part of the Puritan frame of mind.

Right from the beginning the Puritans believed that God had a special plan to bring them to the New World. According to their perception, God's plan was to provide the Puritans with a new centre of power wherefrom they could establish the Lord's kingdom and hasten the Second Coming of Christ. Karen Armstrong quotes on page 476 in her book *Holy War* from the writings of an earlier settler Edward Johnson, who published in 1654 his *Wonder-Working Providence of Sion's Savior in New England*:

> Know this is the place where the Lord will create a new heaven
> and new earth in new churches, and a new commonwealth together.
> Verily if the Lord be pleased to open your eyes, you may see
> the beginning of the fight, and what success the armies of our
> Lord Jesus Christ have hitherto had....

Johnson represented a broad spectrum of Puritan sentiments and aired their perception of the New World as the new religious centre to inaugurate the fight to establish Lord's kingdom. Thus the Puritans not only brought their crusading spirit and hatred of Islam to the New World, but they also cultivated a new zeal in their developing culture which filled them with enthusiasm to start a religious war from their new centre. They had already learned from interpretation of the Bible that Jews' return to the Holy Land was essential in establishing Lord's kingdom, so it became their conscious policy to use the resources and power of the new commonwealth to clear the way for Jews' return. Since Muslims were ruling over Palestine, the Arabs and the Islamic world were seen as obstacles in the way of this scheme. Hence it became a religious duty for the Puritans to oust the Arabs from the Holy Land and deal with the Muslim world severely so it might not be able to oppose resettling of the Jews.

While several branches of Protestantism in Europe had the same feelings and ambitions, the Puritans in America also believed that God had chosen them for this very purpose, and so they were even more determined to start the fight from the new commonwealth. Thus clear motives and specific plans were founded right at the start of Puritans' arrival in America, which became the object of their resolute pursuit throughout the period of their growth and development in the United States. Consequently, acquiring state power of the United States and how it was going to be deployed subsequently became a foregone conclusion for the Puritans. Later their derivatives, the Evangelicals, adopted the same mandate as their own plan of action.

As was already discussed, the Puritans were a deeply religious people. They had also been part of the European crusading against Islam and later utilised their crusading spirit in rebelling against King James and Archbishop Laud in 1618. They were considered a threat by the King's establishment hence many of them were expelled from England. However, their crusading spirit remained a driving force for the ones who chose to stay in England as they subsequently regrouped under Oliver Cromwell and fought against the monarchy as part of his army. The Puritans played an important role in defeating the loyalist in 1649 when Cromwell beheaded King Charles I and established a Puritan republic in England with himself as "Lord Protector." This account of history shows that Puritans were not only religious, but also brutal militants. Puritans' brutal skills were transferred to the New World as they practised them over the Pequot Indians. While the Puritans were settling down in the United States, their objectives were:

1. To turn the New World into a new commonwealth, the "English Canaan." Since they were already seriously impressed by St. Paul 'when he wrote that Christians were the New Israel', they had begun thinking of themselves as the new chosen people and started giving Jewish names to their children as well as to the new cities they were founding in the English Canaan.
2. The establishment of the Lord's kingdom in Palestine and the Second Coming of Christ was their ultimate goal. The resettlement of Jews was the first step hence it became a topmost priority for them. As a result, the seeds for planning the return of the Jews were sown in the consciousness of the growing American religious population such as the Evangelicals, who were spreading all over the country but concentrating mainly in the south, which is the present day Bible Belt.
3. Since the Puritans were experienced in state matters and had the proper zeal for running the state affairs, they began consolidating their position from the south to wield state power so they might use the forces of the new commonwealth to serve the will of the Lord.
4. They chose the Republican Party as their ladder to the state power

because their affinity with conservatism matched with the philosophy of this party.

Hence the religious south began playing an important role in the American politics. Most of the America politicians became aware of this developing power bloc, and all modern aspiring presidents, particularly from the Republican Party, showed closeness to the southern religious leadership in order to win the important southern states. The Democrats also reiterated their sympathy with the agenda of the south and toed their line as demonstrated by President Woodrow Wilson's wholehearted support for the Balfour Declaration in 1919 even contrary to his own famous Fourteen Points which 'proclaimed the principle of the self-determination of people.' President Jimmy Carter affirmed the Democrats' support for the Jews when he spoke before the Knesset in 1979 and assured the Jewish state of his commitment to the special relationship with Israel that had been demonstrated successively by seven presidents.

Thus implementing agenda of the old Puritans to resettle Jews in Palestine had been gaining momentum in America for a long time under the auspices of both political parties. It has now also become the mainstay of the Republican Evangelicals.

The British use of force to take over Palestine and dissolve the Ottoman Empire was regarded as an important step towards implementing the Balfour Declaration and realising the dream of Protestantism. Many American senators and political leaders have since been pleading that more force be used against the Arabs and the Islamic world to dislodge the Muslims from the Biblical Israel, including the whole of the Jordan Valley, Lebanon and Syria as far as the Euphrates. Therefore, the mainstream American politicians and influential Evangelicals leaders have never favourably viewed the Arabs and the Islamic world. This is why the United States follows two distinct policies, one highly favourable to Israel and the other antipathetic towards the Arabs and the Islamic world. As President Jimmy Carter said in 1979 'Seven Presidents have believed and demonstrated that America's relationship...is a unique relationship...because it is rooted in the consciousness and the morals and the religion and the beliefs of the American people themselves...'. Since this statement was made, more presidents have come to power with the same commitment of unique relationship and a mission to dislodge the Muslims in order to complete resettlement of Jews that would hasten Second Coming of Christ. It is important to note that it has been a consistent policy of most American presidents since the time of President Woodrow Wilson's support for the Balfour Declaration, who considered it as an important first step towards altering the socio-political scene of the Middle East to fulfil the religious aspirations of the American south.

Although this goal had been the wish of most modern American presidents, who were covertly working towards achieving it and increasingly showing willingness to use military force to overpower the Islamic world and oust the Arabs from the Biblical Israel, they were hesitant to take action openly in order to avoid adverse world opinion as well as not to endanger their strategic and economic interests. American ideological conflict with Communism had created a new exigency to their interests in which the Islamic world was seen an important factor and ally. Hence politically it was not expedient to take action against the Islamic world until America was finished with the more pressing enemy, the Communist Soviet Union. Consequently, any concerted action against the Islamic world was put on hold. However, after the Soviet Union was scuttled in the late 1980s and effectively the danger of Communism was warded off, President Ronald Reagan took the opportunity to bring the Evangelical agenda to the forefront by publicly announcing soon after the Berlin Wall came down that Islam was America's next enemy. Thus he laid a foundation for military action to accomplish the mission that had been developing in the consciousness of American presidents for a long time. This was the first time that an American president approached the task of dealing with the Islamic world in a practical way by taking a warlike position openly against Islam. It had been coming for a long time owing to the pressures from the Bible Belt, but no president was ready enough to take military action until President Reagan fortuitously scuttled the Soviets in the late 1980s and took the bold step to declare war against Islam. It will be recalled that President Reagan was also the first American president to mobilise voters in the religious south and was instrumental in bringing a large number of religious leaders (over a hundred) into the political arena, which became backbone of the Republican Party in the Congress. Evidently, President Reagan was overwhelmed by the Bible Belt agenda, and so his own religious proclivity combined with the ambitions of the south made it most opportune for him to declare Islam as America's next enemy despite the fact that there was no apparent sign of any enmity or any ongoing conflict between the United States and the Islamic world. His pronouncement was enormously shocking, but consistent with the notion of 'fight' for which the Puritans had laid a foundation long ago. The time had now come to use power of the 'new commonwealth' and unleash the 'armies of our Lord Jesus Christ' to achieve success. President Reagan earned the privilege of inaugurating the fight that Puritan settler Edward Johnson had espoused in 1654 when he reminded the growing Puritan population in the New world 'Verily if the Lord be pleased to open your eyes, you may see the beginning of the fight...'. President Reagan clearly saw the beginning of this fight and took a practical step to inaugurate it, because now was the most opportune time.

According to the bureaucratic protocol, a presidential declaration usually becomes state policy, which in turn becomes a mandate for the establishment. Hence, as soon as President Reagan's declaration was made,
Pentagon officials routinely made it a government mandate and began
preparing to start the fight as espoused by the Puritans and now pursued by
the Evangelicals. Consequently, the war strategists in the Pentagon assumed
this task and set about finding ways and means to start a war against Islam
and defeat this enemy before it could threaten America. Finding a pretext
to inaugurate this war is the backdrop of 9/11.

What was intriguing in Reagan's declaration, however, is that Islam had
not posed any real threat to America, since almost all the Muslim countries
and their rulers, the kings, emirs and presidents, were pro-American and
friendly with all administrations. Hence the question of Muslim or Islamic
animosity did not arise to make Islam or the Muslim world an enemy of
America. Bin Laden's radicalism did not start until 1995-96, but President
Reagan had already declared Islam as the next enemy in the 1980s. Therefore the Republican insiders, as well as the war strategists in the Pentagon,
faced a dilemma, since they did not have a credible or intensely provocative
pretext to inaugurate war against Islam. It is therefore reasonable to surmise that under such unjustifiable conditions, the Pentagon strategists had
no option but to harness a plausible pretext by contriving warlike conditions, so that President Reagan's mandate to attack Islam might be fulfilled
before this enemy (Islam) could ever become strong enough to thwart
resettlement of the Jews or challenge American exploitation of Muslim
natural resources. Consequently, the strategists' task was to insinuate warlike conditions and contrive a pretext to convince the American public as
well as the so-called international community that Islam was indeed an
enemy and a war was necessary to avert its threat to America. Hence they
improvised a pretext to start this war in such a way that it could be taken to
every Islamic country to defeat the polity of Islam and transform the
religious and cultural heritage of Muslims in the name of modernity and
democracy, so that they could never pose a threat either to the United
States or its satellite, the State of Israel. This will be a two-way fulfillment of
the Christian ambitions; one to pave the way for establishing Lord's kingdom, and the other to convert the Muslims who had been evading conversion thus far. A military defeat would corner the Muslims so they might be
converted forcibly through the medium of modernity and democracy,
which will ultimately lead them to Christian-based values as practiced by the
Americans. Thus Muslims could be forced to give up their religious and
cultural heritage in the name of modernity and democracy and effectively
convert to Western or American values, which are Christian values at least
in the view of the Evangelicals.

If we view the 9/11 incident in the Puritan perspective and analyse the war that the Evangelical President Bush is waging in its wake, in the light of the religious ambitions of the south, then we will realise that 9/11 is perhaps the ultimate blessing that the religious Americans had been hoping for ever since they visualised God's special plan to bring them to the New World. 9/11 just did not happen; it was made to happen to provide the new chosen people the opportunity to establish the Lord's kingdom by initiating war against Islam and defeating the Muslims and ousting the Arabs to resettle Jews in the Biblical Israel. The Puritans had always had a burning passion to start the 'fight' and now their successors, the Evangelicals, have acquired power, resources and military might in the new commonwealth, the United States of America, to fulfil their passion for war against Islam. Their coalition with the right-wing, the Judeo-Christian alliance, has the brainpower, the resources and the imagination to improvise warlike conditions to create a pretext in which Muslims and Islam would be portrayed as enemies, which would be sufficient grounds to signal the start of the 'fight'. This is where the need for creating 9/11 arose and this is why this tragedy happened so it may open door for the cherished Christian war against Islam.

Taking this account of history into consideration, we will see how the Puritans shaped the American conscious self and how religious bigotry and brutal militancy penetrated into the psyche of the Americans that has made them so biased in favour of Israel and so averse to Islam. The Evangelicals have inherited the full agenda of the Puritans and now carrying the flag of Puritanism, using state power of the United States to realise their religious ambitions in contravention of the country's constitution, which prohibits the role of religion in state affairs or use of state power to further the cause of any religion or its proclivity. Since President Reagan opened the door for war against Islam, both the Calvinist and Evangelical Bushes, the father and son, have been using state power to wage wars in the Middle East on one or the other pretext.

If we look at all the intelligence lapses in the light of Reagan's declaration and the war strategists' mandate to improvise a pretext to inaugurate war against Islam, then we will realise that these lapses were after all not a failure of intelligence, but rather a success, because the large-scale ineffectiveness of the intelligence services actually facilitated the 9/11 attacks and thereby provided the war strategists with a pretext to inaugurate their preplanned war in the wake of a war against terrorism.

These little mishaps when put together give the clue of a larger picture. The avoidance of a proper judicial inquiry by President Bush, the missing links of the nineteen hijackers with bin Laden or Al-Qaeda and lack of conclusive evidence or proof against bin Laden indicate that something is seriously amiss in the episode of 9/11 plot. The more one looks into the details, the more one gets the impression that 9/11 may be a homegrown venture of the Evangelicals to finally implement the Puritan agenda.

To top it all, the mysterious and simultaneous failure of intelligence in both the United States and Britain brings more clouds of suspicion over the 9/11 plot. Is this yet another coalition between the leaders of the two countries to realise Protestantism's ancient supposed prophecy concerning Christ's Second Coming?

As can be seen currently, President Bush and Prime Minister Blair are intensely co-operating with each other, which reminds us of the first coalition when the British Prime Minister Lloyd George and American President Woodrow Wilson were actively engaged in devising ways and means for Jews' return during 1917-19. Lloyd George managed to produce the Balfour Declaration in 1917 and Woodrow Wilson supported it at the international conference in Versailles in 1919.

Those who are familiar with the history of Balfour Declaration will recall that Lloyd George never put this matter to public debate nor was it ever placed on the parliamentary agenda for discussion. Hence no public support or royal assent was ever given to the Balfour Declaration in any shape or form. This was a private endeavour of a faith-based British prime minister who used cabinet authority to make this declaration otherwise there was no parliamentary or public support behind it. What is even more bizarre is that it was passed by the War Cabinet at a cabinet meeting that was not even attended by Lord Balfour because he was not a member of the War cabinet. Only his name was used to publicise this declaration otherwise Lord Balfour was not part of the process that approved a declaration in his name.

What Prime Minister Tony Blair is doing today is the same what Lloyd George did in 1917 – i.e. pushed a personal religious agenda from the state platform. The drive to resettle the Jews has now entered into its second and final stage, and since the Arabs and Muslims are the hurdles in its way, a war is now necessary to remove this obstacle. Tony Blair knows it. Accordingly he is supporting war even on false grounds so the process of full Jewish settlement may be accomplished and ground prepared for Christ's Second Coming. This seems to be the premise of his support for war and intense co-operation with President Bush, which has now taken the shape of a second coalition between leaders of the two countries. There is a striking similarity between these two coalitions. Like the first one there is no public support for the second one either and the parliamentary support that Prime Minister Blair obtained was largely based on misleading impressions otherwise it would not have come either. Like Lloyd George, this, too, is a private zeal, which is by all accounts a personal venture of Tony Blair.

The case of President George W. Bush is also comparable with President Woodrow Wilson, who supported the plan to return the Jews even against the spirit of his own famous Fourteen Points, which opposed territorial allocation without the principle of self-determination. Such a contrasting move from Wilson could not have come without a strong religious motivation, which is similar to the passion of President Bush who is now also pushing the war against Islam to realise his religious goal of hastening Christ's Second Coming.

So it can be seen that the Bush-Blair coalition is actually the continuation of the first coalition. In both cases public support is conspicuously missing and both ventures are religiously motivated without any true scriptural foundation.

This is food for thought for the people of Britain and the United States who must look at the 9/11 tragedy beyond the smoke and dust of the Twin Towers. Hysteria and assumptions or presumptions is not the way to judge an incident or launch or justify vicious military actions against any country. It is time for the American administration to table a solid proof to justify its war measures against the Islamic world. Without solid proof, the thesis that 9/11 is a homegrown venture as outlined above cries out to be investigated.

In summarising the arguments to support the theory that 9/11 is the outcome of the Judeo-Christian strategy against Islam, the following points may be noted:

1. No conclusive or convincing evidence has been produced to link bin Laden or Al-Qaeda with the nineteen hijackers.
2. President Reagan declared Islam as America's next enemy as far back as the late 1980s.
3. Most of the war strategists who helped Reagan brand Islam as America's next enemy kept moving from administration to administration and now dominate the presidency of George W. Bush. They brought their war mandate into his administration.
4. Accordingly, the war architects like Paul Wolfowitz, Dick Cheney, Donald Rumsfeld and Richard Perle have had profound influence over the policies of President Bush. These veterans have extraordinary talent, brilliant imagination and enormous brainpower and intellectual and material resources to plan any operation, no matter how bizarre, and make it seem convincing. Bin Laden is nowhere near these veterans in either intellectual calibre or technical sophistication.
5. Though Reagan and his advisers had marked Islam as America's next enemy, the war proponents were unable to inaugurate this war owing to lack of credible pretext. This was why President Clinton declined to take the war initiative, even after the bombing of the embassies in 1998.
6. Finding a pretext to start the preconceived war against Islam became an urgent need for the war strategists in 1998-99.
7. The wheels of covert operations were put in motion, and the extraordinary imaginative powers of the war strategists seem to have been deployed to contrive a scheme using the help of friends who have

experience in launching acts of terrorism and may also have had an interest in waging war against Islam.

8. If we look for a motive, there are two chief beneficiaries of this war: namely, the Evangelical Americans, who want to transform Islamic culture by conquering the East, and the state of Israel, which wants to bolster its land claims by defeating the Arabs and eroding the polity of Islam.

9. Such large-scale security or intelligence lapses could not have been incidental. They have the air of being intentional, with a view to facilitating and inaugurating the cherished war against the Islamic world.

10. President Bush's own conduct, his posture, his inert policy against bin Laden, and most of all his less than diligent handling of the security alerts put him right at the centre of the probability that 9/11 was a home-brewed tragedy.

11. Again, President Bush's extraordinary appeasement of Ariel Sharon, unprecedented acceptance of all his terms for land settlement and setting aside of the refugee claims suggest that Sharon may well have been President Bush's covert partner, whom he lavishly rewarded in April 2004.

12. The fact that President Bush had been avoiding judicial inquiry and was less than willing to institute the 9/11 Commission or openly testify before the American public to clarify his position suggests that perhaps there is something amiss that he may have been trying to avoid.

13. Full facts about the nineteen hijackers, beyond their mere names and nationalities, should be made public; including how they were re-cruited and how they were connected to each other or how they communicated as a group with Mohammed Ata or any other ringleader and particularly how Ata, Al-Shehhi and Al-Jarrah were recruited in Germany and who came from Afghanistan to accomplish this task. Is it not possible that some impostors were giving instructions or directing these students separately and independently, so that each knew sepa-rately what was expected of him but they had no knowledge as a group?

14. How much flying skills did the ringleaders actually have to carry out the attacks on the Twin Towers so precisely and perfectly? Can an inde-pendent international aviation board authenticate their skills?

15. What happened to the other two flights? Was their wreckage forensi-cally examined to determine how they came down?

16. Why has nothing been said about the timeline between the time the planes took off and the time they were rammed into the Twin Towers? Examining the time factor closely could unravel the mystery of the entire 9/11 episode.

17. Scrutinising the known facts minutely, the first plan took off from

Logan Airport, Boston at 7.59 a.m. It lost contact at 8.14 a.m. indicating that trouble had started in the cockpit after 15 minutes of flying time. Radio transponder was turned off a few minutes later and at 8.24 a.m. the radio became active again and the controller heard Mohammed Ata directing the passengers to remain calm. It means that between 8.14 and 8.24, a span of 10 minutes the hijackers managed to overpower the plane, killed the pilots with box-cutter knives, unfastened and removed their bodies from the seats, settled down in the pilots seats, regrouped their nerves, familiarised with the plane's instrumentation and began turning the plane around. They changed speed of the engines, switched the climbing mode into the descending mode, figured out flight path to New York, descended from over 30,000 feet to a level of 1400 feet, turned around the plane and precisely hit the tower at 8.48 a.m. without any trial and error. It means that all the sophisticated chores, including the journey to New York, were carried out between 8.24 and 8.48 a.m., a duration of 24 minutes. According to this timetable, Ata's voice was heard at 8.24 a.m. indicating that Ata had taken over the plane and the pilots were presumed either incapacitated or dead. All of it happened between 8.14 and 8.24 a.m. a period of 10 minutes. The in-between period of 24 minutes was used up in turning around the plane and journeying to ram it into the North Tower at 8.48 a.m.

18. The second plane took off at 8.15 a.m. also from Logan Airport, Boston. Marwan Al-Shehhi was supposedly the ringleader of this hijacking. The plane lost contact at 8.37 a.m., indicating that trouble had started in the cockpit 22 minutes after the take off. Then at 8.41:32 a.m. a message was relayed on the mike "everyone stay in your seats", which was heard by the Boston controller. The contact was lost again after about 5 minutes at 8.46:18 a.m. This timetable and silence from the plane indicate that the pilots were out of the picture between 8.37 and 8.41:32 a.m. a duration of nearly 4.5 minutes and then completely gone out in the next 5 minutes. So in a total span of nearly10 minutes the hijackers managed to kill the pilots with box-cutter knives and do all the chores necessary to bring down the plane to 1400 feet and hit the South Tower at 9.03 a.m., which is nearly 18 minutes from the time contact was lost at 8.46:18.

19. Is it possible that strong and physically fit pilots would surrender to 4-inch box-cutter knives so soon and their fight for life would be over in just 10 minutes? Did the pilots not resist desperately and engage in a prolonged fight to save their lives, especially when the assault weapons were only 4-inch box-cutter knives? How could the fight be over so soon? To say that the pilots were doped does not exclude the possibility of a little time span in which they could have cried or shouted to attract

attention of at least the first class passengers some of whom might have responded to rescue the pilots. Furthermore there is no evidence that the hijackers carried any doping substance since they were thoroughly screened and checked at the point of entry.

20. Is it also technically possible for the ill trained hijackers to carry out the complicated manoeuvres of commandeering the sophisticated wide-body 767 Boeing aircraft in this small span of time? Furthermore the fight in the cockpit must also have affected the flying pattern of the plane. Why was any repeated irregularity in the flying pattern not noticed on the radar screen by the control tower?

21. The first time the control tower became aware of trouble was when contact with flight 11 was lost at 8.14 a.m. 34 minutes later this plane rammed into the North Tower. Trouble of flight 175 was detected at 8.37 a.m. when it, too, lost contact with the control tower. 26 minutes later this plane rammed into the South Tower at 9.03 a.m. The authorities were aware of the hijacking problem since 8.14 a.m. and if the military planes had acted within 30 minutes then they would have intercepted not only the first plane but also the second one. The time between 8.14 a.m. and 9.03 a.m. is 49 minutes. Technically the United States was under attack for 49 minutes yet there were no military planes in that period to intercept the hijackings or prevent the ramming into the Twin Towers. Is that how the United States Air Force work? Should there be no question or serious public inquiry into this critical lapse? The American public as well as the rest of the world are entitled to know the full account of these 49 minutes. Who sat on the timeline and how the sequence of actions was recorded in the military logbook to depict where the crucial 49 minutes were lost. Was there any inefficiency or delinquency? If so, then who was responsible and why there is no accountability?

22. These are extremely important and pertinent questions but they were conspicuously left out of the 9/11 inquiry.

23. The war on Iraq has actually spilled the beans – how a false pretext of WMDs was devised to invade Iraq. Could 9/11 not have been a similarly fabricated pretext to attack the Islamic world? The thrust of the religious south and its control of the White House suggest that it is not beyond their capability even to fabricate a tragedy like the 9/11 to pursue their religious goals.

It is time for the American public and, indeed, the rest of the world to hunt down the truth about 9/11 by sifting the debris of wars that President Bush has scattered in the name of his war against terrorism.

9

The Desire for Peace and the Obstacles in its Way

It may sound paradoxical in the current conditions of hostilities, but the fact is that most Muslims yearn for peace and want to bring an end to this cycle of violence and counter-violence. No one needs peace more urgently than the Muslims. They need peace to straighten their lives, sort out their internal affairs, and bring freedom, democracy and social and economic progress to their communities in accordance with their religious and cultural heritage.

However, before getting to the question of peace and contemplating how it could be achieved, it is essential first to discuss the obstacles that lie in its path. Peace is the fruit of virtuous living, which, regrettably, humankind has not been able to reap so far, despite astronomical material progress. Scientists may have harnessed the forces of nature and invented amazing science and technology, but the human race has yet to learn the basics of peace, what constitutes it and how it can be achieved.

This writer's ardent desire for peace made him search for the obstacles that have been impeding it for so long. His aim is to first identify these obstacles as broadly as possible, so that all aspirants for peace may recognise the hurdles and make a concerted effort to overcome them ultimately to establish peace on earth.

Since religion plays a dominant role in a person's life, it became necessary to explore what part it or its misconception plays in creating tension in human society that hinders peace. Hence, more than anything else, religion became the object of intense scrutiny in this chapter. Accordingly, this chapter is dedicated to a broad and open-minded discussion on religion, how faith is derived, what role it plays in shaping human societies and individual behaviour and how it can become a defining force in human lives. Faith is the heart of religion. If it is logically based, then it can work wonders in a person's life. If, however, it loses its foundation in logic or reason or gets corrupted or manipulated to serve the personal ends of political and religious leaders, then faith can also become a devastating force that ultimately ruins peace.

Thus the emphasis of this critique is upon discovering how faiths become faulty and how they misguide or spur believers to oppose each other either for worldly gains or even for supposed spiritual benefits. In any case, when a faith becomes faulty, it takes the shape of a destructive force that profoundly affects peace among humans. It then becomes the single most damaging obstacle in the way of peace. Accordingly, it is essential to analyse faith more deeply, what it is, how it is formed, and how susceptible it becomes to manipulation by unscrupulous leaders.

This critique is not meant to disparage the doctrines of any particular religion or play one against another; rather it is a serious endeavour to learn about human failings that arise from following faulty faiths, which overwhelmingly affect human behaviour. This discourse may become philosophical at times and religious at others, but at no time will it become irreverent. There may be moments of discomfort when one's faith is put to the test, but the purpose is not to cause pain but rather to learn what makes us act the way we do and why we have not learned or found a finer way of conducting ourselves with each other. Given that we are probing into faiths, extensive discussion on religion and God becomes inevitable in this discourse. It will widen our scope in reviewing religion, and the extended study should be well worth the effort.

This undertaking will not be easy, but with dedication and perseverance it may expose the pitfalls lying in the way of peaceful co-existence and eventually help in bridging them to achieve the goal of peace.

Reviewing religions could take volumes of reading to comprehend the doctrine of spirituality and the fundamentals of faith of diverse communities. However, for the sake of convenience, a shorter route may be taken to grasp the basics of religion and the development of faith within Prophet Abraham's monotheistic community.

Since Judaism, Christianity and Islam are the three most influential religions that profoundly affect human society, the faiths of the Jews, Christians and Muslims will form the subject of this critique. What these faiths teach or propagate determines how their followers think and react in relation to each other as well as set trends in international affairs. Hence, faith becomes a driving force in the lives of Jews, Christians and Muslims alike.

In the monotheistic religions faith is linked with spirituality that connects the faithful to God, the Creator of humanity and the rest of the universe. Thus the impact of faith in shaping a person's life is profoundly defining and enduring. It can be a good thing in guiding the faithful to a happy and successful way of living; but if for any reason the faith gets corrupted or becomes faulty along the way, then it can also become a devastating detraction in individuals lives without their even knowing about it. Thus an intelligent and rationally weighing new generation has to be diligent about its faith, or before accepting it or forming a new faith, to be confident that it is founded on logic and reason. Accepting the faith even of one's own heritage without the assurance of evaluation or re-evaluation could involve a person in the same error of judgement that his or her forefathers might have been drawn into owing to their obscure circumstances.

Therefore it behoves an enlightened modern generation to review its faith in the light of the emerging enhanced knowledge that is continually confronting human society. The chances of one's faith becoming faulty are high, owing to the influence that powerful religious and political leaders wield over the unsuspecting citizenry. The risk that that will happen is not limited to any particular group of people. It can affect anyone, even the most matured and learned societies. Hence everyone is at risk of practising a faulty faith, though mostly unwittingly. Since a faulty faith could have a most damaging effect, it is essential to discard any fault(s) that may have infiltrated into the belief system, for whatever reasons. The spiritual component of the faith is the most difficult one to analyse, since it will revolutionise or transform a person's life in a profound way. However, analysing the faith in the context of interaction in human society is highly desirable and essential for the sake of harmonious co-existence. Therefore, while reassessing faith as a whole may be more inspiring, the least a person can do is to test his or her behaviour towards fellow human beings on the anvil of logic.

Religiously speaking, when God created humankind He was aiming to perfect His entire creation by producing the ultimate specimen of what He can do. He created humankind in the image of His own attributes and bestowed upon this unique and finest creature the gift of freedom of choice and the ability to act independently. He has angels and other creatures that worship and serve Him constantly, but none of them is equal to humankind in freedom of choice and independence in thinking or decision-making. This extraordinary gift is unique to humanity, but it is also a test for humankind how they use this gift or apply it in organising their daily lives as individuals and communities. This test is not only good for the human race to keep it on the track of right choices, but it can also be a source of gratification for the Creator, who would like to see how His finest creature fares in making choices. So, to test His masterpiece, God has created two characteristics in human nature, evil and virtue, as the sources of an enduring test of choices. It is then left open to humankind to exercise this gift in distinguishing virtue from evil and choosing what is virtuous or best.

While virtue carries with it strong demands for forbearance, evil is tempting and impulsively active. Thus evil plays a more active role in human lives and becomes the strongest peril in the way of the human race. God's Will has imbedded a tendency to evil in human nature, which poses a constant challenge to humans, demanding restraint. Evil appears in the shape of many perils, such as greed, jealousy, arrogance, egoism (self-centredness), enmity, hypocrisy, murder and wanton killing for power or money, stealing, lust for unspiritualised sex, destruction of property and environment, including cruelty to animals, usurpation of the rights of individuals, exploitation, hatred, racial discrimination, religious intolerance, injustice, denial of freedom and so on. These perils are part and parcel of human nature. However, God in His infinite wisdom has also ingrained the faculties of knowledge, intelligence and wisdom in the human character, to help humankind cope with its perils by being able to discern between good and bad and choose only what is good. God's delight is, of course, to see how the humans apply His gifts of knowledge, intelligence and wisdom and benefit by making good choices. To that end He put in place a scheme of rewards and punishments as an incentive for humans to use His gifts judiciously.

God loves humankind enormously, because they are His most outstanding and distinctive creatures, even superior to angels, who are devoid of independent thinking and freedom of choice. When He dispatched humans to earth, He did not abandon them in the woods of planet earth; He continued to love them and care for their well-being. In His infinite wisdom God knew that the greatest challenge that humankind would face on earth would be the difficulty of living harmoniously and interacting amicably with each other, owing to the enormous power of evil. If not guided, humankind may become its own worst enemy, because of its independence, and destroy the gift of life. Thus God took upon Himself the obligation of guiding the human race. So He had been sending messengers from time to time, to remind humans of the distinction between virtue and evil and point out His scheme of rewards and punishments, which depends on how humans fulfil their obligations in making choices.

Further to help humans live successfully, God has devised a set of *Divine Rules* and sent them through His messengers to guide the human race through the thick and thin of the earth, so that they may draw maximum happiness and joy from the experience of living on this planet. These rules guide them to virtuous living that ultimately fulfils the purpose of life. In view of their importance, it is essential to know these rules and embrace them to enhance the quality of daily life in human society.

The first rule pertains to human fraternity, declaring that all human beings emanate from the same race and have the same heart and soul and the same emotions and feelings of pain and pleasure. Fraternity builds bonds that prove all humans are the same and have common characteristics of desire, passion, hope and despair as well as the feelings of pain and pleasure. Full compliance with this rule inspires compassion, but neglect of it causes fragmentation, double standards and exploitation of the weak and vulnerable.

Flowing from fraternity is the rule of justice. Justice is God's most beloved and favourite rule, and nothing has received more attention from Him than the proclamation of justice in human society. Keeping its importance in view, it is appropriate to discuss this rule in detail.

In the scheme of independence, every person should have desire and passion to better his or her living conditions; and given the expanding perimeter of enterprise, innovation and freedom and knowledge to harness the forces of nature, humans should be able to make incessant strides to move forward. Proper and full utilisation of all its God-given talents could take humankind to great heights, and conversely the neglect of them would leave it backward, even impoverished and humiliated. Disparity in greater or under-utilisation of the talents is unavoidable, owing to human limitations in ability to benefit from knowledge, intelligence and wisdom. Those who move forward owing to their ability to take risks and agility in exploration tend to develop personal and group or tribal power over others, who may be slow or unable to use their faculty of intellect in a similar manner. To deal with this, the Creator inculcated the principle of justice, so that those who manage to move forward should not trample over those who, for whatever reasons, either of their own making or inflicted by outside forces, are sluggish. In His wisdom God knew that such an imbalanced situation would give evil a chance of corrupting and savaging the human race. So He instituted justice, which draws lines that the powerful ones should not cross to encroach upon the rights and privileges of others, regardless of their status in the social fabric. Fundamentally, justice protects humans from the excesses and atrocities of their fellows, secures a person's right to live in dignity and earn a living unimpeded, and establishes laws to protect individual rights and property that no one is allowed to violate. While God's system of freedom leaves wide-open opportunities for the aggressive and forward-moving types, His ordinance of justice prescribes limits to protect the rights and autonomy of others, to ensure that they are not deprived of their share of happiness in this world. Regrettably, humans continually violate this most important rule of God, which is why our world has seen so much unhappiness and atrocity throughout the ages. Men of power have forgotten their responsibilities, which God entrusted to them at the time of their creation, and spoiled the great show of human fraternity, peace and happiness on earth. If we are to reap the fruits of peace, then we must sow the seeds of justice as given to us in the greater scheme of the Creator. There can be no compromise with this important rule of God.

The next *Divine Rule* is the equality of humanity in the eyes of justice. This is the reinforcement of the first two rules of fraternity and justice. Two people may not be of the same social or economic level owing to variance in utilising the intellectual resources bestowed upon them, but in the eyes of justice they have equal rights and privileges. This rule goes a long way to establish harmony in human society, since it eliminates discrimination, double standards and mistreatment of the poor and weak by the rich and powerful. The ordinance of equality outlaws double standards and double-faced policies, which, regrettably, have been the sore part of our civilisation. The equality provision also gives birth to human rights. Islam took the initiative of enacting human rights some 1400 years ago and had since been preaching their adoption to establish a just society. In our times, the United Nations has also taken the initiative to implement human rights, but more often than not the superpowers, who profess to exult human rights, are actually the ones who routinely violate them.

These *Divine Rules* set the pace for a just and equitable social and economic system in a most profound way to enhance mankind's living experience and enjoyment of all the bounties that God has bestowed upon earth. God created diversity in the human race, because diversity in all forms and shapes is His delight. Harmonious living on earth, despite diversity and temptations and choices, may be His way of gratifying Himself for His creativity. If so, He must interest Himself in how successfully the human race uses His gift of knowledge, intelligence and wisdom to cope with or overcome the perils of evil and reap the benefit of a happy and joyful life on earth. This is the ultimate test of humanity. Humans are able to meet this challenge owing to the unique gifts of knowledge, intelligence and wisdom that only they have in the scheme of the Creator. Without a test or challenge, human life would become dull. This is why God has instituted an ongoing strife in human nature and has appointed a Day of Judgement, the day of reckoning when He will take account of how human societies were organised and life was lived on earth. Hence what distinguishes humans from other earthly creatures is their ability to differentiate between good and bad and be accountable for their decisions.

What is good or what is bad is governed by the *Divine Rules*, which basically define the rights of individuals or groups and the need for restraint by way of justice, so that no one is put to disadvantage by the excesses of others. There are other rules, too, but they all aim at providing guidance in establishing harmonious interaction and just and fair co-existence as a fraternal human society. Prayers, worship and all other forms of spirituality are principally designed and ordained by God to keep humanity in contact with the Creator for drawing inspirations and taking help in making prudent choices to live a peaceful and happy life. Worship is entirely for humankind's own benefit. God derives no benefit from the prayers or worship of individuals, for they cannot make Him any greater than He already is. Prayer or worship strengthens human character and helps to improve or ease human living conditions.

Different people have different faiths, depending upon their perceptions about God. Essentially, religion outlines that God is the Creator, the

Provider, the Merciful, the Beneficent, Sovereign, Owner of the entire universe and the One Who has the right to judge humankind on how they exercise their choices and whether they successfully use His gifts to live peacefully and harmoniously on earth.

Faith is an integral part of religion because it establishes a belief system about God and in His attributes as well as in His laws and rules. It also reminds humans that while they have the freedom of choice, they are also accountable for their actions. This is the essence of faith. If humans see God as a god of war, then their faith will lead them into war. If they perceive God as Beneficent and Merciful, then their conduct will show mercy and peace. So it is one's faith and how one perceives God that determines one's behaviour and conduct. In any case, faith is the central force that determines how a person leads his or her life, whether belief in God and His rules or any other system governs their lives.

Applying this brief survey of religion and faith to our own worldly situation to check the conduct or behaviour of the Jews, Christians and Muslims, on the scale of the *Divine Rules*, we can see whether their faiths are healthy or tarnished. If these faiths were not affecting the peace of our world in such a profound way, then we should not have needed to go through this analysis, which may make some people uneasy.

However, from the point of view of peace this evaluation of faiths is too important for us to skip it for fear of offending some. At the outset, however, we may say about the monotheist communities that it is terribly sad that the posterity of Prophet Abraham, the friend of God (may peace be upon him), should have turned out to be such warmongers and so destructive. Prophet Abraham brought the message of peace from the One and Only God, but his progeny and the followers of his faith – Jews, Christians and Muslims – are practising violence, hatred and wars. Prophet Abraham is recorded to have made war once, to rescue Lot, according to Genesis, but his was a war of defence against foreign invaders. He did not fight against his host country, nor did he wage war to press a territorial claim or accomplish a political or economic agenda as his progeny have been doing throughout their history. They have not only broken peace between their own communities of monotheists but have also brought misery and hardships on the rest of humanity. It is, indeed, a setback to the religion of Abraham. These three branches of Prophet Abraham's children are the most dominant factors in our world, but they are also the three most destructive forces on earth. It is, therefore, utterly important to scrutinise their behaviour in the light of their faiths to comprehend how such violence and terrorism has arisen and whether we have any chance of controlling it.

Taking up the case of the Jews first, it is impossible to see how God could change from the God of peace to a God of war and vengeance. There is no historical trail to suggest that Prophet Abraham, the forefather of the Jews, when introducing the religion of One God, ever described Him as a god of war. Likewise, there is no indication that Prophet Moses (may peace be upon him) might have characterised God as a god of war and vengeance. How could God adopt war and become partisan when He is the Creator and Benefactor of the entire human race? Those who submit to Him benefit from His Grace, but those who defy Him suffer from their own evil actions. God's Mercy is equal for all; those who choose the evil bring affliction on themselves. God is not a partisan; rather humans do not benefit from His Grace uniformly owing to their own divisions.

Had God been a god of war right from the start, then He would have demonstrated His warmongering skills or capabilities from the outset on many occasions. For example, when Iblis, the Satan, defied God by refusing to prostrate himself before His masterpiece of creation, humankind, God did not wage war against him; He just cursed him and expelled him from His special domain, paradise, until the Day of Judgement. Again, when Prophet Abraham was persecuted and tortured by King Nimrod in what is now Iraq, God did not declare war on Nimrod or fight against his forces; God simply took his favourite prophet away from the hostile scene and showed him another place where he could live in peace and harmony and continue preaching his faith to others by his own virtuous conduct. Yet again, when the Pharaohs had transgressed in every way and atrociously persecuted the Jews, God did not stand up to fight or wage war against them; again He chose to have His people leave the hostile scene. There is no track record that God was ever a god of war at any time in human history. The destruction of past nations as a result of natural calamities cannot be quoted as God's acts of wars. These were consequences of man's own transgressions and showed that persistent rebellion against the rules of God could instigate God's displeasure and anger, which might erupt in the form of natural disasters and bring about destruction of the transgressors.

Undoubtedly, there are passages in the Bible that represent Moses as characterising God as a God of war and vengeance: "to me belongeth vengeance and recompense" (Deut. 32-35 and also verses 41 and 43); "the LORD is a man of war" (Ex. 15.3 and see the whole song from which the verse comes). Respectfully, the point of contention is that these passages are not consistent with how things happened in Egypt. Assuming that God is the God of war and vengeance, then why did He not fight with the Pharaohs, and why did Moses agree to flee and not demonstrate to the Pharaohs how capable a warrior his God was? We are entitled at least to suspect that the notion of war as an attribute of God first arose when Joshua tampered with the Torah after it fell into his hands as military leader of the Israelites. As was discussed earlier, Joshua may have ventured this move to spur the Hebrew tribes to force their way into Canaan and wage war to kill and drive out the Canaanites as some Hebrew tribes were demanding as a prerequisite to entering the holy land. Thus a military leader may have manipulated the core of the faith of the Israelites about God at the most delicate stage of its inception. All the other deductions that were afterwards made from the Old Testament to depict God as God of war are then under a cloud as being suspect. The difficulty is that believers in a faith are usually reluctant to test their faith on the anvil of rational or logical analysis. Consequently, those in authority, such as Joshua, have an open field to circumvent the word of God however they may wish. Their unsuspecting followers then take their version for granted and fashion their lives accordingly. This is a human failing that had been exploited throughout the history by religious and political leaders. Jews, Christians and Muslims are alike victims of the same phenomenon of manipulation and exploitation by fanatical leaders in their respective communities or religious dominations.

As far as rationality goes, God did not favour war, which was why He summoned Moses to extricate the Jews from Egypt. He also gave Moses a Book to guide the Israelites on the path of peace and righteousness. The whole Law of Moses contains 613 precepts, of which the Ten Commandments are the greatest. Since wars of aggression or for the love of territory are not consistent with the attribute or character of God, it is inconceivable that He would institute the notion of war in any of these covenants. The inclusion of the notion of war for aggression and territory in the scriptures is more likely a venture of man than God. It will be remembered from sura *Maida* in the Quran that God did not promote the idea of killing or driving out the strong people of Canaan, nor did He suggest assaulting the gate. The first part of this action came from the Hebrew tribes and the second from the two men who were discussing the re-entry strategy with Moses and the expedition. As far as God was concerned, He wanted the Israelites to enter and then, if necessary, use a defensive war to secure entry. As Prophet Abraham demonstrated (Genesis 14) and the Quran also affirms, war is permissible only as a defensive measure. Every human being has received a right to defend his sovereignty, religious culture, social and economic resources as well as freedom from invading transgressors who defy the *Divine Rules*.

The insertion of the notion of aggressive war into the scripture seems to have happened after the children of Israel insisted that Moses and his Lord should fight against the strong people of Canaan. This was the time when Joshua was encouraging the Hebrews to make the assault on the proper gate, and realised that they would not do it until they first saw God engaged in fighting. So Joshua appears to have changed the image of God and made Him a God of war to impress upon the Hebrews that God was in fact engaged in war and commanding the children of Israel to join with Him in this war against the strong people of Canaan. Changing God's image to meet the demands of the reluctant Hebrews became possible for Joshua as he assumed command of the Jewish expedition after Moses had passed away. As a result, the books of Exodus, Numbers, and Deuteronomy in particular depicted God as commanding the Israelites to wage a vicious war against the Canaanites. This warring image of God has since been a severe problem for peace on earth, because the Jews have made war a part of their faith. How can the Jews embrace peace when their God incites them to war? As was already discussed in an earlier, chapter the Jews have been waging wars ever since they embraced a new god, different from the God of Abraham and Moses, and made him an integral part of their belief system. Their faith has thus become corrupted, which explains why they are unable to make peace covenants and live in harmony with other communities.

As for the Christians, their dilemma is that Jesus Christ (may peace be upon him) passed away at a comparatively young age without having an opportunity to crystallise his messages in the form of a book. So whatever messages the Christians have received were compiled after his death by apostles and devotees who did the best as they could from memory or hearsay. However, deriving information from the Old Testament was also inevitable to fully construct the Book. Since Jesus was originally a Jew and believed in all the precepts of Judaism, the apostles saw no harm in adopting passages from the Old Testament to complete the Christian scripture. Thus the Christians have gotten portions of their messages from the Old Testament. Accordingly they have close compatibility and affinity with the Jews. What the apostles apparently did not realise at the time, and generally the Christians still do not realise, is that there was a risk in copying or adopting passages from the Torah since it was already suspect owing to Joshua's tampering with it. By emulating or following many spiritual elements of the Jewish faith, the Christians seem to have also acquired the Jewish faith in war despite Jesus' own pacifism. Hence it would appear that the Christians' view about war is derived from the tainted Jewish faith, which they unsuspectingly copied. Many Christians have been heard saying that war in human society exists by God's own design, and therefore war will always remain an active part of human behaviour. That is why many medieval Christian priests and preachers, including many Popes, were warmongers, waging wars of persecution against the Jews and later embarking on crusades against Islam. Pope Urban II at the Council of Clermont, along with Peter the Hermit, was preaching and inaugurating war in 1095. Crusaders under the aegis of Pope Urban canonised violence and made it a Christian vocation. Priests, monks and other clerics, including saints such as Saint Bernard, were actively engaged in promoting wars, believing that war was a commandment from God.

The phenomenon of war penetrated even deeper into the Christian faith when the aggressive and martial people of the northern nations of Europe entered Christianity. They needed a religion that would be compatible with their own martial or warmongering lifestyles. So a new concept came to life, to accommodate them, that presented Jesus as a military leader who waged war against oppression. Once Jesus was associated with war, the aggressive northern nations joined Christianity and continued with their warmongering lifestyles. "Soldier saints like St. George, St. Mercury [sic; perhaps St. Maur or Maurice] and St. Demetrius were looked upon like pagan deities. Jesus was seen as the feudal landlord of the Crusaders who had summoned his Knights to recover his patrimony—the Holy Land from the infidels", to quote from Karen Armstrong's book *Holy War*.

To make matters worse for Christianity, it was not only the infiltration of war from influences of Judaism and warmongers from the Northern nations that turned it into a war-based religion, but the Romans who adopted Christianity had also brought their warmongering and imperialist influences into their new religion. Hence Christianity mostly flourished under the wings of the Romans and the Vikings, who were among history's most savage and brutal people. Consequently, the foundations of historic Christendom were laid not only on warmongering but also inevitably on a Roman culture of imperialism that the Western civilisation practised over the unsophisticated and unsuspecting Third World after the Renaissance. Throughout its conquests and imperial domination, the Christian faith had become so faulty and eroded that its followers had no qualms about practising savagery, plundering, and blatantly violating all the *Divine Rules* of God. The plight of the Third World declares for itself what the Christian imperialists have done to other nations during their ascendancy of the last several centuries.

The priests, preachers and knights, including saints new and old, had succeeded in changing even the perception of Jesus Christ from the Messiah of peace to a feudal lord of the Crusaders and military leader who sent them to wage war to recover his patrimony. This was a horrible transformation of a noble and peace-loving prophet. The warmongering preachers showed no regard for Jesus' pacifism, how he rejected war and even retaliation by telling his followers to turn the other cheek and how he lived in austerity with compassion and devoted his entire life to helping others. How could he be a warrior, killing even the infidels? He was a prophet; his mission was to change the lives of people to a better and spiritually more gratifying path. He did not come to this world to kill people; he came here to transform people and nations to live virtuously and enjoy the bounties of the Creator. "I am come that they may have life, and have it more abundantly" (John 10.10). But the force of corrupted faith is devastating. When falsehood infiltrated from the Jewish book and combined with other forces of imperialism, the religion of Jesus Christ was fundamentally tarnished. From a preacher of peace, human compassion and pacifism Jesus was

turned into a military leader. It is a painful demonstration of how faulty
faiths can destroy institutions and bring havoc upon humanity. First the
notion of war was adopted from Judaism and then it was compounded by
the influences of the Romans and the invading northern nations. Consequently, many Christians now also believe that war is a commandment from
God and it is a Christian prerogative to wage wars against infidels and evil
people. They have forsaken the pacifism of Jesus Christ and ignored how
he practised compassion, peace, austerity and love for humanity in spreading the word of truth. He showed that propagation is only by invitation and
by good conduct, which he demonstrated by the example of his own
pacifist good conduct. Sadly, Christian conduct in general is contrary to
Jesus' conduct and the example he set for his followers.

While the Jewish faith in war was limited to territorial gain in ancient
Canaan and engaged in wars only in the Middle East, the Christian faith in
war has a wider and greater dimension. They have canonised war for export
anywhere in the world for their own reasons which they may deem right
from their own perspective. History is full of accounts of wars waged by
Western Christian civilisation not only on the continent of Europe but also
in other parts of the world, killing tens of millions, perhaps hundreds of
millions of human beings, mostly innocents who were caught in their
vicious vocation of war. Regrettably, the traits of war are now so firmly
embedded in the Western frame of mind that it is difficult even in our
modern times to convince a Christian faith-based leadership to desist from
war and explore more peaceful means of solving international disputes or
controversies. The present-day warring posture of the West is a clear manifestation of how a faulty or corrupted faith can become destructive and
spur its followers to the path of death and destruction instead of resolving
disputes peacefully.

The Christian Church, or at least its leadership, cannot escape responsibility for what the followers of the Christian faith have been doing around
the world for a thousand years or more. Their failure to control the
wrongheaded policies and corrupt actions of their followers is an indication that they have not been able to inculcate the *Divine Rules* or nurture
peace in their congregations, despite preaching Christianity for nearly two
thousand years. Nor have they sufficiently refined or reformed the conduct
of their followers in dealing with people of other faiths. The misery of wars,
imperial domination, oppression, injustice, deception, and double standards happen all the time under the eyes of the Christian Church leaders.
They exercise little or no influence, nor raise their voices against these
transgressions, because they have lost touch themselves with the *Divine
Rules* of the Creator owing to their faulty faith. Another reason for their
ineffectiveness is that after the Reformation the Christian Church was so
severely subdued that it could offer no effective guidance to Christian (now

Western) rulers or plead successfully for reprieve from their excesses for the victims of imperial domination. Hence Western civilisation has become unruly and lives by military power, which has turned it into a powerful despot. To be powerful is one thing, but to be a good human being is quite another, as Nelson Mandela once boldly reminded President Bill Clinton in a face-to-face public meeting during his visit to Africa. Mandela's words of wisdom were, however, of no avail.

Since Western Christian civilisation has replaced the *Divine Rules* with its own man-made rules in the name of modernity, democracy and secularism, it has inevitably deprived itself of the benefits of morality and spirituality that are inherent in the *Rules*. A man-made system predominantly pro-motes materialism and unfettered liberalism, which in turn give birth to greed, jealousy and all the other base emotions mentioned earlier that impair mankind's ability to distinguish good from bad. Consequently, the West is now devoid of the benefits of the *Divine Rules*. The chief victim of their neglect is peace and harmonious co-existence with other members of the human fraternity. Accordingly, many social ills and moral delinquencies now grip Western society and extend their bad influence to other parts of the world.

Economic and material progress has nothing to do with morality and peace, as can be seen from contemporary times, when our world has the highest level of material progress yet peace is alarmingly deteriorating on the international scene. If economic and material progress were the foun-dations of morality and peace, then we would already be reaping the fruit of peace owing to our world's astronomical economic progress. Granted sound economies are essential for prosperous communities, but they can-not supersede the constraints of morality and spirituality. The fact that our world is filled with so much violence, injustice and transgressions reaffirms that it is not economics alone but rather morality based on *Divine Rules* jointly with economic prosperity that forms the foundation of peace.

Nowhere in Christian preaching have there been substantive signs that the church is imparting the virtue of peace or admonishing its followers to give up wars. Consequently, the population has not had real exposure to peace. Nor has it received indoctrination in the *Divine Rules* of God, since the religion has fallen into the hands of warring pastors and priests who claim to be men of God but have turned out in practice to be men of War. Hence Christian civilisation has done little or nothing to benefit its subjects during its protracted ascendancy of the world except wage wars to impose imperial domination. Undoubtedly, the European Christians made much progress in material developments, which helped their subjects to improve their living conditions in some ways, but the majority of the benefit from natural resources and material progress went to the imperialists. The Euro-peans did end tribal warfare in many parts pf the globe but it was mostly to consolidate their own imperial domination. They also helped to end the practice of slavery in the West but the germs of discriminatory treatment of other races still survive. Consequently, their view of other religions, races and nations is still clouded with prejudice. Their most notable deficiency is in peaceful co-existence and fair and just dealing with people of other races and religions. Hence the Third World lacks any real foundation of progress, which is evident from the present-day plight of Africa and many other parts of the globe. The Jews, who also regard themselves as part of the West, are not far behind in moral deficiency since they are also waging wars and inflicting cruelty upon humanity. Their love for territory and their warmongering to grab the whole of Palestine precludes them from ever establishing peace in the Middle East.

The current Judeo-Christian alliance against the Muslims or Islam cannot be a good omen for peace. The Christians have a military power of unprecedented magnitude, which the Jews are skilfully manipulating for their common advantage. Since both the Jews and many Christians appear to believe in war as a commandment from God, they offer no future in peace for the posterity of humankind owing to their faulty faiths.

What emerges from the reflections given above is that when faith gets corrupted or becomes faulty, human behaviour becomes threatening under the immense influence of such a faulty faith.

Looking at the Muslim case, it will be seen that Muslims, too, have corrupted their faith during the course of their own drift from their religion. Before reflecting on how their faith was corrupted and how the noble notion of *Jihad* was transformed into a slogan of offensive war, we must first recognise that Islam also emanates from Prophet Abraham's religion of One God. Its messages are consistent with the ones that Prophets Moses, David, Solomon and Jesus propagated. Unlike the tainted versions of war in Judaism and Christianity, Islam does not preach war, nor does it condone violence or terrorism as a means of achieving political or economic objectives. The Quran specifically outlawed offensive wars. Muslims are forbidden to resort to acts of violence as aids in their struggle.

The Muslims' drift started about a century after the passing away of their Prophet, but it grew wider from the days of their ascendancy in Spain during the eighth and ninth centuries. Muslim teachers or learned social reformers came from Arabia in large numbers to educate the newly converted Spaniards in the message of the Quran, as well as to familiarise them with the Sunnah and Islamic principles and just practices in the realms of social and economic life. Since the Muslim population of Spain was relatively new to the faith, these teachers were treated with great respect, which enhanced their influence in the society and filled them with a sense of importance. They were also aware what their counterparts in the neighbouring Christian states were doing. What they saw was that the Christian priests and pastors were dominating the state affairs of their countries and canonising laws to fortify a theocratic state under their control. It was an enviable position of theocratic influence, which gave rise to temptation in the Muslim teachers, who began emulating the Christian practices to steer their own Islamic state in Spain. Those who were inclined to use state power as a means to impress their teachings saw an opportunity to grab state power as their counterparts were doing in the neighbouring Christian states. Hence, the focus of some overly ambitious teachers began shifting towards the state powers. What irked them most was that a sultan was ruling the state instead of a caliph. They were sceptical about the sultan's knowledge of or commitment to Islam. So they began to interfere with state affairs and intervene with the sultan about the application of the Islamic laws as they saw them. Their status in the eyes of the people got a boost, as they were looked upon as influential and learned scholars of religion. But their increasing influence over the population also made them even more ambitious, because by then they had begun dictating what the sultan could or could not do. The tool they had in their hands was their knowledge of the Islamic laws, but whether they were using them in the true spirit of dynamism of Islam is debatable.

In any case, they made Islam a pretext for controlling the sultan and dominating state affairs. Their interpretations became the final words, since they were supposedly the only ones who were learned in the Islamic principles. Thus a new institution developed that later took the shape of mullahism, whereby the power-oriented scholars became the authority in interpreting Islam and directing state affairs. Not all scholars had departed from the original task of building a true Islamic society in Spain, but the shift became noticeable as the sultan began to respond to their dictates. Successive sultans faced difficulties in governing the state, since the scholars were routinely stirring up the population about the sultans' failure to comply with the *Sharia*. Thus seeing a threat to his rule, the sultan invited many imposing scholars (mullahs) to his council of advisers and put them in charge of supervising the religious aspects of the administration. This was the first time these scholars had tasted state power, and ever since that time the aggressive ones have become power-hungry mullahs. This new phenomenon spread from Spain to Damascus, Baghdad and other seats of Islamic states and ultimately took over the Ottoman Empire. Its legacy now haunts the Islamic world, as any fanatic who claims to be a scholar can lay claim to state power to run state affairs as he may deem fit according to his own interpretation of the religion. If he cannot gain state power, then he resorts to stirring up the population in the name of Islam, which is all too common in contemporary Islamic countries.

The technique used by these power-hungry mullahs is to take away initiative from the people by confining them to rituals and preventing the

enterprise of the citizenry from finding progressive outlets. Islamic precepts have been interpreted in antiquated ways that are regressive and
contrary to the original revolutionary spirit of Islam. Thus instead of
moving forward according to the dynamism originally inherent in Islam to
improve living conditions by harnessing the forces of nature and scientific
discoveries, the Muslim nations began to slip into stagnation, which then
became a serious recession and brought about their downfall. The mullahs
cannot escape responsibility for the Muslim downfall and the deplorable
plight of the *Ummah* as we see it today. It is not enough just to blame the
outsiders or condemn Muslims for not following the religion in its true
spirit. The failure of the mullahs has a great deal to do with the decline of
the *Ummah*. Abdul Wahab in Saudi Arabia is a prime example from nearer
our times of how they pulled back the population and made them stagnant
and backward. The current stagnation and backwardness in the Muslim
world stems from the corrupted faith of the power-hungry mullahs who
believe (erroneously) that sticking to conservatism or adhering to the
traditions of the past is a dictate of the religion. They have ignored the fact
that Islam is fundamentally revolutionary and inspires its followers to move
forward and continue to benefit from any new knowledge and new inven-
tions that mankind can discover using the knowledge and intelligence that
God has planted in the human mind. To keep their own control over the
unsuspecting citizenry, the mullahs have obscured the fact that God de-
lights in progress and innovation as long as they are applied in a virtuous
manner.

While Muslims were still free from the regressive clutches of the power-
hungry mullahs during the earlier stages of Islamic development, they
made phenomenal social, economic and scientific progress. Their Golden
Age is a testimony to how an uninhibited or freethinking Muslim can make
such phenomenal progress in all branches of science, literature and social
theory. Those Muslims did not give up the values or principles of their
religion, but neither did they stay put in any one period of time; they
moved forward taking their values and principles with them; they entered
new horizons of progress. Regrettably, some misguided scholars of the past
and antiquated mullahs of the present times oppose modernity, fearing
that it erodes faith in religion and brings corruption that undermines
human character. They fear that believers will thus stray from the right path
under the confusion of modernity. But they do not realise that human
progress outweighs the risks, which can still be managed by education and
training of the intellect to distinguish between good and bad, right and
wrong.

It is interesting to note that a celebrated Irish thinker, Bernard Shaw,
once made a fascinating comment about Islam and Muslims. He must have
studied both, as he said that Islam was the best religion but the Muslims

were the worst people. It only goes to show how much damage the corrupted faith of the power-hungry mullahs has done to the Muslims as people and as nations. Many newly converted Muslims have expressed similar sentiments, because when they studied Islam from an academic point of view and reflected upon the teachings and life of the Prophet, they were overwhelmed and embraced the faith, but when they see the plight of the Muslim character they are disappointed. Despite this disappointment they keep the faith, because they like the doctrine of the religion and see a personal spiritual gain in adopting and cherishing Islam.

Such is the devastation wrought in the Islamic world by the corrupted faith of some mullahs. As far as the religion is concerned, the Prophet (may peace be upon him) emphasised that the Quran was complete in every respect as an institution in itself to guide believers in all facets of life. Following the Sunnah is recommended to seek elucidation of how the Prophet dealt with certain situations but true authority to guide the Muslims is vested only in the Quran. The mullahs, however, have complicated the interpretations and crushed the dynamism of Islam, turning this vibrant and revolutionary religion into a stagnant embodiment of rituals. Hence the mullahs have done nothing to move Islamic societies forward in the dynamic spirit of Islam for improving living conditions of its followers. They quote the Quran in the light of their own perspectives, especially perverting the noble notion of *Jihad* to arouse Muslims in the name of Islam for their own purposes of politics and power. *Jihad* is a noble concept of constant struggle by Muslims to continually improve their living conditions and bring refinement and reform in society in keeping with the dynamic character of Islam. There is nothing obnoxious in the notion of *Jihad,* as the Western media tend to portray it. The abuse of *Jihad* is, of course, pernicious, but the true philosophy of *Jihad* is laudable.

Karen Armstrong has expounded the full meaning and implication of *Jihad* in the Author's Note to her book *Holy War,* from which we quote:

> The word literally means "struggle" and is used in the Koran (the sacred book of Islam) usually as a verb: Muslims are urged "to struggle mightily in the way of God." The ideas of struggle and achievement are crucial in Islam and the word *Jihad* has always retained this connotation. But most frequently the "struggle" referred to is the war [Prophet] Mohammed was forced to wage against the non-Muslim Arabs of Arabia. Later, by extension, it came to mean "holy war" and in that sense is discussed in the *Sharia* (Islamic Law) in the century after [Prophet] Mohammed's death.

The implication of *Jihad* in the war that Prophet Mohammed (may peace be upon him) was forced to wage is that the Muslims had to struggle in defence of their survival and so they were empowered by the Almighty to engage in a defensive war. *Jihad* as a defensive war is described as *Jihad Fisabilillah,* meaning that it is in the cause of God to defend the believers. Thus *Jihad* is automatically governed by the rules of Allah, which make it a war of self-defence and also prescribe stringent rules of engagement. Massacring civilians or aggression against unarmed non-combatants is strictly forbidden. Therefore Muslims have to be extremely careful not to hurt the civilian population when engaged in a *Jihad.* If for any reason, intentional or unintentional, Muslims happen to kill civilians in wars, then they must beg forgiveness of the relatives and pay appropriate compensation for their error of judgment. There is no such thing in Islam as the "collateral damage" that the West routinely uses to cover up its war crimes of killing civilians indiscriminately as we are witnessing in the wars in Afghanistan and Iraq. Hence, while *Jihad* gives Muslims a right to defensive wars, it does not empower them to wage offensive wars and in any case not against the civilian populations. Besides the example of the Prophet, Sultan Saladin was another example of following the Islamic rules of engagement when he did not take any revenge or massacre civilians or destroy their homes and properties during his victory over the Crusaders.

However, the extension of the meaning of *Jihad* to include holy war (aggressive wars) was made much later, after the Prophet's death. As was alluded to above, it was the new institution of mullahism, which controlled interpretation of the Islamic laws, the *Sharia,* that gave *Jihad* the meaning of holy war consistent with the Christian practice, which the mullahs had emulated in Spain. They were also attracted to the abuses that were practised by the papacy and tempted to adopt them in their own positions. Ironically, the Christian counterparts that the mullahs had been emulating in Spain have subsequently been ousted in the West by the Reformation and the reaction to the religious wars that it sparked. But the antiquated mullahs, who emulated them, are still surviving in the Muslim world and will until Muslims also undertake social and political reforms in their societies to transform their mentality with education and enlightenment according to the true spirit of Islam. Unless the Muslim societies inculcate the revolutionary and dynamic spirit of Islam, they will have little or no chance of moving forward in a rapidly changing world. A change does not mean giving up religious values; it means moving forward in the light of new human progress without compromising with the principles of the religion. This is a challenge that the Islamic world faces today and the mullahs will have to adjust their positions to let human progress take its course. They need to give up nitpicking, hair-splitting or arguing for the sake of argument. They need to focus on the fundamental good of the society and leave divisive arguments which may not be at all relevant either to the times or even to the spirit of Islam. In spite of the criticism it must be recognised that the mullahs do have an important role to play in Muslim societies. The community needs them, because their enlightened knowledge of the spirit of the religion can provide leadership in building strong moral character in the Muslim societies based on social, educational and economic progress. There is a great deal for the mullahs to learn and improve, as their constructive function can help uplift the Muslim societies from current stagnation and backwardness.

Thus we can see how the Muslims have been made to decline from a Golden Age to a period of recession and stagnation by the regressive mentality of the power-hungry and misguided mullahs. We can also see how the notion of *Jihad* was corrupted by the same mullahs to use this phenomenon to further the cause of their power. In the context of today, many disgruntled Muslims have become victims of mullahism, and are now waging senseless "holy wars" in the name of Islam, believing that this is the only avenue now left open to them to counteract Jewish and Christian aggression. *Jihad* in the sense of aggressive war or even violence and acts of terrorism has now been taken up by many disgruntled Muslims as a way to seek redress for their grievances. Undoubtedly the Muslims have a struggle on their hands owing to the exploitation and excesses of the West. What Muslims need is to build internal strengths within their own countries to be able to withstand the Western onslaught. They cannot resolve their difficulties with the West while their own societies and rulers are gripped in dishonesty, disloyalty and exploitation of their populations and national resources to enrich their personal coffers. Building unity, discipline, loyalty, patriotism, education and social and economic strengths, coupled with adequate defence capability, is essential to strengthen the Islamic world so that Muslims can negotiate their positions and resolve their disputes with the West on the strength of their economic and moral power.

Regrettably, very little or no attention is paid by either the mullahs or even the intellectuals in the Islamic world to undertaking internal building of their countries. Usually they become subservient to the rulers, who are generally disloyal to their people and dishonest to the countries. Their immoral character and corrupt régimes are the main causes of Muslim downfall. Anyone who rises to power from either the religious platform or the military ranks or the tribal dynasties of despotic rulers is so grotesquely dishonest and disloyal that he can sacrifice the well-being of his nation to satiate his own greedy appetite. Such corrupt persons are easy prey for the outside superpowers, who patronise them and increase their ability to plunder their own nations even more so long as they also serve the political and economic interests of their patrons. Once the leaders, whether religious or otherwise, have sold their souls to outsider powers, they become callous to their own people and nations and push them into the deep pits of despair. Sadly, this is where most Muslim nations are today. They are trying to come out of these deep pits and taking desperate measures to make their voices heard by their own despotic rulers and their foreign patrons. In doing so they resort to acts of violence, which then become counterproductive. These are internal problems of the Islamic world that Muslims would need to resolve not only by social and political reforms but also by intellectual revolutions that would transform their stagnation and take them back to the dynamism of Islam to improve their living conditions. Using violence as a means to achieve this goal is not only un-Islamic but also counterproductive. Dubbing wars of aggression or terrorism as *Jihad* or interpreting offensive wars as holy is also un-Islamic, because there is no holiness in wars according to the teachings of the Quran and the Prophet.

Historically *Jihad* as a call for war had been dormant in Islamic history for a long period of time. The last time it was used extensively was in the twelfth century by Saladin. Since then it had mostly lain dormant until it was revived in the 1980s by the Americans, specifically by the former National Security adviser Zbigniew Brzezinski, who roused Muslims by calling them to serve as Mujahideen who would fight the Communists in Afghanistan in the name of Islam.

Although the Muslims had a prior exposure to using violence through the British during the onslaught of Lawrence of Arabia, the modern-day use of *Jihad* as a configuration of acts of violence and terrorism was introduced by the American and British secret services during the Afghan war. The Americans and the British are responsible for creating the current generation of Muslim terrorists, which the Western media wrongly dub Islamic terrorists instead of calling them American-trained terrorists. Islam played no part in breeding terrorism or shaping terrorists, but the West unloads its own guilt for breeding terrorism and creating terrorists by assigning the blame to Islam and calling these American-trained terrorists Islamic terrorists. As we have already stated, Osama bin Laden is not a product of Islam; rather he is entirely a product of American training.

So we can see how mullahism was born in Islam and how this misguided institution exploits Islam for its own purposes. The Americans did not spare to exploit Islam either for their own ends in Afghanistan and groomed and nurtured violence and terrorism in the same radical Muslims who have now turned against them. Lightly speaking, this is a situation of Frankenstein's monster devouring his own inventor.

Anyhow, since offensive war has now become part of the faith of radical Muslims, they are taking desperate and extreme actions to make their points, even by blowing up their own bodies. Dying for the cause of religion has opened a new dimension for the disgruntled Muslims. As was said earlier, faith is a powerful phenomenon, but if corrupted, it can become a most destructive force. It is also pertinent to say in the context of today that Muslim populations have suffered economic and social suppression by external and internal forces for a prolonged period of time during the last thousand years, which has brought them to the bottom of the pit of despair. They see no relief from it except to explode their bodies in anger, which is what is going on currently.

What transpires from this study is that all three religions deriving from Prophet Abraham are totally off the mark as far as faith is concerned. Unfortunately, it is also clear that since war has now become part of religion, these three branches of Prophet Abraham's religion are unlikely to give it up. Hence the weakest of the three will continue to suffer, and peace on earth will remain as elusive as it has ever been. Peace in all parts of the world, especially the Muslim world, has now become a myth owing to the faulty beliefs in war perpetuated by misguided Western political and religious leaders.

The only prospect of improvement is if the rest of humanity embarks on a joint struggle to persuade the warring progeny of Prophet Abraham, urging them to cease their acts of violence and terrorism against each other, because it also affects the peace of the whole world. They must be convinced that it is now time to take a step back and re-examine or test their faiths by applying logic and reason to see whether what they are doing is truly following the message of their founding forefather Prophet Abraham.

The Jews need to learn about God all over again, asking whether He could really take someone else's land and property and give to them. Is God not too just to act that way? They need to understand that God would not be God if He went about waging wars against humans, usurping the rights and properties of some to appease others or made massacring humans part of His scheme, finding a homeland for His chosen ones by making others homeless. These are too human characteristics to be attributed to God. The earliest Jews must have got it all wrong and implicated God to satiate their lust for territory. They used His name to annihilate the natives, tear down their cities and destroy their lands and livelihoods in one of history's most atrocious acts of land-grabbing. The Jews are not natives of Palestine. They came as refugees first from Iraq and then from Egypt. God assigned this land to them as a place of peaceful co-existence and virtuous living but they have turned it into a battleground to impose their false exclusive title. Their rebellion against the wishes of God has earned them a troublesome present and a bleak future in addition to a miserable past.

But, again, how the Jews in modern times conduct themselves and behave depends on how they have been taught their faith. It seems that there are two strains running all through the Old Testament. In one, the Jews are God's chosen people in that He has revealed Himself to them and given them His laws and by keeping them they are to be "a light", an example, to all other nations. In the other, they are his chosen instruments for punishing and subjugating the nations that will not worship Him or obey His laws. The Zionists of modern Israel have emphasised the second strain rather than the first.

Being chosen also means carrying a greater burden of responsibility towards other people and nations. However, when we look at Jewish conduct with respect to other people's rights and privileges, we do not see them at all as being any kind of example or light for the rest of humanity. How they had treated the Canaanites and how they are now treating the Palestinians has no semblance to any divine light or example.

Their interpretation that God is a God of war and vengeance is not only contrary to God's own attributes but also the first sign that perhaps the Jews have departed from the chosen path of light. Their belief that God ordered them to kill and drive out the Canaanites as punishment for their idolatry, gross immorality and horrible customs such as sacrificing their children indicates that perhaps the Jews have lost their chosen status and are now behaving just like any other unscrupulous human beings. From the point of view of rationality, one would ask if this is the light that God wanted to shed on the rest of humanity or if this is the example that God wanted to show for dealing with human transgression and immorality. From all other scriptural teachings one gets the message that God's way of addressing human failings is by reforms and education but here we see that the chosen ones have been using brutality and inflicting inhumanity supposedly to deal with human failings. Where are God's mercy, forgiveness, reforms and refinement?

The inconsistency between Jewish actions and God's attributes goes to show that Jewish conduct is not of a chosen calibre. It is so grossly brutal and oppressive that it fits only savages who could not be the chosen people of God.

This is something for the Jews to ponder upon. They need to broaden their spiritual horizon to grasp the scheme of God in the light of spiritual knowledge and intellectual enlightenment and understand that seizing territory could not be His command, whereas virtuous living, peace, harmony and compassion for one's fellow human beings are the objectives of the Divinity. The Jews must also recognise that the true God is not the god of war or vengeance. He is the Creator, Benevolent, Merciful, Loving and Caring for all humanity and would never authorise anyone to invade the land and homes of others and usurp their rights and properties to make a home of their own. Taking refuge in other lands, and also spreading the true word of God by peaceful means and co-existing with other humans, is the essence of virtuous living. Self-defence is one thing but coming in as refugees or invading someone else's land for the love of territory and to dispossess them from their homes is quite another that cannot be justified on moral or spiritual grounds.

At best the Promised Land is meant to be a safe haven for the Jews, but at no time were they given right to expel or exterminate its other inhabitants. God did not give any exclusivity to the Jews, nor did the Balfour Declaration, which, while favouring a Jewish national home, stipulated that it would be "without prejudice to the civil and religious rights of the non-Jewish people already living there." The Jews need to remember this. There is no gain in being dogmatic about a faith that is demonstrably faulty. As intelligent people the Jews must re-evaluate their integral self, who they are, what has happened to them throughout human history, and whether the fault lies completely outside or is at all likely to be partly within. It is crucial for the sake of peace for the Jewish community to take an inward look at their faith and their perception of God. How and when did God become the god of war, and who propagated this notion and for what motives and on what spiritual grounds? More importantly, the Jews must ask themselves whether a tract of land is more precious or sacred than human life. Is it conscionable to kill children, women and old people just to press a territorial claim? Is not the whole idea of killing humans to grab land silly? There is ample room for the Jews to adjust and reform their attitude and philosophy on life instead of blaming the rest of the world for their miserable past and dismissing all criticism of their atrocious and brutal present as anti-Semitism.

It is important for Jews to keep in mind the historical facts about their return to the Promised Land: how there were disagreements with Moses and how demands were made by the children of Israel and how Joshua came up with the idea of "assault" to force the Hebrew entry into Canaan and then wage a war to kill and drive out the natives. They must also remember that God's image as a God of war and vengeance appeared for the first time in the books of Exodus, Numbers and Deuteronomy when these books were in Joshua's custody at a time when he was contemplating an assault on Canaan. These were enough grounds for him to tamper with the scripture and make God the focal point of war to rouse the Hebrew tribes to make a forceful entry into Canaan.

For the Jews to believe that God ordered them to kill and drive out the Canaanites as punishment is to say that God has no other means to reform or educate His misguided creatures. Where is God's great attribute of refinement through education? These immoral customs were also in practice during the lifetime of Prophet Abraham but he never received any such orders from God to kill the transgressors. The Arabs also used to sacrifice their newborn baby girls but Prophet Mohammed never killed the wrongdoers. He uprooted this immoral customs by education and reforms. On the one hand the Jews claim that owing to their chosen status they are light and example to the rest of humanity, and on the other hand they show no mercy to guide the wrongdoers except to kill them or drive them out as an order from God. This is a very cruel way of being a light or example for the misguided. These inconsistencies in the Torah make the credibility of this scripture an issue. Knowing the military background of Joshua, it is reasonable to surmise that he might have had a hand in creating these inconsistencies to serve his military goals. This is indeed a tough situation for the Jews to resolve but if they apply logic and use reason, then they may be able to see the flawed fundamentals of their belief and try to rectify them by changing their own stance on war and territorial claims.

It is also necessary to ask the Christians to take a step back for the sake of peace. While their right to believe in Jesus Christ however they may wish is acknowledged and respected, their thrust to convert adherents of other faiths, as part of a divine mandate, is a cause of concern for the outside world. Spreading the message of Jesus has been defined as a "duty" at the end of Matthew's gospel, but the religious zealots appear to have stretched the meaning of this duty to using force as a commandment of God. Thus, they try to accomplish the mandate even by transforming the religion and culture of other civilisations by coercive means. The current Evangelical spiritual invasion of Muslim Afghanistan and Iraq are two cases in point where force has been used to subdue the Muslim populations, which is then followed by an army of thousands of Evangelicals to impose their religious beliefs on Muslims.

It may not be mainstream Christian belief, but many Christians do appear to believe that only Christians will enter paradise and the rest of humanity will be destined to hellfire. This is a strong motive for them to convert others. In ancient times war was used as a coercive service to humanity to save them from hellfire, but in modern times economic and material inducements are used to entice the poverty-stricken populations in the Third World, which is both repugnant and immoral. Such encroachments have been a cause of resentment and hatred, which over-zealous Christians indulge in without realising that such acts in the name of God cannot be moral or even spiritual pursuits.

Intolerance of other faiths and unwillingness to co-exist with them are major sources of tension caused by the over-zealous Christians. The consequence is that such Christians like to overpower other faiths and nations, which leads them to become imperialists and usurpers not only of other people's faith but also of their wealth and resources. The Christian church seldom intervenes to stop imperial domination or exploitation of other nations' wealth and resources and all the atrocities that are associated with it. For one thing, the imperialists do not listen to the church, and for another, the church may also see an opportunity of converting the subjects of imperial domination. Thus the concept of live and let live is missing from the faith of such Christians, which creates many difficulties that they tend to ignore by assuming their own conduct to be a commandment of God. Hence Christians in general, and the Western Christians in particular, have been spreading wars, injustices and exploitation around the world, because they view people of other faiths with disapproval. What the Christians need to realise is that mere profession of a particular faith will not entitle a person to paradise. Jesus himself clearly and repeatedly taught that only doers of good and believers in God and accountability on the Day of Judgement will be entitled to His mercy on that day: "Not everyone that saith unto me 'Lord, Lord' shall enter into the kingdom of heaven, but he that doeth the will of my Father which is in heaven" (Matthew 7.21). Thus, it can be seen from Christians' own religious point of view that there is no shortcut to paradise except good deeds. Forcible conversion of others is no substitute.

The other contentious part of Christianity is that some at least of the Evangelical denomination look for the Last Days and try to prepare ground to hasten their arrival so they may then claim paradise. This is why those Christians are going to the Middle Eastern countries, levelling ground, growing trees and encouraging Jewish territorial expansion, to facilitate Christ's Second Coming so that he may return to earth to redeem their sins and lead them into paradise. Is it plausible that God would hand out paradise merely on belief and not on deeds or accountability? Or is it conceivable that God would hold back His operation waiting for such Christians to plant trees and clear the way in Palestine so that He could then send His son back to earth to wind up the world? God is Almighty; He has power to do whatever He may please or wish. He does not depend on anyone to pave the way or prepare ground for His actions. The Evangelicals' notions about resettling the Jews, Jesus' Second Coming and preparations for the Last Days of earth make God look like a feeble entity depending on human help in carrying out His Godly functions. Most modern Christians are in fact highly suspicious of the notion that restoring all the Jews to the Holy Land, or even converting large numbers of heathen, will hasten the coming of God's kingdom. They point out that the Bible nowhere says specifically that all Jews must return to the Promised Land before God's kingdom comes, and Jesus himself said that even he did not know when it would come, but only his Father (Matt. 24.36, Mk 13.32).

It is crucial at this point in time to remind Christians in general and the American Evangelicals in particular that the notion of the return of the Jews as a precondition for Jesus' Second Coming cannot be considered a revealed truth, in view of the above quotation from Matthew. As was discussed earlier, the Biblical prophecy was conveniently misinterpreted at the time of Reformation as a political move to escape Christian hostility during the early sixteenth century. It is highly deplorable that Evangelicals are now abusing American military power to try to fulfil an interpretation of the Bible that is demonstrably false and invading and killing thousands of humans in the Islamic world on such shaky grounds. The chaos that

Evangelicals have created now raises a challenge for the mainstream Christians to clarify the factual position of the Bible, so that Christians in general may adjust their faith accordingly. They must also point out to the American Evangelicals that their policy of warmongering in the East to resettle Jews in Palestine is completely un-Christian and based on false conviction. Unless a bold step is taken by the mainstream Christians to clear up the misconception, peace in the Middle East will not come to pass and our world will continue to suffer the perils of death and destruction.

Lastly, the faith of an influential minority of Christians in the Last Emperor, who is supposed to come to conquer the East and transform all other faiths, cultures and civilisations, is a worrisome thought for people of other faiths. It may give opportunity to any military-minded and powerful Christian ruler who may conveniently assume that he is the Last Emperor and abuse the power at his disposal to crush other faiths and civilisations, believing that to be a command from God.

This appears to be the belief of at least many of the American Evangelicals. The notion of conquering the East is totally militaristic, which is why many such Christians are military-minded people, and are now waging wars, crushing other civilisations and bent upon transforming other cultures and religions. They are now using modern concepts such as freedom, democracy and modernity and even fabricating false pretexts to attack the Islamic world to transform its religious heritage and achieve the ancient goal of spreading Christianity in an innovative way. The methods of "high-pressure salesmanship" that American Evangelicals employ seem like a licence to encroach on and attack other religions even on false pretexts. Such compulsion in promoting religion cannot be God's commandment, for it is against His gift to humanity of freedom of choice.

This is an issue that the mainstream Christians must take up to resolve the conflicting views within Christianity regarding resettlement of Jews in Palestine as a precondition for Christ's return, so that the unholy war that some Christians are waging in the Middle East to hasten Christ's Second Coming may be brought to an end.

It is not that the leaders and spokesmen of the mainstream churches have not tried to do this in the past, it is the problem that Evangelicals, who believe in the literal truth of the whole Bible, regard anyone who disagrees with their reading of it as an apostate and just do not listen to such people. The breaking away sects such as the Puritans and the Evangelicals, who emanate from the ancient European Crusaders, have intimate affinity with the Jews and belligerently holding on to the Jewish interpretation of the bible to help Jews not only to acquire a national homeland, but also to take over the entire perceived biblical Israel by driving out the Arabs. Their belligerency has the air of the old crusading spirit, which is why the United States does not make an objective contribution in resolving the dispute between the Arabs and Israelis.

Thus it can be seen that the cause of our world's greatest dispute is embedded in the misconstrued Evangelicals' belief in Jews' return to Israel as a precondition of Christ's Second Coming, which is based largely on false conviction. It is now time that this falsehood be expunged from the Christian belief system so our world may see a new order of peaceful co-existence of various cultures and religions in Palestine.

If the mainstream clergy are unable to take up this task once again, then perhaps a Black preacher, such as Reverend Jessie Jackson, should embrace the mission of streamlining the Christian belief system by initiating a religious debate in the United States to expunge the divisive false beliefs that have crept into Christianity and thereby created unstable conditions in the Middle East, and contributed to war against the Islamic world. As a result the entire world is now plunged into a state of violence and counterviolence. This is a challenge for the Black clergy and Reverend Jessie Jackson could play a leading role to extinguish this flame by changing the course of misguided Evangelical Christian faith.

God is perhaps the most misused or abused phenomenon in human society. His name is used to slaughter humanity, and false commandments are attributed to Him to incite believers to murder fellow human beings, destroy their homes and take away their livelihoods. Humans, who make Him appear as a helpless entity that can be manipulated by powerful men whether to control religion or the state, have exploited God's posture in silence. These manipulators portray themselves as men of God and then use His name to carry out their own ungodly ventures. They hide their horrible deeds behind the image of God and mesmerise the unsuspecting citizenry by chanting supposed words of God that have no moral or spiritual foundation.

The best contemporary example of this tendency is America's faith-based president, George W. Bush. He has been described as a devoted religious man and a born-again Christian and hailed in the United States as a true man of God. But on looking into his actions, we find that thousands of innocent civilians, including women and children, have been killed by his orders in both Afghanistan and Iraq. He set out to avenge the deaths of three thousand Americans and succeeded in killing tens of thousands of Muslims, mostly innocents. Indiscriminate bombing of civilian communities by his army has disrupted the lives of millions of civilians. How killing innocent Muslims could console the grieving American families of 9/11 tragedy is difficult to comprehend. He ordered the invention of the MOAB, the Mother of All Bombs, to kill humanity on a massive scale. He also authorised dropping cluster bombs in Afghanistan and Iraq, which remain long on the ground and kill civilian citizenry in stages, mostly children playing in open fields. He also ordered carpet-bombing from the air that killed humanity indiscriminately. Currently he has authorised the development of small-scale nuclear bombs and claims that the United States has the right to use them to perpetuate its world domination. Newer smart bombs are also being developed to go several layers deep into the ground to kill the enemy. This so-called man of God is demonstrating immense destructive powers and by threatening to use nuclear bombs he is now entering the bounds of insanity. If one takes account of all his warring actions and adds up the number of civilians that he has killed in both Afghanistan and Iraq, then one would see there is nothing godly about this president's conduct. What, in fact, would be seen is gross exploitation of God by killing helpless humanity based on the notion that the hand of a just God is guiding his actions. He has shown no restraint and made no efforts to explore peaceful alternatives to remedy a contentious situation. All President Bush did was wage war in the old Jewish and Christian religious tradition of warmongering. Where is the godly conduct to justify the title of man of God?

God has nothing to do with wars. He has forbidden wars in His last message. How could He kill His own creature that He described as His finest miracle? God gives life; He does not waste life by waging wars. Death is a cycle that comes in its own designated natural turn, without God's hastening it by wars. If we study God's attributes with an open mind, then we shall see that creating life is His greatest miracle. He has given His finest creature the prerogative of independent thinking and freedom of choice. He has also equipped humankind with knowledge, intelligence and wisdom so that they may make good choices in living a virtuous, peaceful and happy life on earth. Whenever He felt the need to admonish humanity or guide the human race, He did not opt outright to kill them; rather He sent reformers and messengers as prophets to educate them and correct their mistakes. He is forgiving and merciful and willing to pardon the misdeeds of humans if they will repent, or else take account of their deeds on the Day of Judgement. His way of dealing with obnoxious situations is through education and reforms. He does not wage wars or authorise aggression in His name. The human mind not only makes wrong choices but also abuses God's name to carry out its sinister enterprises of aggression and warmongering. All the destruction that we read about or see in our present times is the result of human misadventures, injustice and oppression. It is the result of human failing caused by faulty faiths, as can be seen in the conduct of the Jewish and Christian civilisations that have been waging offensive wars throughout their history.

God in His infinite wisdom has opted mostly to remain silent in human affairs, but humans take undue advantage of His silence and attribute their own misdeeds to Him as though they were His commands. Men of God have been killing God's masterpiece creature, innocent humanity, in God's own name. Thanks to His posture of remaining silent, God has become the most abused phenomenon in human society.

It is now expedient, in the interest of world peace, for both Jews and Christians to take a step back, rethink their religious outlook and make amends in their faiths to expunge the notion of offensive war from their religious beliefs. They urgently need to embrace the *Divine Rules* of God for establishing peace on earth. The benefits of the philosophy of live and let live far exceed those of seizing a tract of land or striving for an unsure paradise by practising faulty faiths and imposing religious dogmas on other people or transforming their civilisations.

In view of the present precarious international situation, it is necessary for all peace-loving citizens of this world, regardless of their religious affiliations, to come forward to defend peace. The Americans, by virtue of their power, are at the centre of world affairs. Therefore they are urged to ask not what the world can do for them or how it can serve their economic interests, but what they can do to serve the world's interest in peace and establish the rule of justice and fairness for all mankind.

How could the Americans make a difference to change the course of events? It is not easy to answer this question, because American society is so complicated and driven by so many self-centred groups and vested interests, which control power and money and are able to hamper the right course for America. Nevertheless this question must be taken up, to elucidate what steps the American citizenry would need to take to alter the perilous course that their government is currently following.

The American people need to tell the perpetrators of war, the fearmongers, the proponents of faulty faiths, and the framers of imbalanced policy that our New World does not need them. Western Warriors such as the Bush-Blair crowd have no place in our world of peace and harmony. No matter what they may say about terrorism or how they may twist facts or fabricate pretexts, their posture in aggressive war remains deplorable. If there is a threatening situation, then other ways must be explored to overcome the difficulty. These warmongers or proponents of violence in the name of freedom must be rejected firmly and discarded from the system of power, so that they may no longer control the destiny of our world.

The religious fundamentalists or *resurging crusaders* from the southern United States, who are using modern terminology to accomplish their ancient abominable goals, must also be warned that their religious bigotry has caused more than enough bloodshed in human society. The new generation of the New World is no longer prepared to tolerate them, no matter how patriotic, pious and religious they may pretend to be. Their bigotry cannot be allowed to interfere with other peoples' faiths or revive the old hatred of crusading.

The American citizenry needs to take back charge of its country and assert its right to change the obnoxious direction that its leadership has now taken.

So far the warmongers have been able to thrive by spreading falsehood through propaganda, malicious hysteria and fear-mongering, which impair the judgement of the unsuspecting citizenry and hamper proper evaluation of their covert intentions.

The current trend of war must give way to peace. It can happen only if the new generation takes charge and warns the older generation of warmongers that they now know how the Palestine problem came into being, how the Communists created the Chechen saga and how the British officials created the Kashmir tragedy and left behind this dispute. More importantly, the younger generation now also knows that Al-Qaeda would not have come to life in 1996, and bin Laden would not even be known today, had President Bush Senior been sensitive and respectful to Muslims' religious sentiments and not established U.S. military bases on Islam's sacred soil. His arrogant and aggressive policy of military takeover of Islam's sacred land was the single greatest reason that gave birth to Al-Qaeda and brought bin Laden to the forefront. The peace-loving citizens of the New World are now better informed about the cause and effect and poised to take a new direction to establish a just and fair New World Order of peaceful co-existence between diverse religions and civilisations. The people of the United States have a responsibility and a moral obligation to extricate their country from warmongering and lead the way to a new beginning and a new era of peaceful co-existence.

This is an important message not only for Western civilisation in general but also for the American public, who cannot be reminded enough that their leadership has not only clouded their judgement but has also created so many problems around the globe. In just a few years their faith-based president has managed to undermine institutions that our civilisation took over a thousand years to build. Jurisprudence was a shining milestone of our civilisation's achievement, but President George W. Bush has made it irrelevant by contravening its precepts and undermining its application in such matters as a judicial inquiry into the September 11 tragedy to determine whodunit and how it happened.

Human rights were another outstanding milestone that our civilisation had reached after hard work and many centuries of toil. By his atrocious treatment of the Muslim captives in Guantanamo Bay, and now by proposing to give his government the "right" to torture captives to extort "useful information", President Bush shows that he is bent upon undermining all the fundamentals of a civilised society. It was not easy for our world to establish universal human rights, including the rights of captives, nor was it easy to save humanity from organised torture by tyrant rulers or atrocious states. There are now many conventions and many resolutions with legal force that forbid torturing of captives. Torture is outlawed in virtually the whole Western world except the United States. Regrettably, the Bush administration still practises it in the Guantanamo Bay prison camp in defiance of international law. Keeping suspects in prison is one thing but torturing them and denying them all human rights is quite another. The U.S. now also wants to restore its right to torture new captives who may be apprehended on unfounded or frivolous charges. The American citizenry need to understand that their president is taking the world back to the Dark Ages that our civilisation left behind so many centuries ago.

Since the last paragraph was written, the revelation of the abuse of the Iraqi prisoners through photographs has shocked and stunned the whole world. The American citizenry is dazed in disbelief that members of their army could be so inhumane and cruel to the captives. The blame is being put on a few criminally-minded soldiers, but that is not true, in view of the above statement that the Bush administration had established its right to torture captives to extract "useful information" in spite of bans by so many conventions and international laws. The six or so soldiers could not have decided on their own to do what they did unless it had come to them as a military order through the chain of command. It is not an isolated case of limited abuse of prisoners. It is a widespread problem, as is indicated by a recent military report, which leads us to believe that it is the result of a policy rather than individual acts of brutality. The policy of torturing the captives started from the very top of the administration, which is now evading responsibility and making a few soldiers and a woman general the scapegoats for the consequences of a policy that was initiated at the highest level. Defence Secretary Donald Rumsfeld has testified that there are more photographs and videotapes showing even more horrific images of abuse of prisoners. It has been said that when released they would show raping of women detainees, brutal beatings of prisoners and even murder of captives. These are far more inflammatory than the first photographs. Regrettably, they would start retaliation by Muslim extremists, who might brutalise American captives even more savagely, as indeed and most regrettably has already happened in the case of young Nick Berg.

What has happened to America and its values? Everyone, including the president, is scrambling to defend America and pleading, especially to the Islamic world, that what a few soldiers had done does not represent America and what it stands for. But when Muslims were in a similar situation and pleaded that the actions of Osama bin Laden did not represent Islam, President Bush ignored their pleas, and attacked the whole of Afghanistan and killed tens of thousands of civilians in the name of war on terrorism. He has targeted whole Islamic countries and Muslim nations for the misdeeds of a few radical Muslims. Now President Bush is pleading with the Muslim world not to view America adversely as a nation because of the wrongdoings of a few soldiers. Why did he not give this advice to himself before attacking the Muslim countries and killing tens of thousands of innocent civilians and destroying their homes and livelihoods? He devastated Iraq just because of one person, Saddam Hussein, but he does not want others to have a dim view of the American nation just because of a few bad soldiers. How ironic!

Is President Bush on the track of peace, or is he off the track in the old warring Christian tradition, and waging wars of aggression to annihilate the "infidels" (the Muslims)? This should be food for thought for the Americans, because they need to grapple with this question to form an exact opinion about their own president and the direction that his administration has taken.

The United States constitution does not empower the president to invade other countries for the purpose of altering the religious and cultural heritage of the fallen states and transforming their religious civilisation. Nor does international law contain any provision that would give any superpower the right to transform the cultural or social heritage of other civilisations. Neither did the United Nations give permission to President Bush to invade Iraq for any reason whatsoever.

President Bush's policies in Iraq are illegal from the standpoint of international law and in conflict with the American tradition and value of freedom of choice. His denial to the people of Iraq of their right to frame their own constitution and to choose their own system of government contravenes international law, which upholds the right of all nations to choose their own form of government. He is also in conflict with the principle of self-determination that President Woodrow Wilson proclaimed in his Fourteen Points and fought for at the Paris Conference after the First World War. The essence of democracy lies in freedom of choice, because it prescribes that a nation should be governed by the people, for the people and of the people, without outside interference. Thus dictation or imposition by an occupying power is both unlawful and undemocratic and contrary to the American values of self-determination as put forward by President Woodrow Wilson in 1919. Imposition of a foreign doctrine, the convictions of Communism, used to be the way of the Soviet Union. The American people and the rest of the free world fought hard to end Communist usurpation of the rights of other nations by dictatorial imposition. Denying the people of Iraq their right to choose their own form of government is now akin to the Communist practice of usurping the rights of other nations. Regrettably, President Bush is now practising the very core of this Communist ideology by imposing a foreign doctrine upon the Islamic world in contravention of the Woodrow Wilson doctrine.

The dictatorial and undemocratic policies of President Bush should be enough provocation to move the constitutionalists and all law-abiding and freedom-loving citizens of the United States to challenge his Iraqi policies in the Supreme Court of the United States. His policies are aimed at

interfering with the Iraqis' religious culture (Islamic civilisation) and denying them their universal human rights, contrary to the constitution and
international law as well as America's own values. These are compelling
constitutional and legal challenges that ought to be taken up to restrain
President Bush from the path of clashing with other religious civilisations
and making religion the target of attack instead of battling against brutal
dictators like Saddam Hussein.

The argument that President Bush was forced to invade Iraq to oust
Saddam Hussein because he posed a threat to the United States is baseless,
since the president has failed to demonstrate how Saddam Hussein posed a
threat to America. Giving the president the benefit of the doubt, at best he
may have been justified in ousting a dictator, but having done that, he has
no constitutional or legal authority to stay on in Iraq to alter the Islamic
character of its civilisation. The allied occupation of Germany and Japan is
an example of how occupation was wound up soon after the war. If he
continues to impose his will upon the people of Iraq, then he will create a
legally contentious situation. From where has President Bush derived legal
or constitutional authority to transform Islamic civilisation in Iraq? Or is his
policy in Iraq the result of another "call"? If a supernatural call is his only
authority, then the American people need to be wary that their president is
bent upon using their economic and military power to serve his bigoted
beliefs to alter the religious heritage of other nations. His actions are not
only a breach of the American constitution and law but they are also a threat
to world peace. It is now a test for the American constitutional lawyers, how
they will deal with a runaway administration that is tearing down America's
own constitution and its laws and values of self-determination.

There is much for the Americans to learn from history and do for the
sake of establishing a harmonious co-existence where all nations could live
and let others live by the precepts of true freedom, justice, fairness and
recognition of the rights of all to practise their own traditions. These are
the essential ingredients that would constitute peace on earth.

The Americans have a particular responsibility to know both sides of the
story. They have a daunting task to sift the truth from the pile of media
falsehood and the debris of the hysteria and fear-mongering that their own
government has generated. Indeed, they have much to learn and do for the
sake of ushering peace in our world. The ball of peace is, indeed, in
America's court, and the world will be watching with expectation and hope
to see if America will play the ball.

Our world needs a new generation of leaders that would be free of not
only religious bigotry but also the disease of imperialism that has been
devouring and eroding the human fraternity for so long. War as a route to
peace, as promoted by the Judeo-Christian or right-wing leadership in the
United States, is unacceptable.

Learning from the example of the peace treaty that King Richard I and Sultan Saladin concluded in 1192 A.D. would be a refreshing development in resolving the tension that currently prevails between the West and Islam. The first lesson is that King Richard realised that warring against a religious civilisation was of no avail, since no people like to give up their religion. Hence such a war would have no end. Therefore, he decided to trade war for peace, to open a new chapter in human relations based on mutual respect for each other's rights and a peaceful co-existence. Both he and Sultan Saladin jointly called for recognition of the rights of all parties and respect for the sovereignty of the Muslims over Palestine and the rights of the Christians and Jews to practise their religion in freedom under Muslim ascendancy. King Richard proposed no dictatorial conditions and opted for co-existence as a way to overcome the contentious issues. He was so inspired by the idea of co-existence that he even proposed a marriage between his sister and Saladin's brother, Adil, so the East would have had a Muslim king and a Christian queen. It was a most remarkable display of desire for unity and co-existence of diverse religions and civilisations. Though neither the Christians nor the Muslims approved his suggestion, King Richard nevertheless did demonstrate how peaceful co-existence was more important than the religious or racial divide. Sultan Saladin was already a man of clemency, compassion and peace. He did not let this opportunity slip away and showed the world how compromise and truce could be made for the sake of peace. Hence both King Richard and Sultan Saladin concluded a landmark treaty of peace in 1192 A.D. and established an outstanding milestone in the realm of co-existence. Our world is again in need of two heroes of their kind. The West needs to produce another King Richard. When a true proponent of peace emerges from the Western horizon, the Islamic *Ummah* may also put forward a new Sultan Saladin to complete the equation of peace. Modern peace advocates from both sides may look to this example for inspiration.

While both the Jews and the Christians are battling with their faulty faiths and grappling with their misguided leaders, the rest of the world can help them to go through this painful re-evaluation and arduous journey from war to peace. The international intelligentsia has a responsibility to speak about these matters, debate them openly, and engage in a defining discourse to develop a consensus that would encourage especially the Jews to emerge from a gloomy and perilous past. A combined and concerted effort by the international community can usher in a new era, in which our world would become peaceful and living on this beautiful planet would become happy and joyous. While we may keep looking for new planets, it is vitally important first to learn how to live peacefully on the planet earth that we already have. Otherwise, what will the outer worlds' aliens, if any, say when we arrive in their world with our baggage of war, cruelty, inhumanity and injustice? What good is finding a new planet, when we are bent upon ruining the one that we already have?

Sitting on the sidelines, watching the atrocious scenes of bloodshed and feeling depressed over the news coming from Baghdad will not help anyone. It is now time to take steps to stop all the nonsense that has gripped our world. Aliens will not come to solve human problems. Humans will have to do it themselves. They have all the talents and capabilities to accomplish the task; what they lack is the will to act jointly and judiciously with mutual compassion. This has to change now.

The Muslims also need to re-examine their faith and make adjustment to bring it in line with the teachings of their Prophet and the dictates of the Quran. The problem with the Muslims is that they have been suppressed so much and for so long that now they are nearly giving up the spirit of their own religion and wandering around in vacuum in a confused state of mind. Hence they have acquired many corrupt habits and a passive attitude of waiting for good things to happen instead of making them happen peacefully for the good of their society. They have a mistaken kind of trust in God that somehow He will change their condition, but God has said clearly in the Quran that He will not change condition of a people unless they change it themselves.

The difficulties in the way of changing the Muslims have been compounded by many factors, especially by lack of their own actions and distrust in the Western civilisation. Thus approaching the Muslim mind has become increasingly difficult, because it feels and views, owing to bitter past experience, that perhaps the West has a trick up its sleeve and is looking for an opportunity to undermine the polity of Islam and crush Islamic civilisation. The current climate of hostility and the unsettling rhetoric of President Bush have completely eroded their trust.

Continuous suppression of their aspirations, especially during the twentieth century and now peaking in the twenty-first, has been the main cause of tension between the West and Islamic civilisation. Muslims resent how the British and the French, after scuttling the Ottomans, undermined the caliphate and how the Muslims are not allowed to re-establishing an Islamic form of government. The fiasco of how the army ignored the results of Algerian elections, to prevent an Islamic Party from coming to power through a democratic process, is a bitter source of frustration not only among the Algerians but also throughout the Muslim world.

The Western aversion for an Islamic state or caliphate system of government is based primarily on religious prejudice. The West may also be apprehensive that Islamic civilisation might again overtake it, as it once did during the Islamic Golden Age many centuries ago. Thus it has now become a competition, which the West is trying to win by applying military force against Islam since it cannot match it in the realm of applying morality and spirituality to the social and governmental systems.

The Islamic Golden Age has demonstrated how successful the Islamic principles of governance and Islam's enlightened approach to education and progress have been in bringing about extraordinary success for the Muslims. Their Islamic philosophy of life based on justice, equality and compassion for the human fraternity, coupled with the Muslim practice of morality and spirituality in worldly affairs, took them to great heights. Unable to match these qualities, the West finds it convenient to oppose the Islamic form of government and undermine the polity of Islam, as the only way to win the competition. The Muslims, on the other hand, are equally determined to regain their system of caliphate, so that they may again be on their way to success by once again embracing its progressive economic and education policies.

Much blood has already been shed in this strife. It is time for Western civilisation to realise that suppressing the polity of Islam is of no avail since the Muslims will resist it passionately. It is not worth the hassle. It is therefore in everybody's interest that instead of battling with the Islamic civilisation, the West should learn to live with it in harmony. If there are concerns for "our raw materials", then there is other more reasonable and commercially honest way to go about securing it. War is not a conscionable way, and it is clearly not businesslike to accomplish a commercial transaction by force. The world would see that as an act of plundering and looting, which surely is not the objective of the new Western generation.

If we are all to co-exist, others need to know more about the Islamic form of government, the caliphate system, to appreciate its merits and benefits. Resisting the aspirations of the Muslims will not lead to harmonious co-existence.

To dismiss the idea of an Islamic form of government out of hand by citing the examples of the Saudi régime and the last Taliban rule is unfair and shows a lack of due diligence. The misdeeds of the Saudi government cannot be blamed on Islam, since it did not come into being on precepts of Islam or the traditions of the first four caliphs. The way was paved for it by the British intervention in Hijaz; conceptually the Saudis adopted imperialism from the British. The despotic behaviour of the Saudi kings and the exploitation of the national wealth by the royal house demonstrate its imperialistic character, which is totally un-Islamic. As for the last Taliban régime, the force of passion and emotion drove the Talibans to revive the Islamic form of government, but they badly lacked adequate education and knowledge of the true Islamic spirit. Hence they could only produce an illiterate and backward régime that had no similarity with a true Islamic state. The real model to judge an Islamic state is the one that Caliph Omar bin Khattab introduced and practised, which is what the Muslims ardently strive for. It has the entire infrastructure of a just society based on compassion and moral and spiritual values. It also has a mechanism for obtaining consensus of opinion by consultation, which could be brought up to date by introducing an electoral process. There are many good points in this system to commend its application in the Islamic states. Doubtless it would not be easy to revive Caliph Omar's model or an Islamic state given the many constraints, mostly external, but it is worth a try and Muslims deserve a chance at it. They should be allowed to discover their own destiny and develop their own systems to fulfil their religious and cultural aspirations. This system has proved its merits, as it has once been so successful. If the Muslims were left alone by the West, then they could at least try to regain success in governing their societies and have a chance to overhaul their system by bringing it up to speed with modern progress. On the one hand it would inspire Muslims to improve their conditions using their own system to take their place of honour in the community of nations, and on the other hand it would take out heat or Muslim resentment, which would be conducive to peace and highly desirable all round.

Historically speaking, the Western world recognised the inherent qualities of the Islamic form of government and its services in uplifting the quality of life for the Muslims. While the West was still struggling in the Dark Ages, Islam was making progress by leaps and bounds in the social, economic and scientific fields. This is why so many Christian scholars came to Islamic Spain to learn about the Muslim progress and copy their books so they could take this knowledge to Western and Northern Europe and initiate their own progress on the basis of Islamic achievements. Muslims were ahead in many branches of science and engineering including medicine, mathematics, chemistry, physics, astronomy, architecture, shipping and shipbuilding and navigation. The West copied the Islamic books, some of which are still preserved in the Oxford University libraries, and emulated Muslim knowledge to build the base for its own scientific progress that we so happily see in the West. The West took full advantage of Islamic achievements, its principles and innovations. History gives undeniable proofs of how profusely the West benefited from the Islamic progress.

Islam was also ahead in introducing an organised system of jurisprudence and social welfare. Since the Islamic system of jurisprudence was the only functioning model free from imperialism and discrimination, the West must have derived its modern system of jurisprudence from the Islamic state and adopted its concept of an independent judge and proof of the case by evidence and witnesses. Omar bin Khattab's innovative social-welfare system was also copied by the West and then refined over time to suit the growing needs of the Western citizenry. If one looks back in history, then one can see how much the West has learned and acquired from Islam.

It is unreasonable, rather reprehensible, that the Western powers should now be suppressing the rebirth of the very government system from which they benefited so much in the past. Muslims dearly want to re-establish the caliphate so they may rebuild their social and political infrastructure once again on its moral and spiritual principles, but they face opposition from the domineering West. It is ironic that the West now stonewalls the Islamic system after having once benefited from it so profusely. The caliphate system could not have been a bad system; otherwise the West would not have adopted so many of its achievements. Undoubtedly, there is room for improvement in it just as there is in any other system. But it does not follow that it should be disbanded or replaced by a foreign system, which may not be acceptable to the Muslims or appeal to their sense of a fair and just society based on the *Divine Rules*.

The essence of freedom of choice is that one should be able to embrace whatever system suits one best. If the Muslims want to live under their own system of government, then give them a chance, so they may practise it and improve it through their own experience. By stonewalling Muslim aspirations or imposing a foreign system of governance on them, the West is creating a perpetual rift that will lead to an enduring conflict. Besides, what authority, moral or otherwise, has the West got to dictate what other religions or civilisations can or cannot do? To say that the Western system is the best is to show lack of appreciation for others. There are many flaws in the Western democratic system that make it unsuitable for the Muslims, who want to found their system on moral and spiritual values of their own religion. Besides lacking moral and spiritual basis, the Western system is too materialistic and suits mostly the rich and the powerful. This is not to say that it is not serving the needs of the Western societies, but it may not be suitable for the Muslims. To oppose the Islamic system on the grounds that it is a threat to others is not factual, as is evidenced in Spain, Palestine and other Islamic countries where Jews, Christians and other minorities have enjoyed full religious and social and economic freedom. The Islamic system has been successful once and it has the potential to be successful again if the West would lift its iron hand and let the Muslims shape their own social and political system.

This is not to say that some Muslim rulers in subsequent dynasties have not resorted to excesses over the minorities or their own populations. That only goes to show how all societies, including the Muslims, are prone to human failings. In spite of these failings it cannot be argued that the whole system be discarded because of the misdeeds of a few rulers in any given system.

Since the Islamic system of governance and Islam itself have been made the object of opposition, a sort of antagonist, it is relevant to explain for the new generation in the West more about this alleged adversary, what really it is and what it truly stands for. So, at the risk of digression, a short study of Islam is in order to enlighten a Western audience about Islam's religious and social principles and its philosophy of governance.

What is Islam and What does it stand for?

Islam is not just a religion; rather it is a complete way of life, which is called the *Deen*. Spiritually Islam originates from Prophet Abraham's monotheistic belief in One God. Hence, in spite of some fundamental differences, there are many similarities between Islam, Judaism and Christianity. Basically the Islamic doctrine is based on two parts: one relating to God, known as *Haqooq-ul-Allah,* and the other pertaining to human relations or interaction within the human community, known as the *Haqooq-ul-Ibad.* It was revealed to Prophet Mohammed (may peace be upon him) and its message has since been preserved in the Glorious Quran. A direct way of learning about Islam is to study both parts of its doctrine.

Haqooq-ul-Allah is the spiritual core and mandatory part of the faith. It declares that God is one. He is the Supreme Being and has no partners, nor is He begotten or has begotten anyone. He is Beneficent and Merciful, Loving and Caring for the goodness of humankind. He is Sovereign, Omniscient, and Creator of the entire universe, Sustainer and Provider for all beings, and has appointed the Day of Judgment, when all creatures will return to Him for accountability. Briefly, this is the permanent spiritual element of the Islamic faith that cannot be altered or changed in any way.

Haqooq-ul-Ibad outlines the principles of human relationships or interaction within human society to achieve the goal of virtuous living. Its applications may change with the times to accommodate the progress of the human mind, but its principles of righteous interaction will remain in force forever. Muslims are required to comply fully with the precepts of both *Haqooq-ul-Allah* and *Haqooq-ul-Ibad,* which is a complete submission of one's life to God in both spiritual and worldly affairs.

Accordingly, Prophet Mohammed (may peace be upon him) delivered this new message so that human beings might fully comprehend their commitment to Allah as well as recognise and realise their responsibilities to each other in human society. Islam shows that a balanced practice of the two sides of religion leads to a virtuous and blissful life in this world and hereafter.

Since daily living must conform to submission to God, Islam has laid down elaborate codes or values of life, comprising the *Divine Rules,* to make *Haqooq-ul-Ibad* easier for the human race. Hence the Islamic values cover every aspect of human interaction. For example, they prescribe the rights of all human beings as well as animals. Parental rights, the rights of children and their obligations to their parents, the rights of individuals in society and with each other, the rights of women, the aged, the sick, widows and the poor are fully secured in Islam. Even the rights of captives and criminals are recognised.

Recognition o these rights leads Islam to place a great deal of social responsibility on its believers. Every Muslim must pay an annual levy of at least 2.5% on his total accumulated wealth as *Zakat* to support the social infrastructure and care for the poor, the sick, widows and orphans. The *Zakat* funds may also be used to build schools, hospitals and other social amenities, so that every citizen can better his or her life. Muslims are strictly warned against usurping the rights of others, whether in property, monetary or personal matters. Lying, stealing, cheating, dishonesty, betrayal of trust and hypocrisy are strictly forbidden in Islam. Accordingly Islam has instituted a system of jurisprudence to deal with infractions to protect individuals from the excess of others. The Islamic laws apply equally and justly to everyone, without regard to the position or power of individuals. Islam views character reformation and moral correction seriously, and proposes maximum deployment of resources to improve believers' standards of morality and character. Wilful and repeating offenders are sternly dealt with, but not without first being offered help to refrain from their crimes or overcome their bad habits with assistance from the state.

Building morality is very important in Islam. Hence Muslims are not allowed to consume alcohol, use drugs or indulge in gambling, because these habits undermine the human character. Ramadan is a unique Islamic practice of fasting for a month to fortify believers' willpower and spirituality to help them build a strong character. Prayers five times a day have been enjoined as a spiritual duty. The benefit of prayer is manifold. It protects individuals from the temptation to mischief that surrounds them due to freedom of choice. It also keeps a person in contact with the Creator, to draw strength to live righteously. Therefore the main theme of these prayers is to praise God for His greatness, as well as to seek His help in avoiding wrongdoing and following the straight path. A Muslim repeats at least seventeen times daily in his prayers that he worships only Allah and seeks His help to find the righteous path that He showed to his noble men and not the path of those who have strayed. A Muslim does not ask for riches or material gains as the main theme of his prayer, which should be entirely dedicated to seeking help in finding the righteous path. Material needs and other wishes may be sought at the end of the prayer.

Islam deals with social matters, especially sexuality, in a very special way. While it recognises the natural force of sex, it does not permit illicit sexual relations, nor does it tolerate lewdness and promiscuity. Islam strictly forbids exploitation of women for sex or commercialisation. Islam rejects celibacy and promotes the institution of marriage (between man and woman) as a means of procreation as well as gratification of the natural urges. It has permitted polygamy, to take into account the shortage of men created by wars in older times as well as to accommodate local customs. It was expedient to allow men to have up to four wives, to ensure that every Muslim woman would have a husband and a home, instead of leaving large numbers of them unmarried and exposed to exploitation in prostitution. However, the religion warns Muslim men that having several wives will place a huge burden of responsibility on their shoulders, because they must treat them all fairly and justly. Thus Muslims are reminded that one wife is better for a cohesive family, and accordingly, the majority of Muslim men have only one wife.

Islam favours development of trade and commerce and promotes economic prosperity among its followers. The Prophet himself was a merchant and showed his followers that development of sound economies was essential to attain prosperity and earthly happiness. Islam recognises that supporting and sustaining the social infrastructure of education, health care, the welfare system and other services to improve the living-conditions of believers requires ample monetary resources. Therefore it promotes economic growth through development of trade and commerce and industry and encourages its followers to engage in commercial activities to pave the way for social and economic prosperity. Islam sees no harm in enjoying material comforts, so long as honest means are used to acquire them and provided the affluent lifestyle is maintained without arrogance or affront to decency.

There is much more to learn about Islam. Prophet Mohammed lived as a role model for twenty-three years, to show the Islamic ways and demonstrate the spirit of the Islamic lifestyle. A comprehensive study of the Prophet's conduct in life will illustrate the principles for building a just, fair and moral society according to the Commands of Allah.

Looking at Islam as an alternative for establishing peace on earth, a wider view is necessary to grasp its position on war, its approach to settling contentious issues with antagonists and its relationship with other faiths. Also, a review of its system of governance will demonstrate whether Islam is a viable alternative for establishing peace and harmony in human society.

Beginning the review with Islam's approach to war, it can be seen that it is different from those of Judaism and Christianity. As has already been stated, Islam strongly forbids offensive wars, including wars for greed or love of territory, whether sacred or not. From the Islamic perspective God is not a God of war but the Lord of peace, mercy, forgiveness, love and care for all his creatures. Therefore, offensive wars and killing any living being without a just cause is a sin in Islam – so much so that Muslims are not allowed even to slaughter animals without reciting the covenant of permission, which Allah has mercifully approved to provide food for mankind. This is why Muslims can only eat meat from animals that have been slaughtered in accordance with Allah's permission (*halal*). Creation of life is a miracle of God, and Islam does not allow its followers to destroy this miracle unnecessarily. Unlike the Torah and the Bible, the Quran categorically outlaws wars of aggression and wanton killing for settling claims of one sort or another. Life, including the life of animals, is precious in the Islamic faith. But that has not stopped some Muslim sovereigns from waging wars, sometimes war of aggression, because, in spite of the teachings of religion, human failings still dominate individual Muslims just as they do in other cultures.

According to the Quranic dictates there are only two grounds for resorting to war. Allama Iqbal, an Islamic scholar, has summarised these conditions and said:

In the first place, in self-defence and, in the second place for the establishment of conditions of universal peace or to enforce the regime of law in human society. When believers in the Islamic faith are tyrannized over and driven out of their homes, they are permitted to appeal to arms. War may also be waged for collective security. In no other circumstances is war obligatory. War simply for the love of land or appeasement of land-hunger is unlawful in Islam.

The régime of law includes abiding by treaties and honouring the terms of settlement to respect the rights of all signatories to an agreement. Violation of treaties is seriously viewed by Islam and gives rise to grounds for war. It would be considered a war in the defence of law in human society. Pre-emptive wars for ensuring collective security from threatening states or empires are also treated in Islam as self-defence. Wars for imperial domination, political or economic exploitation, or for the purpose of imposing a particular social or religious doctrine or even taking revenge of any sort, are not permitted in Islam.

Islam does not regard any land or territory as worthy or sacred enough to kill humanity for its sake. According to Islamic teaching the whole world is the land of Allah, and wherever a Muslim may reside, that piece of land becomes his cherished homeland. Love of land is meaningless for Muslims, since land is only a transitory path in life's ultimate journey. Love of virtue and a life full of righteousness is the goal of Islam, for it will help believers to complete their journey of living a happy and joyous life successfully and also attain a blissful life hereafter. So when it comes to territory, true Muslims would not wage wars or kill humanity; they would rather migrate to avoid suppression and retaliation, as did their Prophet when he migrated from Mecca to Medina.

The Prophet was very emphatic about showing peaceful ways to his followers. Migration was one way, and covenants of peace and treaties and pacts with antagonists were another way of accomplishing peace and harmony. When conditions became unbearable for Muslims in Mecca, the Prophet preferred to migrate to Medina. One of the first things he did there was to enter into a peace treaty with the three Jewish tribes of Yatrib, assuring them of peace as well as obtaining assurance from them of peaceful conditions for the Muslims within their territories. This was a remarkable beginning of peaceful co-existence by Islam. It established the tradition of treaties to ensure peace. Subsequently, through the Treaty of Hudaybiyya, the Prophet of Islam also demonstrated how the principle of give and take could be applied to overcome tedious and contentious issues. The Prophet promoted co-existence with other faiths by way of treaties and pacts.

Prophet Mohammed (may peace be upon him) lived strictly by the Commands of Allah. Later, when he returned to Mecca to reclaim Muslims' right to perform religious rites in this holy city, he could have waged war to end the tyranny against his people, but instead he chose peace and made the landmark Treaty of Hudaybiyya to negotiate terms with his opponents that would also allow Muslims their right to perform the *Hajj* in Mecca. Even though the terms were not entirely favourable, as Omar bin Khattab and other companions of the Prophet complained, the Prophet chose peaceful means to settle the differences and accepted even unfavourable terms to set a milestone in peaceful settlement of explosive situations. Though the Muslims had enough military power to wage war over Mecca, they preferred negotiations to end the conflict. While recognising the rights of others, the Muslims also obtained recognition of their own rights.

This is a historic example of give and take. The Islamic doctrine of compromise as adopted in the treaty of Hudaybiyya is a beacon showing humanity the way to avoid bloodshed and wars. It also showed that no territory could be more sacred than the sacredness of human life. Mecca had been a sacred land and supremely important for Muslims from the very inception of Islam, but the Muslims did not wage religious war for its sake. They made a peace treaty and went back to take their turn for pilgrimage the next year, according to the terms of this agreement. However, the Quraish violated this treaty in later years, which forced the Muslims to appeal to arms to enforce law in human society. Even when the Muslims were forced to resort to war, the Prophet forbade wanton killing, revenge or pillage of any sort. When the war was over, everything was settled humanely and peacefully. Amnesty was granted to all opponents, and protection was assured even to non-believers. As was quoted in an earlier chapter, the best example to illustrate Islamic teachings about humane treatment of adversaries is found in the instructions that Prophet Mohammed gave to Zaid, his freedman, when he sent him to Syria to undertake a war for collective security against the threatening Christians: "He told them to fight in the cause of God bravely but humanely. They must not molest priests, monks and nuns or the weak and helpless people who were unable to fight. There must be no massacre of civilians nor should they cut down a single tree or pull down any buildings. This was very different from the wars of Joshua (as well as the Crusaders)" (quoted from Armstrong's book *Holy War*).

Islam began its journey by outlawing wars of aggression, but it also showed its opponents that in case of injustice, tyranny and violation of treaties, and for the purpose of collective security, Muslims could appeal to arms to defend their rights, as was revealed later in the Suras *Anfal* and *Tauba*. It may be emphasised that these two Suras do not incite Muslims to wage wars in any way except for defence as outlined by the Prophet. Even in case of war, stringent rules were established to avoid unnecessary destruction of life and property and inhumane treatment of the vanquished. Islam never fought wars against any religion, and there is no concept of war being holy in Islam. Islam's wars have been only against people, because people threatened the survival of Muslims, violated peace treaties and transgressed on their rights. All wars that Muslims fought had been defensive in one way or another. Even the few pre-emptive wars undertaken during the reign of Caliph Omar were primarily for the purpose of collective security and to fortify the defence of the Islamic state from the surrounding threatening empires.

Islam does not permit wars for the sake of spreading its religious message. It acknowledges other peoples' right to follow the customs of their own faith. God clearly commanded his Prophet to declare to the non-believers that Muslims do not believe in what they worship, just as they do not believe in what Muslims worship. They can choose to worship whomever they wish, just as the Muslims would worship whomever they believe in. Your way would be different than our way, but you could have your way and we would have our way. Words to this effect are narrated in one of the most beautiful *suras, Kafiroon,* as it lays a foundation for a tolerant and harmonious co-existence. Unlike the Torah, the Quran does not teach annihilation or extermination of non-believers or even forced conversion as some Christians demand as a means to salvation. Although the Bible nowhere commands forced conversion of unbelievers, leaders of various denominations of Christianity have been seen effectively demanding such conversions. The most notable example was the forced conversion of Muslims in Spain and Jews in Western Europe between the eleventh and fifteenth centuries, when they were given the choice either to covert or to accept death. This is another case of human failings, when individuals defy their scriptures and yet believe their conduct to be religious.

The Quran and the Prophet are very emphatic in stressing tolerance, which is truly the key to peace on earth. Who would go to paradise or who would be consigned to hellfire depends entirely upon the deeds that one has done in this world. Conversion to any religion or faith to avoid accountability or ensure entry to paradise without good deeds is totally rejected by

Islam. You could be a Muslim and yet go to hellfire if your deeds are not righteous. Similarly, in the eyes of Islam, you could be a Christian and if your deeds are not righteous, you may very well end up in hellfire. Good conduct on earth is the only assurance of receiving God's grace for entering paradise; otherwise there is no shortcut in simple redemption of sins, as some Christians believe.

The Quran teaches that all doers of good and believers in God (Allah) and the Day of Judgement and Accountability are entitled to a reward including paradise, even though they may not be Muslims per se. Islam emphasises righteous living and a basic faith in God and the Day of Judgement and Accountability as a means of attaining salvation or receiving His mercy on the Day of Judgement. Each individual is responsible for his or her deeds. Islam has no notions of compulsion, since everyone in Islam is responsible for his or her conduct or deeds. Once the message is announced, the task of following or not following is left up to the individual to make a free choice. Freedom of choice in religion is important in Islam. There is no requirement to convert others against their will. Its tolerance of other faiths is unmatched, and its desire to co-exist in a pluralist world is its best approach to peace on earth. Alas, human failings undermine religious teachings in all cultures and hamper tolerance of other faiths in establishing peaceful co-existence.

Besides opposing offensive wars, Islam also fervently advocates adherence to the *Divine Rules* of fraternity, equality in the eyes of law and application of universal justice in the social, economic and other spheres of life, which are essential in building harmonious societies. The first four Caliphs enacted these rules and were able to demonstrate the merits of Islamic governing principles, which took Islamic civilisation into its Golden Age of progress and prosperity.

Lastly, it can be said that corruption of democracy and politics has little chance of breeding in the Islamic system, given its complete openness and strict accountability as demonstrated by Caliph Omar bin Khattab. Allah is the Sovereign and the Caliph of an Islamic state is His vicegerent carrying out His rules and implementing His laws as laid down in the Quran. Therefore in a truly Islamic system the Caliph's ability to make his own laws or devise a system to abuse power is virtually nonexistent. Hence an Islamic head of state takes office on the premise of serving and not becoming a power-oriented ruler. So, of course, do the Christian rulers in truly Christian kingdoms. But when the rulers depart from the truly religious states, their oath does not always prevent them from abusing their power, just as many Muslim rulers have done in the course of their history.

A Caliph or head of state is only a trustee of the responsibilities entrusted to him by Allah to do good for mankind without corruption and personal gain. Therefore a Caliph's approach to running the government should be based on building spirituality and morality, improving the living conditions of the people, working for social and economic prosperity of the country and strengthening its defences to protect it from aggression and invasions. As long as Muslim heads of state followed this concept of governance, they were able to achieve outstanding success, which is known as Islam's Golden Age. Regrettably, over the course of time many Muslim rulers began decaying in spiritual and moral values and thus strayed from sound Islamic traditions and began devising their own obnoxious systems that brought about their downfall. In the modern times some Muslims are advocating adoption of the Western political system of governance. However, there are internal conflicts over doing so, which creates even more difficult situations. Thus currently the Muslims can neither keep their own system, nor fully adopt the Western system of governance. In the meantime many Muslim rulers have created a pernicious system under which kings, emirs and brutal dictators became oppressive rulers, contrary to Islamic tradition, which brought about the steep downfall that Muslims are currently experiencing all over the world. Islam had left the system of governance open to development, since the Prophet did not prescribe any form or limitations; apparently, the idea was to leave the system open to progress so that the followers could improve it according to the growing needs of their times. Muslims' neglect in developing their system according to the needs of the time and inability to move their modes forward produced the pernicious systems and un-Islamic practices that currently dominate the Islamic world. The institution of mullahism is also un-Islamic. Like the un-Islamic monarchs and dictators, the mullahs are also un-Islamic agents of power.

Notwithstanding the Muslim downfall, the true Islamic system of governance still holds the best hope for peace and prosperity for the Muslim world. The Islamic system of governance was taken away from the Muslims a very long time ago. It is still not available to them for several reasons, but mainly due to their own negligence. Their current deplorable plight on the international scene stems from their failure to maintain the system that would have shaped their lives and set the pace for their progress and prosperity. Having lost their system of governance, the Muslims became disoriented and disillusioned, which has made them stagnant as we see today. Their vulnerable position is now encouraging certain Christian rulers, especially the American Evangelicals, to overpower them militarily and transform them to a Western system based on Christian values in the name of modernity. However, the Muslims are resisting it, since they believe that the only way that could truly make progress is through their own way of life, which is why so many of them are struggling against and even confronting the West, to regain their own system of governance. It is crucial for the powerful Western nations to recognise the Muslims' aspirations and help them to rebuild their lives in their own way, so that they, too, may become progressive. The true Islamic way of governance has proved highly beneficial for the Muslims once before, and it may do so again if the Muslims are not hindered in readopting it. Islam is a dynamic and forward-moving way of life, so it will offer opportunities to the Muslims to modernise their way of life according to their own social and cultural needs. They do not need people like President Bush or Secretary Rumsfeld to move them forward by imposing a Western modernity that is flawed in many ways itself.

Islam has its own value system and all the ingredients or infrastructure of viable and successful statehood. It can be successful again based on its teaching of *Haqooq-ul-Ibad,* provided that internal and external forces do not thwart Muslim nationalists' efforts. Undoubtedly, the Islamic system would need reforms and modernisation, but that is no reason to discard it. Its principles teach tolerance, freedom of choice in the matter of religion and peaceful co-existence with other faiths, as explicitly enunciated in the *sura Kafiroon* and practised by many Muslim sovereigns. The fact that non-believer minorities have lived peacefully and prospered in Muslim states corroborates Islam's philosophy of co-existence. These and other attributes of Islam can be nurtured further by studying the life of the Prophet and emulating the period of Omar bin Khattab, while bringing their models up to speed with modern times.

Opposition by the West to Islam or Islamic governments is totally unnecessary and based on ignorance and prejudice. Undoubtedly, every system has its crudenesses, just as the Western system of democracy has its own problems. So the Islamic system may also have its share of crudeness, but there is also a mechanism in Islam known as *Ijtihaad,* meaning adjustment or refinement according to the needs of the times without transgressing from the spirit of the precepts. Muslims have the ability to make adjustments and refinement, provided the West gives up stonewalling the development of their systems and lets the Muslims establish their own Islamic way of life. Coercive opposition is causing greater problems than any crudeness in the Islamic system might pose. Initially, there would be difficulties, but given the chance, the Muslims would eventually overcome them. Besides, as has already been stated, what moral authority has the West got to dictate or impose its will on the Muslim world?

Islam still has much to offer the West in establishing peace on earth. As was noted above, it helped the West once with enlightenment in education and sciences to pull itself out of the Dark Ages. It can do as much again by helping to pull the world out of the pits of violence and terrorism by applying its moral and spiritual values to solve contentious disputes and establish a fair and just social order on the foundation of harmonious co-existence. Regrettably, the Western superpowers, having given up their true Christian character, have rendered themselves devoid of morality and spirituality. Hence the West has become blind not only to the merits of an Islamic form of government but also to the values and merits of a true Christian state.

This emptiness is evident from its day-to-day conduct on the international scene. Even the West's treatment of its own people is not always equitable. Thus our world has a dominant civilisation that has made astronomical economic and material progress but badly lacks the foundation of being a good human fraternity. As we said earlier, to be powerful is one thing, but to be a good human being is quite another. This simple logic is, however, sadly missing from the character of Western civilisation.

It is now time for the West to regain the morality and spirituality that are missing from its governing system, so that our world may have a better chance for peace. This can be accomplished by reverting back to the Christian values of the past or learning from Islam once again, as the European did many centuries ago. Whichever method it adopts, the West urgently needs to begin inculcating morality and spirituality in its governing system so it may conform to the *Divine Rules* of justice, fraternity and equality. If it chooses, the West can deputise its scholars and intelligentsia again to study the Islamic moral values and principles of tolerance, justice, respect for rights of others and fair and equitable treatment of people of all nations regardless of their caste, creed and colour. As in the past, Islam can help Western civilisation once again if the West will lean on it for enlightenment. How and when morality and spirituality can be brought back to guide the governance of human societies will depend on how the New Generation of our world views this need and accepts the challenge to change the bad with the good.

Resuming our earlier discussion, suppression of the Muslims' aspirations, coupled with exploitation of their natural resources and military occupation of their lands, has worsened the chances of turning the Muslims around. Now the trust between the West and the Islamic world is completely eroded, thanks to President Bush's invasion of Iraq.

Iraq could have been a beautiful feather in America's cap had President Bush been sincere and genuine in his intentions towards its people. Apart from the fiasco of falsehood regarding the WMD, President Bush also made strong statements about bringing liberty and freedom to the people of Iraq. Ostensibly, he said he was liberating the country from a dictatorship and giving the people of Iraq their right to freedom, but in practice he has refused to give the Iraqis freedom to choose their own form of government. Hence that has become another of his false declarations. Freedom from a dictatorship was a welcome move, but imposing another kind of dictatorship or even contemplating imposition of martial law is just as abhorrent as the previous one.

When America occupied Iraq it glorified freedom, and the people of

Iraq were excited, believing that the time had come at last for them to take charge of their own destiny. They expressed a desire to establish an Islamic state on a modern pattern of democracy and freedom, so that they could rebuild their lives on the pattern of their glorious past. However, by freedom the American leaders did not mean full freedom for Iraqis, but only a controlled freedom according to the will of the Bush administration. Hence Donald Rumsfeld was quick to denounce the Islamic form of government and reject the Iraqi aspirations outright. President Bush publicly concurred with him and rejected the idea of an Islamic system of governance in Iraq. Thus on the one hand President Bush was beating the drums of liberty and freedom for Iraq, and on the other hand and in the same breath he was denying freedom of choice to the Iraqis. The Iraqis were confused and began distrusting the United States. This was just the beginning of the tension between the liberators and the liberated.

The Iraqis began to think that the invasion of Iraq could not have come out of love for them; rather it appears to them to have sprung from hatred of Islamic culture and heritage, which is why the Bush administration is denying them the right to establish an Islamic form of government. Misgivings about President Bush's intentions are the reason why the Americans are failing in Iraq.

President Bush's dubious intentions began to show up when Ayatollah Hakim, a moderate Shiite cleric, returned from exile from Iran. He said no to Saddam Hussein, no to America and yes to Islam. He was emphatic about establishing a modern democratic Islamic state and assiduously began working for Shiite-Sunni unity, so that both factions could live peacefully within the framework of an Islamic state. Ayatollah Hakim produced a compromise formula that would have bridged the gap between President Bush's plans for democracy and the wishes of the people of Iraq. He proposed making the Islamic state modern by enshrining the Western tradition of democracy and freedom as an integral part of the constitution. He was aiming at accommodating the American demands for modernity and democracy as well as complying with the wishes of the Iraqi people. His approach soon became popular in all quarters of Iraq, and for the first time Shiite and Sunni factions were united and ready to work with Hakim's constitutional proposal. There were high hopes of success, but the Bush administration flatly rejected the proposal and sternly said no to Islam in any shape or form. This led to a serious impasse between the Iraqis and the military occupiers. While the Ayatollah was moderate and willing to negotiate mutually acceptable terms, the Bush administration was totally inflexible. The Ayatollah became disheartened, but he did not give up, owing to his very strong position within the Iraqi society. However, his popularity and strong appeal to the Iraqis became a problem for the Bush administration, because it saw no prospects of slackening in the Ayatollah's determination for an Islamic state. Mysteriously, the Ayatollah was killed in a car-bomb attack. So far there has been no formal inquiry or report from the civil administrator or the military authorities to throw light on who might have killed him and why. It reminds us of the Beirut car bomb in the 1980s, which was also aimed at killing a Shiite cleric. It was believed at the time and has since been widely thought to have been a CIA operation aimed at eliminating a threatening cleric. It would not be preposterous to suggest that the CIA might have re-enacted the Beirut car bomb to eliminate yet another uncontrollable cleric.

Ayatollah Hakim was the man who would have filled the leadership vacuum in Iraq and overcome the stalemate on Iraq's future. Sadly, President Bush was so averse to the idea of an Islamic government, even on modern footings, that he not only rejected the compromise formula of Ayatollah Hakim but also sat passively to watch his elimination from the Iraqi political scene. Hakim had become a hurdle in the way of diverting or transforming Iraq, owing to his popularity among the Sunnis despite his Shiite affiliation. His flamboyant leadership may have appeared as a formidable obstacle and a difficulty in containing the notion of the Islamic state. His departure from the political scene was perhaps the only way of thwarting his prominence in Iraqi politics. His demise has now created a void in Iraq that is impossible to fill. It also meant the beginning of tormented and precarious times, not only for the Iraqis but also for the Americans.

The people of Iraq had never trusted the Americans from the very beginning, but they had been willing to give them a chance. However, when President Bush's intentions began to become clear, it dawned on the Iraqis that he had not come to liberate them in the true sense of the term liberation; rather he seems to have invaded Iraq to impose his own perception of Christian values, or more exactly Evangelical values, in the guise of modernity and democracy, whereby he would transform the Islamic religious and cultural heritage of the Iraqis and undermine Islamic civilisation in Iraq. The Iraqis fail to discern any other reason for his coming to Iraq except an onslaught on their religious heritage. The spiritual invasion undertaken by his co-religionists, the American Evangelicals, who have descended upon Iraq in the thousands to convert Iraqis to Christianity, spilled the beans of President Bush's plans. The Iraqis now sense an ulterior motive in his policies, and feel that they may be out of the frying pan but they are now in the fire. This is how the Iraqis lost faith in the Americans, and troubles began spreading like wildfire, as the world is now witnessing.

President Bush's intentions in invading Iraq had been suspect right from the start. His reason for not handing over control to the United Nations can be explained by saying that he seems afraid that the international community will give the people of Iraq their right to choose whatever form of government they may wish. This would mean an Islamic form of government, which President Bush opposes intensely. Therefore, he wants to retain the control in his own hands, to ensure that the Islamic form of government is not instituted in any way. He would also like to keep American forces in Iraq for an indefinite period of time to stonewall the re-emergence of the polity of Islam. He mentioned in his speech of April 13, 2004 that the United States would enter into an agreement with a new government of Iraq, subservient to the United States, to allow the American army to stay in Iraq. Since he talked about other victories in the region, he may even be contemplating a leasing agreement with the Iraqis like the one at Guantanamo Bay, which would virtually make the American presence in Iraq as permanent as it has been in Cuba. All these premonitions cast serious doubts on the prospects for peace in Iraq.

Denial of the Iraqis' wishes and obstructing the notion of a democratic Islamic state became the flashpoint of hostilities between the Iraqis and the Americans. What might have been a beautiful feather in America's cap has now become an ugly blot on President Bush's Iraqi policy.

Currently Americans are confused and worried about the turn of events in Iraq. They blame the insurgents and other Islamic zealots for creating troubles in Iraq. What the Americans are unable to grasp is that the policies of their own president and the government of the United States are the root cause of all the troubles that they see in Iraq. They do not have to go far to look for the answers. Just look at President Bush's motives, and the answer will become clear. He attacked Iraq on false pretexts. He made a false promise of liberating the Iraqis and giving them their freedom but in fact denied them the freedom of choice. He opposes Iraqi aspirations for an Islamic state without even knowing what an Islamic state is all about and why it is important for the Muslims to live under this system. When the American policies are so acrimonious and cynical, how could there be peace in Iraq?

President Bush seems to be unaware of how much the West has learned and gained from Islam and how much Islam could still offer to the West. He does not seem to know that his co-religionists went to Spain to learn from Islamic achievements and copy the Muslims' books to acquire their knowledge. He does not seem to have a clue about how much the West owes to Islam as far as innovations and knowledge are concerned. Now he wants to obliterate the same civilisation that was once a benefactor of the West in so many ways. How ironic! Stonewalling the Iraqis from deriving benefit from a system that so profoundly benefited the West makes no sense. There is no moral or logical reason for blocking the wishes of the people of Iraq, unless President Bush and his administration are driven by an immense religious prejudice against the polity of Islam. What he appears to be doing against Islam is the same as what the crusaders did during the Middle Ages, and so

he is consciously sowing the seeds of hatred and bringing to life the old
religious rivalry that our world had left behind so many centuries ago.

It is worth noting that Iraq is renowned in history as the cradle of human
civilisation. It pioneered the development of civic principles to build civilised societies based on recognising the rights and needs of fellow humans
in an atmosphere of trust and mutual respect. Many trading institutions,
such as the letter of credit, are just a few examples of what emanated from
Iraq. Development and refinement in literature, philosophy and arts and
science also owe a great deal to Iraqi ingenuity. The people of Iraq are quite
capable and well enough educated to look after themselves and build their
own social and economic infrastructure. In all sincerity, while keeping in
mind the deference due to the high office of President of the United
States, we cannot avoid saying that the people of Iraq do not need an
intellectually lacking President Bush or his hawkish administration to tell
them how to sort out their internal difficulties. President Bush's intrusion
into Iraq's future or internal affairs is unwelcome and unwarranted. His
efforts to remove Saddam Hussein are appreciated, but now he must leave
Iraq to the Iraqis.

The Iraqis' difficulties lie not so much in their inability as in their
misfortune that foreign invaders have long been destroying their infrastructure and ruining their lives. First, the Mongols came to inflict their
savagery on the population and destroy the cradle of civilisation. Then for
several centuries the Ottoman Turks oppressed them, using the old technique of divide and conquer to set the Arabs against the Kurds and both
against the Yezedis and the Assyrian Christians. Then, many centuries later,
the British came with a dubious agenda. They severed Kuwait from Iraq to
weaken its territorial and political power. They also disrupted Iraq's civic
and political systems by implanting an outsider as king, a son of the Sharif
of Mecca, who had no experience or talent for leading Iraq into social and
economic progress. Thus monarchy was established in Iraq instead of
allowing an Islamic form of government. The Shiites mounted a massive
revolt to recover their freedom from the British, but their rebellion was
severely put down and they were slaughtered in droves. The British left
behind a legacy of imperial rule that ultimately paved the way for dictatorships and a brute like Saddam Hussein emerged to grip the nation. Now,
eighty-five years after the British intrusion, the Americans have appeared
on the scene to do their part in dehumanising the Iraqis, undermining
Islamic civilisation to fulfil their own religious ambitions and capture Iraqi
natural resources. The poor Iraqi population sees no end to the suffering
that foreign invaders have been causing it for so many centuries.

Everything now seems to go back to square one. It is now imperative that
these people of a great centre of civilisation should be left alone to find
their own way and discover their own destiny by applying their knowledge

and using their ingenuity in developing their own social and economic system. They do not need hypocritical world leaders like Bush and Blair meddling with their future. The ploys of Saddam Hussein's supposed threat to America and Iraq's supposed involvement in international terrorism have now outlived their usefulness and cannot excuse suppressing the people of Iraq any more.

The American public has to ask the question all over again: Why did President Bush invade Iraq? If he did it to enrich the people of Iraq with freedom, then why is he now standing in the way of their freedom of choice? Or did he go there to conquer the East, annihilate the evil people and eradicate the wicked civilisation of Islam? By probing the heart and soul of President Bush, the American public will be able to see his motives and finally take steps to free the Iraqis by ending the invasion and giving them true freedom of choice, leaving them to sort out their internal problems by themselves. Iraqis are educated people, quite able to discover their destiny and accomplish their goals of peace and happiness for themselves. All they need is to be left alone.

By frustrating the Iraqis' wishes President Bush has opened the way to a never-ending saga of tension between the West and Islam. If he resolves to station American troops permanently in Iraq, then the greatest victim of his imprudent policies will be peace. His fantasy that he can change the Muslim frame of mind by beating up on Islamic civilisation or spending America's tax dollars in the hundreds of billions, if not in trillions, to bring about a social and religious change is a dream that will quickly turn into a nightmare. Someone has to stand up and tell him "Mr President, you are dead wrong about Iraq or transforming the Islamic civilisation. Force can only change situations, but it could never change minds, nor could it ever win someone's heart." This is a simple fact of logic that President Bush has to get. And he simply hasn't got what it takes to change minds or win hearts; he must get that, too.

The American leadership has to learn that there are other ways, besides use of force, to appeal to the intellects of members of other religions and civilisations. Until he learns this, President Bush will continue to mar the political scene and peace of our world by continuing his failed strategy of waging war against Islam in the wake of the war on terrorism.

Thanks to the ambiguity created by President Bush, there is now no credible leader in the Western World who can appeal to the faculty of intellect of the Muslim World to bring about a change in their attitude. This is also the dilemma faced by Muslim moderates, who may wish to play a role in defusing the situation, but have only had hollow words without any substantive leverage.

If there is ever a chance of turning around the Muslims' frustration and anger, then only the Muslims themselves can do it with their own intellectual resources. However, before they can make a move, the West must first demonstrate meaningful goodwill towards the Muslims and change its posture of war into an extension of its hand in peace by showing appropriate sympathy to Muslim causes. That would require a dramatic change in American foreign policy, which President Bush may not be able to implement, given his offensive posture against the Islamic world. So he should be set aside to give America a chance to pursue a new policy of peace, which is the only way to get rid of the terrorism. Having said this, the big question becomes, Will the next man be any better? Whoever he is, he will need to grasp that war and an oppressive posture against the polity of Islam will only aggravate tension and result in more terrorism, such as we are currently witnessing in Iraq and elsewhere. America does not need just a change of face; it needs a fundamental transformation of its outlook on the world as a community of diverse faiths and civilisations that deserve to be treated justly and with respect.

On the bright side, if the American people can once establish an atmosphere of goodwill, then other things will start falling into place, and the Muslim intelligentsia could also come into full swing to convince and persuade the militants that the conflict is now over and the time for peace has arrived.

With enough goodwill on the part of all parties and plenty of will to succeed, several things may begin to happen simultaneously. The Jews will have to give up on their drive for territorial expansion. The Christians will have to discard wars as a means to peace. The Muslims will have to emerge from their state of stagnation by rallying around the real teachings of their Prophet and returning to practising *Jihad* in its true meaning of a dedicated peaceful struggle to improve the living conditions of their people. They must give up militancy and become constructive and productive, to contribute to building a peaceful and harmonious human society.

Each member of the Monotheist Community has a responsibility to change its view and discard faulty faith. Only then can they become ambassadors of Prophet Abraham and a model of peace for the rest of humanity to emulate. Without a change, they will only bring more disgrace on their creeds and tarnish the religion that their founding forefather, Prophet Abraham, brought for the goodness of humanity.

In addition to the Monotheist Community there are others, too, that need to change for the sake of peace. The Russians must give up their Communist mentality of suppressing the Chechens and restore sovereignty to these victims of repression. The Indians also need to realise that suppressing the Kashmiris is not going to work forever. The Hindus used to take pride in promoting themselves as the people of *shanti* (peace), and now is the time for them to demonstrate that they mean it by ending their military occupation of Kashmir and giving the Kashmiris their right to self-determination.

This may appear a simplistic approach or an idealistic or optimistic ambition. However, what the sceptics are missing is that there are already ripples of peace among the younger generation of the New World that may become a wave of change to make it happen and that new winds are slowly gathering under the wings of peace. A change is in the air, especially in Europe, that will bring a fresh breath of peaceful co-existence between civilisations based on religious tolerance, respect for the rights of others and justice and fairness for all. Peace is beautiful; it's worth a try.

10

Epilogue

You can be a Jew, you can be a Christian, you can be a Muslim and, indeed, you can profess whatever other faith you may wish or choose. What you cannot do is fail to be a good human being. What good is there in being religious when there is no goodwill and compassion for fellow humankind?

As has already been illustrated, the *Divine Rules* determine what is good or bad, which in turn is governed by the power of logic. Hence logic ultimately establishes justice and leads to truth, which is the core of spirituality. A logically founded spirituality can be very beneficial, whereas illogical faith can undermine the human character.

Logic is like a spring from which flows the stream of knowledge, intelligence and wisdom. The easiest definition is that logic is a process whereby the faculty of intellect sorts out fact from fiction and establishes prerogatives for the surrounding realities. Living by logic gratifies the soul and leads the practitioner to reforms and progress that ultimately bring peace, prosperity and happiness in human society. Equally, adhering to illogical faith leads to altercations, divisions, and even death and destruction by wars. The key to harmony in human society is therefore to live by logic, because everything is truthful if there is logic behind it. However, where logic is missing or ends or fails, truth also ends and fails. Then corruption or evil takes over human conduct and plays up in individual faiths that so profoundly mar the relationships between humankind.

Thus, logic is the only potent intellectual power that can save humankind from futile strife and endless conflicts or clashes. Regrettably, logic is also the most neglected factor in human conduct. Having neglected logic, faiths become vulnerable and get corrupted by illogical beliefs and notions that somehow manage to creep into the body of religions. Such subverted religions then become threatening because they create tension and wars between their diverse believers. What we are witnessing in our present-day world in the form of injustice, atrocities, oppression and bloodshed and all the resulting violence and terrorism, are the consequences of corrupted faiths. If we delve deeper into the woes of our world then we can see that corrupted faiths and subverted religions are at the centre of this deplorable state of affairs of our times.

Jews, Christians and Muslims are often dogmatic about their religious positions, but the grim reality is that they are the insinuators of our world's miserable plight owing to their faith-based perverse conduct. As a result humanity has suffered and continuing to suffer because these three warring dogmatists show no signs of improvement in their spurious beliefs, nor do they listen to neutral voices from within their own communities pleading for change of positions.

Since violence and terrorism and counter-terrorism are predominantly faith-based, it is necessary to probe religions to see where logic is missing in them and present a critique showing how subversion penetrated into their belief systems so that the practitioners of corrupted faiths might see the need to re-examine their positions. Optimistically such a critique might touch the imagination of the warring Jews, Christians and Muslims and stimulate changes in their positions.

Although religions have already been discussed in a previous chapter, there is still a need to revisit faiths to grasp how corrupt beliefs were allowed to penetrate into the scriptures and how meddling with the word of God has affected the believers, which in turn leads to their pernicious conduct causing so much misery and death to humankind.

Since the case of Judaism has already been covered sufficiently, it suffices here to say that lack of peace and restlessness of the Jewish people, even in the State of Israel, is a clear indication that something is fundamentally wrong with their beliefs. Theirs is a history's worst example of a subverted religion and corrupted faith that has not only harmed their neighbours and others but also the Jewish people themselves. It is now in their own interest to apply logic to reassess their beliefs and reform their positions.

The case of Christianity is even more complex as it impacts our world most profoundly owing to the economic and military power of Christians. It is the most powerful of the three branches of monotheism and perhaps the most worrisome, because, as a religion, it has so little of its own yet it is so overbearing due to its followers' indulgence in wars, imperial domination and exploitation of wealth and resources of others, especially the assailable Third World countries. Hence its followers were able to amass wealth and military power that has mostly caused hardship and inflicted injustice and misery on the weak and vulnerable cultures and civilisations that fell victims to its imperial domination. It is now imperative that we review Christianity thoroughly and examine the outside influences that penetrated into this religion and affected its character, which in turn are now affecting lives of the others, especially the Muslim world.

If we look back on the evolution of Christianity and study how this religion was developed, then we will realise that Christianity of today has very little or no bearing with the teachings or religion that Jesus of Nazareth, may peace be upon him, had inaugurated as prophet of God. A step-by-step study of the evolution of Christianity is very revealing.

In the scheme of God when any religion becomes flawed or ineffective to serve the causes of truth, justice and peace then God replaces it with a renewed message through a new messenger or prophet. This was the case with Judaism since the children of Israel had embraced offensive wars and changed the character of God by portraying Him as the God of war and vengeance. Their atrocious treatment of the Canaanites transgressed them from being a light and example. And so God superseded their corrupted faith with a new message of truth and peace through Jesus of Nazareth. The greatest infraction of the Jews was the adoption of Joshuan notion of war as part of God's commandment, which disturbed the equilibrium of peace and ruined chances of peaceful co-existence in the Promised Land. Despite efforts by King David and King Solomon to water down the Joshuan notion and expunge war from the mental frame of the Jewish people, the Jews remained entrenched in their subverted beliefs and carried on with the acts of brutality against fellow humans instead of becoming example of virtuous conduct and light so others might emulate them and turn to the righteous path as ordained by God. Undoubtedly the Jews also suffered in this process but they cannot absolve their part in creating misery for others as well as for themselves.

When the Jewish faith in war became incorrigible, God decided to replace their corrupted faith with a new message through a new prophet. This task was assigned to Jesus and his mandate was to start the Divine endeavour all over again to guide the children of Israel back to the path of truthfulness and submission to the *Divine Rules* of justice and peace so humans might attain peace, prosperity and happiness that God so dearly wishes for them. It necessarily meant that Jesus would discard the orthodox creed of Judaism and reform the Jews by expunging perversions that had crept into their Book. His challenge was to extricate the children of Israel from the notion of war, brutality, injustice and oppression against humanity so they might live as an example of good conduct and truly become light for humankind. Accordingly Jesus' ministry started by rejecting the notion of war and engaged in teaching a new message of pacifism, peace, compassion and austerity to help humans to succeed against hatred, oppression, injustice, poverty, disease and hunger. Essentially he discarded the old flawed convictions and replaced the bad with the good but the Jews did not accept this new prophet and rejected his mission of reformation. Like all the other new prophets, Jesus, too, faced brutal opposition as the Jews denounced him for starting a new creed by rejecting their own orthodox beliefs. He was called a heretic and subjected to harassments.

Consequently, Jesus became a target and subsequently fell victim to a brutal conspiracy that took his life prematurely causing interruption in his mission at a very initial stage of his ministry. In the short period of his ministry he nevertheless did demonstrate the truthfulness of his prophet-hood by the sincerity of his message, which was backed by miracles that he was able to perform with the help of God to convince the strayed Jews of his genuineness. As a result many Jews from his close surroundings accepted him as a new messenger of God and believed in his teachings as true revelations from God. His followers, though few in number at the time of his passing away, were fully convinced of divineness of his message and committed themselves to carry forward the torch of his mission. They gave him the title of Christ and called themselves Christians.

Hence the task of spreading Jesus' message was taken over by the few devout followers or disciples who did their very best to construct a religion based on Jesus' teachings. However, they also faced brutal opposition not only from the prevailing Jewish tribes but also encountered oppression from the domineering Romans. Their challenges were many but sparseness of Jesus' teachings was also a hurdle in shaping Christianity as a new supplanting religion. Therefore they were compelled by circumstances to adopt portions from the prevailing Orthodox Judaism to construct a pre-sentable and comprehensive religious doctrine that would contain the spiritual teachings of Jesus as well as incorporate principles of moral laws for building a righteous society. Hence they made a decision on their own to lean on the Torah to shore up the new religion and decided to melange much of the Old Testament with the several messages of Jesus and produce their own Book called the New Testament. Thus the Old Testament be-came part of the Christian faith. This was the first ideological strain put on the religion of Jesus because something had been incorporated into the scripture for which there was no authority either from God or Jesus. It was entirely a decision of the disciples who unwittingly negated the purpose of supplanting the flawed Jewish faith with a new doctrine in peace. Surpris-ingly the Jews did not object to their book being used by the so-called heretics or the followers of a creed that Jews called heresy.

When a new religion comes it essentially replaces or discards the old one, which Jesus was ordained to do. But the disciples unconsciously neutralised Jesus' endeavour by incorporating the old doctrine, which had apparently become flawed and prompted the need for a renewed spirituality. The very purpose of Jesus' advent was to replace the flawed beliefs of the old book and start building a new book of reformed precepts. The disciples, how-ever, nullified Jesus' mission by involuntarily clinging on to the flawed book. Consequently there was no material change in the outlook of the emerging Christians who, too, began following the tainted path of the Jews by believing in wars as commandment from God as described in the Torah.

Hence Christians' attitude and conduct developed in ways that were contrary to Jesus' teachings of pacifism and peace largely due to the inclusion of the Old Testament in Christian doctrine.

Unauthorised adoption of the Jewish creed also created confusion in other matters such as the Old Testament's prophesy about the coming of a Messiah. The Old Testament is truly the Book of the Jews and refers to the Jewish Messiah who would come to rescue the Jewish people and lead them to their ultimate salvation. The Jews do not know who this Messiah would be or when he will come as they are still waiting for his coming. However, when the Christians adopted the Old Testament, they interpreted the advent of Jesus Christ as the coming of the Messiah as predicted in the Old Testament and began preaching that this Messiah had come to reform and convert all Jews to the new faith of Christianity. The Jews, however, never believed in Jesus of Nazareth in any shape or form and categorically rejected him as a heretic. They were far from accepting Jesus as their Messiah as claimed by the Christians. The Christians, nevertheless, remained steadfast in their belief that Jesus was the Messiah as prophesied in the Old Testament. It may be noted that during the lifetime of Jesus he was asked to elucidate the coming of God's kingdom. His response was that he did not know when it would come, but only his Father (Matt. 24.36, Mk 13.32). Jesus thus clarified that establishment of God's kingdom prior to the coming of the Messiah did not depend on Jews' return to Palestine as he said that he himself did not know about it. Jesus' statement should be enough to convince the Christians that establishment of God's kingdom is not conditional upon Jews' return to Palestine.

Since Jesus had passed away the Christians inferred from the Old Testament's prophecy that it referred to Jesus' Second Coming to complete his mission of reforming the Jews and redeeming sins of all believers in Christ. However, the notion of Jesus being the Messiah for the reformation of the Jews is a bone of contention between the Jews and Christians because the Jews have not agreed to take Jesus as their Messiah. A further complication arose about the interpretation of the Messiah at the time of Reformation in the sixteenth century when the Bible was translated into English by Jewish scholars. While Jewish view of Christ remained unchanged, the interpreters merely said that the Messiah, as prophesied in the Old Testament, could not come until the kingdom of the Lord is established which will happen only when all Jews would return and resettle in Israel. As said earlier Jesus did not allude that Jews' return to Palestine was a condition of coming of God's kingdom. This is purely a Jewish point of view made in the perspective of Jewish Messiah.

In any case the Jewish interpretation can be explained in two ways. First the Jews were interpreting the prophecy only in the context of their own perspective and belief in the Old Testament and referred to the coming of their own Messiah when they would be resettled in Palestine and establish the kingdom of their own Lord. The Christians, however, appear to have misconstrued this interpretation first by believing that Jesus' Second Coming was actually the coming of the Messiah of the Old Testament and then that it would not happen until all Jews return to Palestine to establish Lord's kingdom. Hence Christians committed themselves and began facilitating the return of all Jews to Palestine to pave the way or hasten the Second Coming of Christ.

The second explanation of the interpretation is that confusion about Jesus' Second Coming and its link with Jews' return to Palestine might have been a political move to appease the Christians and spur change of their minds and attitude towards the Jews to mitigate their intense persecution. Since Christians' eagerness to relate the Jewish interpretation to Jesus' Second Coming was helping the Jewish cause, the Jewish scholars did not attempt to clarify the delicate difference between the Jewish Messiah and Christians' understanding of their interpretation. Consequently, Christians mistakenly took what was Jews' interpretation about their own Messiah, as a prediction of Jesus' Second Coming and construed that it was contingent upon Jews' return to Palestine. This misconception is the heart of the problem that Christians have been creating in the Middle East since the seventeenth century by scheming to clear out the Arabs and Muslims from the path of Jews' return to Palestine.

Seemingly there are two Messiahs; one belonging to the Jews according to their Book, and the other is the Christian inference that Jesus is the Messiah as predicted in the Old Testament. Consequently they have associated Jesus' Second Coming with the Jewish interpretation.

This is a fascinating confusion but also a most devastating one because the break away sects of Protestant Christians began using this interpretation to hasten the Second Coming of their Messiah by waging wars to displace the Palestinians and defeat the Muslim world's resistance to resettling the Jews in the full boundaries of Israel, which extend to Jordan, Syria and Lebanon. As a result of this confusion and misunderstanding, the domineering Christians have been using their economic and military power since the seventeenth century to find ways and means to return the Jews to Palestine so that Christ may come back to convert Jews and others and lead all new and old believers to paradise. They see Palestinians, Arabs and Muslims as obstacles in the way of fulfilling their religious convictions, and so they are waging war against the Islamic world on one pretext or the other to gratify their religious beliefs, which are in fact totally unfounded. This is the backdrop of current hostilities going on between the West and the Muslim radicals.

The impact of this erroneous belief was the greatest on Britain, which was actually the centre of Reformation where break away sects such as the

Nonconformists, Puritans, Baptists, Methodists, Presbyterians, Congregationalists and most of all the powerful Evangelicals were born. The belief
that Jesus' Second Coming was dependent upon Jews' return to Palestine
was widespread in Britain during the seventeenth century because the
monarchy and ruling religious and political leaders believed in it and were
able to propagate this conviction by use of state power. Consequently a law
was proclaimed that it was mandatory for every British citizen to attend
church regularly. Missing church services was a penal offence punishable by
a fine. Daily reading of the Bible was also a strict discipline in every British
household. Thus the British political leaders and the public were thoroughly indoctrinated in the Old Testament and familiar with the Jewish
traditions and their history owing to Old Testament's domination of the
New Testament. As a result the British felt a profoundly close affiliation and
compatibility with the Jews. They knew far more about the Jewish history
and tradition than their own and had developed intense emotional attachment with the Jews and the Holy Land. Such close affinity with Judaism
aroused a warm passion in the British consciousness to recreate the Holy
Land by resettling the Jews to gratify their religious conviction of seeing the
return of Jesus Christ to lead them to paradise.

As a result prominent British personalities from the days of Queen
Victoria were involved in the idea of creating a Jewish homeland. People
like Prime Minister Palmerston and Lord Ashley began taking practical
steps in this matter in the early nineteenth century. Although a serious
movement was already afoot in Britain during the early seventeenth century, it took the religious proponents of Britain over two hundred years to
come to the stage of actually doing something practical about fulfilling
their religious conviction of resettling the Jews. The religious zealots like
the Baptists, Methodists, Presbyterians, Evangelicals were controlling most
aspects of the British life including the government. Accordingly the ball
was set rolling by Prime Minister Palmerston in the 1840s and carried on by
many, including Disraeli, Gladstone and finally it landed in the court of
Prime Minister Lloyd George during his reign in 1916-22 to turn the
religious passion of the British people into a reality. Lloyd George was a
devout reader of the Old Testament, which swayed him overly on the side
of the Jews. He was also a passionate believer in the return of the Jews as a
means of hastening the Second Coming of Christ. As a result of official
leaning of the British government towards Judaism a strong breed of
Christian Zionists began emerging who used state power to fulfil their
religious convictions. In doing so they trampled over the rights of the
Palestinians and started a crusade against the Islamic world.

It is an irony that prior to the Reformation the British monarchs, religious and political leaders were filled with intense hatred of the Jews who
were brutally persecuted and expelled from most parts of Western Europe.

Britain was particularly cruel to the Jews as it expelled every Jewish man, woman and child and strictly blocked their re-entry into Britain. But all that changed after the Reformation as religious proponents, most political leaders, the prime ministers and a wide spectrum of public began believing that the Jews were actually a means and accessory to the fulfilment of their religious conviction about Jesus' Second Coming. And so their attitude changed.

This was not only a turning point in the history of the Jewish people but also for the people of Britain as the very same British now began using their economic and military power to help the same Jews regain their national identity and a national homeland in Palestine. With changing attitude, their passion grew stronger to see the resettlement of the Jews in Palestine. It broke all barriers of old hatred and a new Judeo-Christian fervour took birth in Britain to make return of the Jews to Palestine a reality.

Consequently Britain increasingly put its economic and military power behind the effort to resettle the Jews in Palestine. This drive was first made in 1621 and the momentum steadily gained until Lord Shaftsbury persuaded Prime Minster Palmerston to take tangible steps in the 1840s to initiate British presence in Palestine and negotiate with the Ottoman regime for increased Jewish immigration and better living and trading conditions for the Jews as a first step to consolidate and strengthen Jewish presence in Palestine.

The British leaders, prime ministers and pastors and priests as well as the masses, by and large, became intensely one-sided, biased and prejudicial when viewing Palestine or thinking about the Holy Land. They shut themselves from the realities of Palestine since all that their eyes could now see was that this land is Jewish and Jews alone shall reside in all of its boundaries so Christ may return and redeem their sins. The views of the British *Gentile* were obscured by the shadows of religious prejudice, thanks to a confusing interpretation and unquestionable reading of a tainted Bible. Hence the British leaders and public were totally biased and oblivious of the hopes and aspirations or even presence of the people of Palestine who existed in this tract of land much before the children of Israel came there to seek refuge.

Thus Lloyd George, a faith-based prime minister of Britain and intensely pro-Jewish owing to his religious upbringing, used power of the British government to throw out the Turks from Palestine and declare Britain's intent to create a national homeland for the Jewish people. This was the zenith of fulfilment of religious passions of the British people but this was also the beginning of bloodshed of the innocent, the human tragedy of the Palestinians and the start of an enduring conflict that would not go away. The British tried a clever move to soften the blow on the region by saying that the Jewish homeland was without prejudice to the religious and civic

rights of the people already living there. Lloyd George must have known
the worthlessness of this rider because he did not put in place any monitor-
ing mechanism to ensure that indeed the rights of other inhabitants would
be safeguarded. America's President Woodrow Wilson had been a steady
supporter of Lloyd George's drive to create the Jewish homeland, but the
jumping of the American Christians in this arena in 1948 changed the
character of the Balfour Declaration from the notion of a homeland to the
statehood of Israel. President Harry Truman, a Baptist, was the main
architect of this transformation as he used influence and power of the
United States over the United Nations to pass resolution that created the
state of Israel.

By supporting creation of the state of Israel the British and American
Christians have together created a great deal of upheaval in the region and
turmoil in the Middle East which has taken lives of tens of thousands, if not
hundreds of thousands, of innocent people including women, children and
old folks. They created all of this bloodshed, misery and human tragedy in
the name of religion and for the sake of gratifying their peculiar convictions.
What they, or for that matter the Western Christian world, consistently fail to
understand is that this is not what Jesus of Nazareth was all about. Jesus had
rejected war of the older creed and started a new faith of pacifism building a
new community of believers in peace. Why would his return be so blood-
stained and dependent upon the very people that he had separated from?
Reiterating once again, that Jesus denied any knowledge of how and when
kingdom of God will come. The inference that it will come after the return of
the Jews is unfounded in the mainstream of Christian doctrine. To say that
Jesus wanted the Jews to be in one place so he could transform them as one
group or a nation does not measure up to the powers of a prophet because if
Jesus were to have divine powers on his return then it makes no difference
where the Jews might live as he could reform them wherever they might be.
This notion of regrouping the Jews in Palestine so Jesus might return and
reform the Jews in one sweep and establish kingdom of God seems more like
a political move than a divine scheme.

But the troubles of Christianity and its resulting devastation on the
Middle East and the Muslim world were not all related to the inapt adoption of the Old Testament into the new religion, or the confusion about the
two Messiahs, there were other serious strains, too, that drastically strayed
the religion of Jesus. For example the miracle of the Roman Emperor
Constantine pushed Christianity even further away from its original axis of
pacifism and peace. As the legend has, Emperor Constantine saw with his
own eyes about noon time 'the trophy of a cross of light in the heavens,
above the sun, and bearing the inscriptions, Conquer By This. At this sight
he himself was struck with amazement and his whole army also, which
followed him on this expedition and witnessed the Miracle', quoted from

Jill Hamilton's book God, Guns and Israel. Such a dramatic vision of a flaming crucifix on the eve of a fierce battle overwhelmed Constantine and converted him to Christianity in the early fourth century. Subsequently as builder of Christianity, he made Christianity the state religion of the whole Roman Empire. It also meant that many ill practices of the Romans infiltrated into the religion, which drifted it even further away from the religion of pacifism and peace that Jesus of Nazareth had inaugurated.

The advent of the Viking Warriors on the political scene of Western Europe in the ninth century was another blow to the religion of Jesus because when Christianity was married with the warriors this religion became the religion of the imperialists who were ruthless and brutal warriors and practiced imperial domination, exploitation and plundering of their subjects' wealth and resources. Thus the religion of Jesus became just as a victim of war and imperial domination as a helpless subject or an assailable Third World country. And so Christians lost touch with humanity as their religious leaders played no role in admonishing the monarchs or at least the political leaders that imperial domination of the weak and vulnerable and plundering or exploiting the resources of the subjects was unchristian and unlike Jesus' teachings of compassion, pacifism and peace and human dignity, which were routinely marred by imperial domination of the Christian rulers.

The imperial rulers of Western Europe, the descendants of the Viking Warriors and the Crusaders who are now resurging from the United States in newer forms and those who are still lingering on in Britain such as Prime Minister Tony Blair, have created volatile conditions of war and instability in most parts of the world in the belief of pursuing religious convictions that have neither scriptural foundation nor any moral grounds.

Sympathy with the Jews or compassion for their miserable plight is not in question. What is in question is that it is insane to alleviate misery of one by inflicting worse misery on the others. The British and the American Christians seem to have lost sense of proportion as their policies and actions are so blatantly biased and unjust that they could only be categorised as medieval fanaticism and outright unchristian or unworthy of Jesus' name.

If there is a moral dilemma for the West to repent or regret for their sins against the Jewish people, then committing more sins against the Palestinians and the Muslim world is not a wise step or an intelligent way of redressing a wrong or seeking repentance. If the international community or the so-called international community is truly interested in resolving the Palestinian issue and looking for a model that would satisfy all sides and create an open country where Jews, Christians and Muslims could live in peaceful co-existence as equal citizens, then there are two examples from which the world community can create a third and lasting one.

The first example is of Caliph Omar who entered Jerusalem in 632 and outlawed persecution of Jews and Christians. Both Christians and Jews were able to run their churches and synagogues and practice their faiths without interference or hindrance. The Jews, too, flourished in spiritual and intellectual activities in addition to their traditional trading and business ventures. This peaceful co-existence lasted for three and half centuries until the first crusade was launched from Europe to disturb the peaceful co-existence.

The second example of tolerance and co-existence is from Sultan Saladin who followed in the footsteps of Caliph Omar and succeeded in creating a viable and united Palestine after his landmark peace treaty with King Richard I in 1192. Despite some rough patches here and there Saladin's model of peaceful co-existence and religious tolerance for all believers in monotheism, lasted for over eight hundred years until Britain, under the biased leadership of Lloyd George, violated King Richard's peace treaty of 1192 and seized Palestine in 1920. Britain and the United States have since ruined its peaceful status of co-existence by creating an unnatural state of Israel. The consequences of this unwise venture are all too well known.

But the status quo must change for the sake of peace and justice. The only way it can happen is if the Christians would re-examine their faith and realise the impact of subversion in their religious convictions and abandon their pursuit of seeking salvation through resettlement of Jews in an exclusively Jewish state of Israel. Our world has enough intellectual talent and historical resources to recreate a united Palestine equally open to Jews, Christians and Muslims to live again side-by-side in a peaceful co-existence. Once it happens and justice becomes rule rather than the exception then we could see immediate cessation of Muslim radicalism and our world could return to normality. This is not a wishful thinking. It is an optimistic scheme that all good-hearted and peace-loving citizens of the world can make come true. Their power is far greater than the powers of Britain and America and even the authority of the Security Council if they would only realise or feel its potency and decide to use it to change the course of war in the Middle East to euphoria of peaceful co-existence of Jews, Christians and Muslims.

This is the only course of satisfying the three warring branches of Prophet Abraham and a logical approach to resolve an enduring dispute. It is thus an opportunity for our New World to apply logic and use its entire available intellectual and political resources to resolve the contentious issues that have divide humanity for so long.

The outcome of logic depends upon the degree of enlightenment of the intellect of an individual. Hence different people of varying intellectual enlightenment and diverse social and cultural backgrounds come to different logical conclusions about the same proposition of spirituality. This is natural and totally inevitable, owing to varying enlightenment and diverse impacts. Therefore the blueprint for a harmonious and tolerant fraternity is to accept the fact that there will be different logical conclusions in the realm of spirituality and people would follow different religions, which must be recognised and respected without necessarily agreeing with them or losing one's own convictions. One can live with other conclusions while adhering to one's own. Once individuals' right to conclusions was upheld without contempt or denunciation or interference or imposition, then the tension of faith would automatically diminish, as no one would be afraid of others' meddling or clashing with their belief. This is the most beneficial and healthy result that a logical view of other peoples' spirituality can produce. It can also be a prescription for tolerance and a recipe for peace and harmony amongst diverse communities. This is the essence of live and let live.

Hence what is needed in today's world is to appeal to the powers of logic to overcome the divisive issues and control the conflicts. Our world has made much progress in modern communications to open opportunities for learning and acquiring knowledge about other faiths and religions through peaceful means. We do not need forcible introductions by religious zealots who create rifts in the name of spreading their particular doctrines.

Therefore, if we apply logic to the plight of our tumultuous world, we will see that there can be no tract of land more sacred than the sacredness of life. Logic will also show that there can be no message noble enough to deserve to be spread by coercive means or against the will of the recipients. Propagation by invitation is one thing, but imposition by military actions and coercive means or material inducements is quite another. Still more logical analysis would illustrate that there can be no social system worthy enough to be imposed by waging wars and killing innocent human beings. Most of all, since logic also establishes the prerogatives of the surrounding realities and defines the precepts of justice, it will not then be logical to usurp the rights of others or encroach upon their lands and properties or deprive them their livelihoods. The power of logic is designed to supervise human interaction in a just and equitable manner.

The crusade to transform other civilisations by acts of war and spiritual invasions, as is happening in Iraq today, is as outmoded and obsolete as the crusading itself. Our New World does not need these antiquated beliefs or corrupted faiths. The essence of progress and modernity is to give up antiquity and embrace modern and more congenial convictions that will still adhere to the spirituality of a belief but eliminate the practice of corruption from faiths. We are now more educated and enlightened and have greater resources of information to help us transform faiths logically while still maintaining the privilege of abiding by our own individual spirituality.

We do not need warriors of the Bush-Blair kind. We need reformers who can appeal to the good sense of the human fraternity and apply logic to reduce tension and solve contentious issues justly and amicably. We do not need imposition of any ideology or system by the force of military operation. It is an antiquated vocation of imperialists that has failed a thousand times and will fail again. We need leaders who can appeal to the goodness of others by the example of their own goodness and touch their hearts to embrace the philosophy of live and let others live. We need leaders who cherish and value peace even in the most trying circumstances and who can pave the way for a harmonious and tolerant world, free of turmoil, so that every people can live by their tradition and customs and practise whatever spirituality they may wish or choose.

Who is an American president or a British prime minister to decide that the Middle East or the Islamic World needs a Western-style democracy in the name of modernity? It is not their call; it is the prerogative of the people of the Middle East.

And how can we be sure that Western democracy or modernity is the right way to go? This may be an overly materialistic way, benefiting only the rich and powerful, since it provides no moral or spiritual refinement, as is all too clear in Western society. One only has to look at the degeneracy that is creeping into American society and other Western countries to see the point that is being made here. Regrettably, this moral and spiritual degeneration is now spreading all over the world through the electronic media of the West.

No, thank you Mr. President; the Islamic world does not need your modernity imposed by military force. Islam has its own set of values and system of governance, which is what the Muslims are striving to regain. Undoubtedly, that system needs refurbishing, but this modernising must come from Muslims and within themselves, so that they may once again benefit from the polity of Islam in modern times as they did many centuries ago. Western interference has upset the balance in their societies. Now your war measures have disrupted their countries and are hindering their struggle to re-establish the polity of Islam or a synthesis of moral and spiritual values in the daily affairs of their lives. There is no point in your trying to impose Western modernity on the Islamic world, because the Muslims may ultimately reject it, or else there will be too much enduring internal strife against it. You must understand that your plans will not solve any problems, but they may create greater ones. Surely our world does not want to see any more countries like Turkey and Algeria, which are so unsettled by the strong undercurrents demanding re-establishment of the polity of Islam. The turmoil in both Turkey and Algeria is a warning of an ongoing contradiction and conflict that can grip a state if the aspirations of the people are suppressed. Egypt and Pakistan also have symptoms of the same strife. If you create another situation in Iraq like the ones in Turkey and Algeria, and then repeat it in Syria or any other country, then you will only be creating greater number of unstable states in the Islamic world, which will ultimately jeopardise world peace. Your plan to keep an American army in Iraq is suspect, for you may want to use it against other Muslim countries in the region for the same purpose of suppressing the Islamic aspirations of the populations. These designs will serve no good ends, but they may generate more disgruntlement and resentment that will affect international peace.

If Western civilisation wants to see a change in the Islamic world, then the West will first have to change itself. It will have to give up its imperialistic mentality, stop waging wars by military and spiritual invasions, disband its economic exploitation of the weak and vulnerable, and desist from patronising or implanting dictators or CIA-backed prime ministers (as in Iraq) or anchoring friendly presidents (as in Egypt and Pakistan). It is futile to try to change the Islamic world without first changing the Western outlook. Iraq was invaded on one pretext or the other and finally in the name of freedom and democracy. When the so-called sovereignty was transferred and a CIA-backed regime came into power, one of the first few laws it proposed enacting was to impose martial law in Iraq to suppress the population's movement in the name of law and order but really to thwart its aspirations to gain true freedom from the Western domination. How ironic the free Iraq under the aegis of the United States is talking about Martial Law and establishing an internal spy agency to check the people! Where is the freedom and liberty of the people? This shows how the American backed regime is disconnected with the people of Iraq.

The Muslims or Islam are not the only ones that need a change. The West itself is in dire need of a change to correct its course of wars and imperial domination that has caused so much exploitation, grief and resentment in many parts around the world. Instead of outward denunciations, a look inward is now needed in the West.

Therefore it is crucial that Americans look inward to first take stock of their own conduct before they point fingers at others. Looking inward, however, can be difficult owing to personal limitations or inhibitions due to self-consciousness or self-respect. Hence an objective view through the eyes of an outsider may be in order to enlighten oneself about one's own bearings. If Americans would take this approach to learn about themselves then they would realise that it is not only the legacy of violent nature that needs to be replaced in their character, but it is also the impaired psyche that they have acquired over the centuries of their developmental process as a nation that needs to be addressed. Impaired psyche emanates from corrupted beliefs, which give the dogmatist an arrogant sense of being right and utterly partisan. Americans go to great lengths to support partisanship without conceding to the rightness or wrongness of the issue. This makes them arrogant and obstinate negotiators who use the weight of their power, as opposed to constrains wisdom, to impose their will without regard to merits of the other side. Since Americans do not listen or care for other peoples' point of views or even their rights, their partisanship or obstinacy makes it harder even for their friends to instil a sense of proportion into their disposition to restore equilibrium in their attitude and take a balanced view of the issues.

Consequently the impaired psyche and corrupted faith is widely spread in the Western societies but deeply entrenched in the American character. Hence the Americans are not likely to change in any constructive way to alter the course of their reprehensible policies or usher a new hope of fairness, justice and peace and prosperity for the human fraternity. Since Americans currently control world's deadliest military and economic powers and are overwhelmed by their psychological and faith-based idiosyncrasy they are not likely to become the builders of lasting peace on earth. Their impaired and subverted entrenchments are beyond remedy so they cannot be repaired; rather they must be replaced by a new psyche and new faith that will be based on the philosophy of live and let live by respecting the beliefs and rights of others. A complete overhaul of their psyche is needed to replace the entrenched notions of "our rights", "our interests" and "our raw materials" that have been the source of great injustice, resentment and bitterness in many parts of the world. Americans also need a new faith so they could see other human beings in a new light and start treating them with fairness, justice and equality in the true spirit of human fraternity and co-existence. Their flawed faith in resettling Jews to hasten Jesus' Second Coming has caused far too much bloodshed and human tragedy. This is not what Jesus would have liked as a prelude to his return. This was a fiendishly clever political move that Americans have fallen for owing to their subverted faith. These are harsh realities but Americans need to know them so they may learn about themselves from an outsider because they cannot see these flaws by themselves.

What transpires from this study is an urgent need for a serious review of the Christian faith by the Christians so they may deal with the subversions of their religion and chart a new position based on the philosophy of live and let live. The least that Christians can do is to rediscover the religion of Jesus of Nazareth and separate it from the subverted dogmas that have managed to creep into Christianity. It is in Christians' own interest to recognise the differences between Jesus' teachings and the positions of the breaking away sects such as the Evangelicals who are waging wars and practicing other unlike-Jesus characteristics in the name of Jesus.

Life is precious and this world is too beautiful to waste in wars based on bigoted and corrupted faiths. The Jews must also learn by now that there is no point in blaming others or taking cover behind anti-Semitism or playing the sympathy card. These tactics have outlived their usefulness. Now the time is for real thinking and talking. Jews must rise to this test and show to the world what it means to be light and example for the rest of humanity in order to claim even remotely their suggested status of chosen people. A change of dogma to a peaceful co-existence is long overdue from the Jews. Once this change would happen then many other changes would follow to make our world a better place. Since Palestine is the key to a new world, a united and open Palestine for all branches of Prophet Abraham is the way to go about it.

A change of passions and emotions is also true for the Muslims who must strive for a peaceful and harmonious co-existence as their religion teaches them.

When these three branches of Prophet Abraham reform their conduct and rejuvenate their faiths in the true Divine spirit of religion then chances of our world becoming happy and peaceful would increase by leaps and bounds. This is our hope and ultimate goal of our New World.

Index

civic and religious rights under,
97–98

Basayev, Shamil, 112, 113–115, 116

Begin, Menachem, 100, 148

Berezovsky, Boris, 112

Berg, Nick, 203

bin Khattab, Caliph Omar, 208–209,
215, 216, 217

bin Laden, Osama, 21–23, 140. *See also*
Al-Qaeda
CIA surveillance of, 123, 124–125,
157–158
as foil for war against Islam,
146–147, 153
hostile views of U.S., 134, 144
Mohammed Ata and, 126
9/11 plot and, 122, 126, 128–129
product of American training, 192
Saddam Hussein and, 48

Black, Conrad, 138

Blackwell, Robert, 150

Blair, Tony, 53, 95–96
morals and Iraqi invasion, 106
personal religious agenda of, 168

Bosnia, Muslims and Jews in, 2–3

Brezhnev Doctrine, 19

Britain
intelligence failures of, 155
partition of Middle East by, 14
and partition of Punjab, 102–103,
105–106
subversive attacks on Ottoman
Empire, 12, 13
support for despotic rulers, 16–17

British Commonwealth, 103

Brzezinski, Zbigniew, 37, 138
and American strategy in Afghanistan, 19–21, 192
and the "Islamic Card," 20–21,
147–148
Islamic Card and the Soviet Union,
139–140
Wolfowitz and, 146

Buinaksk, Dagestan, 113, 115

Bush, George H. W., 130
anti-Islamic policies of, 144–145
first Gulf War and, 144, 155
and U.S. military bases in Saudi
Arabia, 202

Bush, George W. *See also* Evangelicalism
and Al-Qaeda threats, 45, 131,
153–154
anti-Islamic views of, 28, 53–54,
151–152
Arafat and, 158
and attack on *USS Cole,* 44–45
9/11 Commission and, 129
Defence Policy Board and, 152
Evangelical religious beliefs and
Jewish resettlement, 95
on freedom and democracy in the
Middle East, 55–57
imposition of American values on
Iraq, 56–61, 204–205
"liberation" of Iraq, 220–221, 222
motives for invading Iraq, 34, 52–53,
154, 222–224
political ambitions of, 41–42
preparation for war against Iraq,
46–49, 51, 52
Presidential Daily Briefing (PDB),
August 6, 2001, 43, 45, 47, 48, 153
religious convictions of, 41–42,
49–52, 152
response to 9/11, 45–46
role of advisors on foreign policy,
137–138, 150–151
Rumsfeld and, 160–161
Saddam Hussein as threat to U.S.,
52–53, 154, 205
Sharon and, 158–160
Soviet tactics and, 57–58
as threat to world peace, 225, 230
and torture of Iraqi prisoners,
202–204

involvement in 9/11 plot, 133, 159

pro-Israel media activists in U.S., 138

territorial and religious goals of, 135–136, 159, 194–195

terrorists' attacks on U.S. facilities, 131–132, 148, 149–150

U.S. anti-Islamic furor beneficial to, 135, 147–148

Wolfowitz Cabal and, 138, 146–148

Israelites, migration to Egypt, 70–71

Jackson, Reverend Jesse, 199

Jacob/Israel, 68

Jaffa, terrorist attacks in, 100

James I, King of England, 26, 90, 163

Jerusalem, 8, 9

David's conquest of, 81–82

Solomon's temple in, 83–85

Jesus Christ

on Day of Judgement, 197

as military leader, 183

pacifism of, 182, 183–184

status in Islam, 1

Jews. *See also* Israel; Judaism; Zionism

defiance of *Divine Rules* of God, 96–97, 100

Evangelical support for claim to Palestine, 30, 67–69, 89–93, 99–102, 197

as God's chosen people, 96–97, 193–194

impact on American character, 27–28

persecution in Western Europe, 85–87

Puritans and, 27

treatment by medieval Christians, 2

treatment by Muslims, 2–3

treatment of Palestinians, 3, 94, 96

tribes of Yatrib, 215

wars against Palestinians, 77–78, 100, 101

Jihad Fisabilillah (as defensive war), 72–73, 190

Jihad (holy war, struggle)

in Afghanistan, 20–21, 22, 141–142, 192

concept of, 21, 186, 188–190, 191–192, 226

John, Gospel of, 183

Johnson, Edward, 162, 165

Johnson, Lyndon B., 130, 141

Jones, Jim, 50

Joseph, Prophet, 71, 97

Joshua

conquest of Canaan, 71–72, 74, 75, 77, 79–80, 180–182, 195

emendation of Torah by, 74, 80–81, 99, 180, 181–182, 195

Joshua, Book of, 75, 98

Judah, fall of, 75

Judaism. *See also* Israel; Jews; Zionism

Christianity's debt to, 87

God as warmonger, 179–182

influence on Christianity, 182, 183–184

re-examination of faith and conduct, 193–196

Kashmir dispute, 63–64

Britain and partition of Punjab, 102–103, 105–106

Kazakhstan, Chechens in, 107–108

Kennan, George, on raw materials and American foreign policy, 36

Kennedy, John F., 104

KGB (Russian counterintelligence service), subversive activities in Chechnya, 111–112

Khachilayev brothers, 112, 117–118

Khalid Shaikh Mohammed (KSM), 127–128, 136

Khattab, Emir, 112, 113–115, 116

Khrushchev, Nikita, 108

Kissinger, Henry, 37